# THE CHURCH
# AND
# THIRD WORLD REVOLUTION

## Pierre Bigo

Translated by
Sister Jeanne Marie Lyons

ORBIS BOOKS

Originally published as *L'Eglise et la révolution du tiers monde* by Presses universitaires de France, © 1974

---

**Library of Congress Cataloging in Publication Data**

Bigo, Pierre.
    The church and Third World revolution.
    Translation of L'Église et la révolution du Tiers Monde.
    Includes bibliographical references and index.
    1.   Church and underdeveloped areas.   2.   Sociol-
ogy, Christian.   3.   Christianity and politics.
4.   Communism and Christianity.   I.   Title.
BR115.U6B513        261.8'09172'4        76-55388
ISBN 0-88344-071-7
ISBN 0-88344-072-5 pbk.

57892 .

# Contents

*The Church and Third World Revolution*

# INTRODUCTION

"Third world" is an expression people hesitate to use.[1] So many changes have taken place since "the young nations" suddenly became conscious of their solidarity when in 1955 representatives from twenty-nine recently emancipated countries of Asia and Africa met in Bandung, Indonesia. Since then new empires have sprung up: Europe little by little affirming its unity; Japan becoming a rival of the American giant;[2] and the Chinese colossus, a challenger of the U.S.S.R. Among less developed countries, Brazil and India are causing their neighbors anxiety.

Call it what you will, the reality is unquestionable. A different world has come into existence.

First of all, because of the spectacle of its misery. See it with your own eyes and you cannot forget it. It changes your life. If factory work is a revelation to those who "don't know," how much more revelatory is it to move into that other world you meet when you leave behind the great city centers and emerge into their neighboring shantytowns or go out into a bush region or climb up into the *altiplano,* where the earth can no longer feed the families who still cling to it.

Then, because of its critical state. It is a convulsed world, shaken by the rumblings of revolution. Doubtless, in nations called developed, whether of this or that block, people are experiencing a feeling of oppression, of asphyxia. Perhaps the crisis there goes even deeper, although basic needs are largely satisfied. In the third world, upheaval is constant. Nothing is stable. Catastrophes, as well as long-suffering patience, are predictable. Revolution is everywhere.[3] A symptomatic trait of all third-world governments is that they call themselves revolutionary. Plainly, the word no longer has its authentic meaning.

3

As I understand it, revolution in the third world means something else. It means liberation from a lack of basic necessities; liberation from malnutrition, from slums and shantytowns and hovels, from illiteracy, from unemployment, from flagrant social injustice—the great gaps between the privileged and the marginated; liberation from political repression in every regime where it is exercised; liberation from already existing bureaucracies and technocracies.

Above all, it means liberation from the dependence that spells enslavement to the great industrial metropolises and abolition of the racial discrimination that maintains a well of separation between peoples. To sum it up, the third world calls the whole world into question, a challenge addressed to every human being within it. What is difficult for rich and proud people to grasp is that they themselves must change in order to change the third world. It will cease to be marginated only when the lords have abdicated. What is needed is a commune of peoples.

The struggle involved in the third-world revolution makes its way into the very depths of human hearts. Brother is separated from brother in collective enmities that adopt cruelties of a kind unheard of until now and assume forms of unawareness almost as inhuman. Man is separated from himself by a division that reaches the very marrow of his being. In truth, the third world means death to man.

The Church. Unlike "third world," the term "Church" is not disputed. But what of the Church as a reality? Is there still a Christian community? A Christian faith? The crisis of the world is reverberating throughout the Church. The death of man appears to be bringing about the death of God.

Yet the Church lives on in its poor. To testify to that would doubtless mean penetrating the secrets of peoples' hearts and lives. Unknown to anyone, there battles are fought, lives are dedicated, and hope is provided for the Church. And hope for the world. What kind of a Church would make no response to the appeal of the third world, to the question that the whole world is being asked today?[4] The Church is more concerned than anybody else. By the small number of its believers, by its very poverty, it is pledged and involved.

Perhaps the third world does not feel that the Church is concerned for it. Is that so sure? Whence come the ferments at work in the world not only where people are Christian but where the faith has scarcely been planted? From whom did the world learn that man is free? Who is the one we think of when we say the simple words, "Love one another"? Who was the first one to speak of that love and, not content with simply talking about it, died to give testimony to it? Is humanity, wearied as it is by misery and war, ready to forget that man? "In the one Spirit we were all baptized, Jews as well as Greeks, slaves as well as citizens," Paul proclaims (1 Cor. 12:13). Every person has the same worth as every other. This is the revolutionary principle for the third world.

The Church would not be saved were it not already and did not continue to be a leaven for this kind of revolution. But how far must it go in the conversion that has begun to work within it?

The third world—the Church: here is a relationship, a symbiosis written in history.

In an earlier book, *La doctrine sociale de l'Eglise*,[5] I wrote: "The problems of underdevelopment have not been directly treated in this book. Called to become acquainted with them experientially in Latin America, I shall some day perhaps take up a consideration of them based on the foundations laid there." Ten years of work in Latin America led to the present work. Several stays in Africa had already given me the idea for it. I know that this study, carried out chiefly in third-world regions, must of necessity admit of limitations. If differences between the Latin American countries hardly allow us to make generalizations about them,[6] how can we use the same terminololoy regarding the young nations of Asia, Africa, and America?

Nevertheless, there is no dearth of analogies between them. An economist who devoted all his studies to underdevelopment in Asia was asked to interest himself in Latin America and was astonished to learn that the same kind of problems arise there.[7] Are not the phenomena of margination, dependence, and liberation observable everywhere? A third world exists and that is why my thoughts are not limited to the continent where I spent the most time and covered almost completely in my travels.

In this new work, few references to official documents of the Church are to be found. So forewarned, the reader will not misunderstand it, but will find the authoritative statements of others.[8]

The reader will also discriminate between what is only sociological analysis and is not drawn from the faith (Part One); what is a theological approach and constitutes the strong points of a Christian community of thought (Part Two); what is a dialogue with Marxism, in which reflections already published[9] are taken up again and elaborated (Part Three); and, finally, what is research conducted in the Church and in the light of faith (Part Four).

The book calls upon so many different disciplines that one might well hesitate to write it. Yet, does not every option we take cut across every question studied individually by specialists in the human sciences, in philosophy, and in theology? After an expert has spent a long time in study and finally comes to pose the question as to what action is to be taken—the only thing that really matters—is that person to leave its resolution to empiricism? Or are not experts to bring their reflection to its term, even though they may lack the capacity to grasp the ever new and ultimately elusive character of reality? If the human sciences and theologies are often still useless for a person caught up in involvements, is that not due to the fact that the human sciences lack the means to arrive at the truth about humankind; and that philosophy and theology are deficient in social analyses? Are ideologies alone, then, to solve global questions regarding action? Do they have the vocation for that? Is their reach great enough to encompass mankind itself?

If any conviction is expressed in the following pages it is that life is indeed one, existence is one. There is no spiritual doctrine on one side and social doctrine on the other. Both spring from the same source. Humankind is not here and God over there. They are but one. Such is the essence, the uniqueness, of the Church's faith.

The present work is, more than anything else, a testimony to that. The world is one. The third world is a laceration in the heart of our one world. Beyond the noblest, the highest, the most immanent energies operating to bring human beings together, there is a force at work which is absolutely not humankind's. The world will establish its unity only in acceding to this other which is not itself. The Church is among us to testify to that truth. If the Church isolates itself, it no longer possesses the élan, the breath of the Spirit. Today the Church's mission among us all is to give its blessing to the kind of revolution that the third world needs and longs for.[10]

# NOTES

1. The written form "third world" is being used because it seems preferable to "third-world" and even more so, to "Third World," which is often used in France by a dubious analogy to the Third Estate. "Third world" corresponds to expressions in use in other languages.

2. The gross national product of Germany, France, Italy, Great Britain, and Japan together represented 60 percent of the gross national product of the United States; in 1971 it represented 85 percent. *The O.E.C.D. Observer,* Organization for Economic Cooperation and Development, no. 63 (April 1973).

3. In recent times, uprisings have shaken only one rich country—France in 1968— but have created shock waves in 48 percent of the countries with average incomes, 69 percent of the poor countries, and 87 percent of the very poor countries. "Mission au temps des révolutions," Semaine missiologique de Louvain, 1972, *Documentation catholique* (March 19, 1973), no. 1628, col. 250.

4. " . . . the expectation of a new earth must not weaken but rather stimulate our concern for cultivating this one." *Gaudium et spes,* no. 39, *Documents of Vatican II,* ed. Walter M. Abbott and Joseph Gallagher (New York: Guild Press, 1966), p. 237.

5. 2nd ed. (Paris, P.U.F. 1966).

6. See, for example, Betty Cabezas, *América una y multiple* (Barcelona: Herder, 1968).

7. Gunnar Myrdal, the Swedish economist, a specialist in the problems of South Asia, writes, "When I had to give attention to conditions in other regions [Latin America] I was surprised to find that with all the obvious differences, not least in historical background, economic and social conditions were relatively similar and had resulted in policy prob-

lems of much the same character. *"The Challenge of World Poverty: A World Anti-Poverty Program in Outline* (New York: Pantheon, 1970), p. 452.

8. No restatement of the analyses of documents made in my work *La doctrine sociale de l'Eglise* will be made here. The reader can find an up-to-date and less technical exposition written from the point of view of the third world by Françoise Esquerré, *Comme une étincelle: la vocation sociale de l'Eglise* (Paris: Ed. S.O.S., 1971).

9. *Marxisme et humanisme*, 3rd ed. (Paris: P.U.F., 1961).

10. Like my two previous works, this book is the outcome of twelve years of teaching carried out in different places in Latin America and at the Institut Catholique de Paris with students of a variety of national backgrounds—a dialogue needed for my research, which often resulted in modifying my way of thinking. I am grateful to those numerous auditors and also express my appreciation to Sister Bénédictine, who helped with the revision and completion of the manuscript, no easy task, due to my having to be so much on the move because of circumstances and to the very nature of the work itself.

# PART ONE

# A READING FROM HISTORY

## *A Confluence of Revolutions*

The Church has no original instrument of its own for studying and analyzing the general process that transforms, particularly in the third world, mental and social structures. No confessional social science exists. Like everybody else, the Christian can share in the research within this field through means gradually found by each of the human sciences to discover the different aspects of the mutation that humanity is undergoing.

There is an essential difference between Christian faith and the scientific disciplines. The sciences take a general point of view. Authentic faith is eminently concrete and tends to the actual. It touches and changes people in a conversion, a *metanoia,* that modifies their lives. Faith does not simply contemplate the world but changes it. If a scholar in the human sciences cannot abstract from the subject, much less can the believer. For the believer, processes of revolution are not a subject for analysis but a drama in which he or she has a part to play. Nobody is in a position to modify reality without having somehow grasped the whole of it from all its aspects.

A person who undertakes some action, implicitly or explicitly, adopts a global view, and does so whether or not he or she wishes to or is conscious of doing it, but it is much better for one to put it forward openly. Authentic faith tends to action; it is a synthesis.

Faith appears to have more in common with ideology than with science.[1] An ideology is a mediation between thought and action; it results from their convergence and is grounded on a will to change humankind and society in line with certain fundamental ideas. The Church has no analytical method of its own; much less is it identified with any ideology. Not at this level are its research and its role to be found. So each Christian, together with other people, works out a political conception that seems best suited to guide mutating societies. But the faith does not completely coincide with any of the choices that Christians may come to adopt.

There is, however, a given, an element, proper to faith, an option that does not set Christians apart but brings them into communion with other human beings in a process of world transformation. What is it? A love for fellow human beings and understanding of their misery. Above and beyond all ideologies and strategies, a Christian, if consistent with the faith, identifies with people's misery, the whole of their misery, not what they suffered yesterday and may know tomorrow but the misery that they are experiencing right now. A Christian begins at that point and always comes back to it for two reasons: misery goes on propagating itself without end and it reappears in forms ever new. Along the course that ideologies and strategies follow to put an end to these distresses it often happens that they lose sight of the aim that they had in mind and come to put themselves forward as the end in view. Then they no longer ask themselves if they have put the ax to the root of evil but only if they have put into operation the means which they have thought up, without questioning themselves about the distance that continues to separate them from their objective, the elimination of misery in all its forms.

Beyond what all the scientific disciplines and ideologies offer, the resolute choice of faith gives new life to the global view that humanity takes of its own suffering, conflicts, and mutation. Faith must still continue to immerse itself so deeply in the present reality that it will not lose itself in vain prophecies. The analysis proposed in this first part has one purpose in view—to ground faith in reality. The section contains nothing specifically Christian but seems necessary as a preliminary to a faith approach.

## *NOTE*

1. The word "ideology" is in general use and occurs frequently in this book. Here it has two different meanings. One is positive: an ideology is a necessary mediation for which a definition will be given later. The other is negative: an ideology is a totalizing view, claiming to take in the whole of existence. The context will prove sufficient to indicate in which sense the term is being used.

# I

# MARGINATION

The misery of people today cannot be measured, cannot even be named. Figures speak but say all too little.[1] Descriptive words do a little more. But the only way to take the measure of destitution, of hunger and malnutrition, of sickness, of illiteracy, and, to sum it up, of a life lived under the threat of death and at close quarters with death, is to live it. As far as they are able, some people, some Christians, have chosen to do just that. Yet they themselves know, much better than anyone else, how far they remain from really sharing the fate of tens of millions of people today; their participation in wretchedness always lacks something, not only because they come from areas of good living but for a more fundamental reason. Anyone who has chosen even extreme poverty does not see it, does not live it, in the same way as someone who has had it imposed by necessity, like the pitiless fate of Greek tragedy.

Another thing that makes it difficult to become acquainted with misery is the fact that its face is continually changing. In the nineteenth century it wore the face of the proletariat in the rising industry. All analyses, whether Marxist[2] or Christian,[3] agree on that. Misfortune has a way of singling out the weak; in the nineteenth century, hundreds of thousands of women and very young children were chosen as preferred work-hands by the textile industry because of their docility and fine fingers. Now almost everything has been said about the unfathomable misery, the price paid by humanity to bring about the development of the forces of production.

If one compares the lot of a proletarian worker at this initial stage with some other century-old situations that preceded the industrial era and can still be seen in some regions of Africa—in some sub-Sahara countries, for example—the person today does not perhaps seem quantitatively more miserable than they. But people today exhibit two entirely new aspects that make the reality that they face more insupportable. They are what they are as the outcome of disintegration. And they are in violent contrast to the wealth of which they are, nevertheless, a necessary condition.

The agrarian populations have had an existence at least as precarious as industrial workers, but their structures and cultures have assured them a life that makes us wonder if developed countries are at all familiar with their authentic richness. What characterizes proletarian workers at the beginning of industrial capitalism is that they were violently uprooted from one structure and culture without, however, being integrated into the new industrial and urban society, built up by them but not for them. These shifting populations, migrating and marginal, expelled from an old society but not yet integrated into the new, are at one and the same time at the end of a period of disintegration and in expectation of a process of socialization and acculturation, all too slow in coming.

After more than a century this figure of misery has completely changed. It is true that the proletarian populations of the world are always in migration from an agrarian society that is no longer aware of them to an industrial society that has yet to become acquainted with them. But now the mass of wage earners do not always constitute the major part of the proletariat.[4] More than a century of social legislation and labor-union agitation have created a network of security for workers that is little by little integrating them into a new society. This has been a slow process which, in developing countries, still leaves the great majority of wage earners in precarious circumstances but in developed countries has frequently transformed their situation. In great modern cities only newcomers and foreigners, obliged to accept work which others do not want, constitute a proletariat.

In reality, misery has not diminished; it has, on the contrary, increased. Nor has it changed its nature; as always, it is the result of the decomposition of structures and cultures. Places and names may change. What we call these populations in transition, in migration, matters little. They are a fact. Their misery is a fact.

We must look into its nature, analyze it, for today misery has the huge dimensions of the structural and cultural mutation from which it originates.

## The Migration Phenomenon

Scientific discovery and technical progress have opened up to humanity perspectives unheard of heretofore. They have changed the world from an agrarian to an urban and industrial type of society.[5] This has been a slow and painful parturition with a few emerging into new hope and the many shut away from any hope at all. It has proved the source of yesterday's misery and today's as well, a result of disintegration and a cause of violent contrast.

If by revolution we mean the conscious and willed change from one society to another, the process in question is not a revolution, for it has not been conscious and it has not been willed. What has been conscious and intended are the conquests of science and technology, not the mutation that resulted from them. We human beings never reckoned on the changes these conquests would make in our lives; at each stage we let ourselves be surprised by the event. Fifty years ago only a few theoreticians foresaw the demographic explosion. Ten years ago nobody found the pollution of the earth, the sea, and the air and the destruction of the environment a problem. Now the exhaustion of natural resources, although foreseeable for a long time, suddenly arouses anxiety among the experts. The known reserves of oil, for example, are calculated to last for thirty-one years if the present rate of consumption continues.[6] We are faced with a phenomenon that develops with the implacable dependability of natural processes and carries the authority of the exact sciences; we are not faced with a revolution, although what we do see may well be at the origin of every revolution in the present era.

My intention is not to analyze, as many others have already done, this absolutely new historical event but to show how it has engendered a hitherto unknown form and dimension of human misery—margination.[7]

The disintegration of societies of the agrarian type begins when the customs and structures which gave them equilibrium are undermined by urban models of social existence. The attack is all the more deceptive because it is always presented as an aspect of undeniable progress.

Medical personnel are often the first involuntary agents of disintegration. Nobody would dream of making little of the admirable and totally disinterested work of great foreign doctors working in the African bush, for example. But neither can anyone underestimate the consequences of their intervention, no matter how desirable it may have been. It destroyed a centuries-old equilibrium between a high birth rate and a high mortality rate. At the same time, the instability proper to urban society was undermining the social foundations of patriarchal society. A long phase of transition will be needed before people of such societies regain their balance on the basis of a family of mother and father and two or three children. All over the world there are millions of human beings still attached to the principle of the patriarchal family and the generous begetting of children and at the same time affected by the lightning-like progress of modern medicine. And so they live in misery with their large families and swell the great masses of "marginal" populations without stable employment or decent housing. Time is needed before they modify their attitudes in regard to fertility and before the family becomes reconstituted on a new basis. Meanwhile, what is happening is the demographic explosion and the dissolution of the family.[8]

Schoolteachers followed medical personnel. Their work too was fruitful but with an unexpected, if transitory, consequence—illiteracy. As long as a culture is communicated orally, schools are not necessary for its transmission. Cultures called "primitive" have great richness, as all those can testify who have overcome their prejudices and come to know them at first hand by living in them. They also have great cohesion for, in the geographic area where the human group lives, it finds all the elements needed for its existence—housing and work, initiation and education, celebration and religion. These elements are not dissociated as they are in urban society but interpenetrate one another. One and the same wisdom, one and the same lore in living and doing is inherited from the ancestors and inspires the entire life of the group. In conditions of this kind, illiteracy does not exist. Mary, the mother of Jesus, did not know how to read or write. However, she possessed the full richness of the culture of her group. Joan of Arc learned all that she knew of her religion at her mother's knee and from the Sunday sermons in her country church, yet she contended on equal terms with the subtlest theologians. And she could boast of knowing as much about spinning and weaving as the most expert women in Rouen.

In the polyculture of urban society, on the contrary, culture is transmitted in writing through the schools, by books, by the press. The audio-visual means of communication do not retain what belonged to the old culture; they presuppose literacy. Incidentally, the areas of daily life, the home, work, leisure, and religion, are henceforth dissociated and each of them dispenses different, and even contradictory "wisdoms." Mobility, a condition of the culture, serves at the same time as a factor in its disintegration. "Marginal" populations, while waiting to be integrated into a new world and having little or no schooling, no longer find in the milieu where they live models for thought and life. They are in all truth ignorant and illiterate. The disappearance of the customary wisdom that used to dictate their choices leaves them in confusion and disorder. Cultural contrasts between members of the same family can be such as to destroy their unity.

Industry arrived on the scene after the doctors and teachers. It too came with good intentions. It too helped to destroy the balance of the existing society. In a subsistence economy, in an agrarian and artisan society, work has but little productivity. Children at an early age, old people within the limits of their strength, are integrated in production. Primitive agriculture in all climates often requires only a hundred working days a year. As to artisans, their methods are extremely complicated, their apprenticeships often last six or seven years and their output is mediocre. Nobody spares himself trouble; nobody dreams of estimating how much he or she produces in an hour's work; time has no value. Similarly, necessities remain defined by elementary needs and wisdom counsels people to measure their desires by their condition. Then industrial techniques arrive and upset the age-old harmony. Norms of high productivity impose a logic of accelerated growth. Needs and wants augment at the same rhythm. The new techniques compete with and overwhelm primitive agriculture and craftmanship, reducing masters of proud trade guilds—ironsmiths, weavers, and potters—to the humiliating condition of wage earners in the service of persons who own machines. On the outskirts of great cities, a whole world of peasants whom the land can no longer support accumulate, in search of the hard work and unstable employment which the people who live in the city no longer want. The overindustrialized nations are magnets. Huge migrations from nations with little industrialization flow toward them, supplying them with work-hands that they cannot find within their own borders.[9] The sum of suffering represented by this mutation is incalculable. And inevitable. "Progress" is not to be stopped!

The most remarkable feature of this transformation is the extraordinary network created among the countless workers collaborating anonymously in the production of the same commodity. Formerly, in agriculture, whether on a great estate or on a small holding, work was carried on by a small number of persons. It was the same with the crafts. Wool, for example, was sheared, washed, combed, spun, and woven in the same locality where it was grown. In modern agriculture and industry, each product is the work of millions: those who raise the sheep, those who comb, those who spin, those who weave the wool with improved machines, all making up a whole working world, not forgetting those who transport the raw materials and the semifinished and finished products. Today a whole humanity constitutes a single unique network of production and each product contains millions of work particles. The explosion of the small work cell into planetary dimensions can justly be regarded as the most characteristic phenomenon of modern times. It is not surprising that such a disruption in the infrastructure of humanity has produced a series of revolutions. A confrontation between cultures that has resulted has led to their relativization, so that people seek for a "wisdom" that they no longer inherit from the past and no longer receive from their group. While waiting to be integrated into industrial society, which is essentially society in general, whole populations are torn from familiar ways and surroundings and wander, without structure or culture, in quest of a future of which they know nothing.

From then on, social insecurity is their lot. In clan society, the community never abandons a member in need. Custom assigns to some clan member or members the care of the sick, the old, the orphan, the insane. Very strict norms organize "social security" in the bush. It is going to take a long time for modern societies to reconstitute at another level a comparable kind of social security, particularly one that will include everybody in need. The proletariat of the world are the white elephants of that immense organization. At one epoch, the proletariat were identified with industrial wage earners; today they no longer exactly coincide. Except in cases that still occur too frequently, wage earners with some stable employment, especially if they work for a powerful company that provides them with complementary social advantages, are today relatively well off, however modest their salaries may be. Where misery reigns supreme is chiefly among those who come to make camp outside the cities because they have no regular employment.

Irreligion and moral laxity are the almost inevitable consequences of this huge migration. The primitive group used to assure the acculturation of each of its members, prescribing its own wisdom and religion. When the group breaks up, individuals have to establish for themselves their own religious convictions and their own life norms. Religious and moral insecurity is not one of the lesser tragedies of marginal populations. At first still attached to ancestral practices, they gradually let go of them. The scandal of the Church is to have lost the working class.[10] Today whole populations of "the secular city" have abandoned the faith. This is not the place to study the problems that migration poses for the Church, but at least its most tragic aspect must be pointed out; a huge, a worldwide proletariat that has lost its direction and is floundering in despair.

## The Third World: A Destiny of Its Own

Not only is misery today analyzed as a phenomenon of migration in every country but the third world as a whole is marginal. Cut loose from its customs by new modes of existence, it still lives on the margin of industrial society. It is not just a poor relation, it is the stranger at the gate.

The components of misery today are not difficult to enumerate. They are all too evident and recognizable. Ancestral customs remain but are slowly disintegrating: high birthrate, patriarchal family, oral transmission of culture, crafts that endure, a subsistence economy, social solidarity of the clan, religious convictions linking the group together. But the new ways of life are already causing upheaval: a falling mortality rate, the beginning of schooling, the sudden invasion of modern factories, the cultivation of food for export, some attempt at social security, the calling into question of religion. Between the two civilizations the third world forms a sort of no-man's-land marked by the disintegration of the family together with a galloping population growth, illiteracy, social abandonment, loss of cultural identity, decline of the faith, and a vast number of young people either unemployed or, in most cases, engaged in unsalaried work.[11] Here is the full picture of the third world, the outcome of migration.

The fact that some classes with a good income have succeeded in climbing up the social scale does not change the nature of the phenomenon. They comprise a vanguard of industrial civilization; they do not signal the integration of the third world into the new society; on the contrary, they demonstrate its failure. Between the privileged classes in the third world and those in the developed world, there is less distance than between the former and the other people where they live. For this reason, a visitor in the third world can fall into an illusion, apparently finding his own ways of thought and life in these privileged social groups, who have no more fervent desire than to participate in scientific progress and have almost reached the culmination of their migration. But it is not long before the visitor begins to feel the difference and knows that the third world does exist, a world no longer agrarian but not yet urban. The clash between two civilizations forms a moving front and the third world is the field where it takes place.

Under these circumstances, a question inevitably arises. Caught between two worlds, one that drives them away and the other that attracts them, have young nations a destiny of their own? In the movement that has caught them up and sweeps them along, can they remain themselves?

No subject is debated more frequently, especially in Latin America and black Africa. It concerns the enormous problem of the continued existence of cultures. The Asian and Arab worlds have perhaps less fear of losing the originality of their age-old and prestigious civilizations in an industrial world.

A number of writers, marveling with good cause at the riches to be found in many old customs,[12] are rightly concerned at the dependence of third-world countries on what are called the "developed" countries of the West.[13] Young nations rightly fear to see their original worlds founder and disappear forever in the maelstrom of industrial society—somewhat like the endangered animal species which people are trying hard and sometimes in vain to protect from the invasions of technological man.

As a matter of fact, confusion reigns in the debate on this subject. The destructive effects of colonialism can never be sufficiently emphasized, whether it be colonialism in direct or indirect form (the latter being, for instance, the intervention by one nation in the political affairs of another by the expedient of economic pressure of every kind). Young nations protest against situations that involve dependence—an evidence of their healthy nationalism. A surprising number of the aftereffects of colonialism continue to exist. In metropolitan circles, public opinion frankly ignores them because it is thought that they have been completely eradicated. In this context, people are right in referring to Europocentrism[14] and in speaking of the egocentrism of other empires that have satellite nations which cannot do without them because either need or force keeps them within their orbit.

When we move from political and economic to cultural dependence, we enter, although not always consciously, upon a different terrain. There is no question that a country which is subjected to either direct or indirect colonialism experiences a certain cultural coercion, all the more penetrating when not obvious. The ways of life and thought of dominant nations tend to impose themselves on dominated nations; more than that, they are accepted and even sought. Patterns spring up that prove to be real

| CHARACTERISTICS | AGRARIAN SOCIETY |
| --- | --- |
| Demographic | High birth and death rates. Great fertility (an average of eight children) needed for the survival of the species. Patriarchal family. |
| Cultural | Oral transmission of culture: no schools for the mass. Richness of the culture. A one-culture society: a single culture in each group. |
| Economic | A subsistence economy: agricultural and artisan. Productivity based on work, very limited marketing.<br><br>Feudal agricultural structure, divided into *minifundios* and *latifundios,* corporate organization of crafts. |
| Social | A community of customs which abandons no member in need. |
| Political | A feudal system of personal rules. Rise of free "bourgs." |
| Religious | Integration of the whole of existence and religious life; no dissociation. Religion is tied in with the group. |

This list is an attempt to summarize very sketchily the mutation that has been presented in broad strokes in order to bring out the situation of the marginal man, a being in transition from one society to another.

| | |
|---|---|
| Disequilibrium between a high birth rate and a diminishing death rate due to advances in medicine. Galloping population increase. Progressive dissolution of the patriarchal family. | New attitudes in regard to fertility. Birth control. Family reduced to the couple as a result of mobility. |
| Illiteracy: while culture is being transmitted by the school and the means of social communication, the "marginated" continue in an oral tradition. | Many new means of transmitting culture: school, press, cinema, radio, television. Pluricultural society: in each place (family, work, leisure, worship) contradictory wisdoms are taught. |
| Progressive ruin of agriculture and crafts occasioned by new techniques. Disappearance of the feudal and corporative structure. | Division of work on a planetary scale. An economy of high productivity. Increasing necessities. World markets. The birth of the enterprise, based on economic computation. A total structuring of the economy at the national and plurinational level. |
| Disintegration of the community: appearance of proletariats, social contrasts. | Socialization: social security and a collection of agencies providing for the basic needs of all. |
| Intermediary systems: populism, *caudilismo,* personal power behind a façade of democracy. | A democratic system of a state with economic and social roles. |
| Disintegration of the local religious community. A mixture of still extant traditions; confusion in the religious sphere. | Confessional faith: only those with personal conviction and ties with the universal church keep the faith. |

servitudes for the people who adopt them. This devastating form of dependence must also be denounced.[15]

That being said, techniques are universal.[16] No great wall of China exists to ward them off. No people in today's world can renounce medicine, school, car, radio. Even if they wanted to, they could not.[17] And none are disposed to give them up. Technology brings with it certain cultural modifications, if only because of the consequent clash between cultures. The result is not uniform and consistent conduct, far from it, but the unavoidable unity of a world tied together by the same information, the same images, dispensed at the same second by the same media.

Ideologies themselves reach everywhere. No bulkhead exists to turn back their shock waves. The battle fought against the revolutionary idea of 1789 was a lost cause, even if Jacobinism had not been the outcome. Resistance to the idea of socialism is also quite useless, although communism has not prevailed everywhere. Is not the prestige enjoyed by Marxism in countries which jealously insist upon their cultural independence a proof that they are not trying to defend themselves against an ideology that is a completely foreign import? If some day the third world, whether in Africa or Asia or Latin America, were to have a revolution, nothing would prevent the ideology inherent in it from being diffused to the ends of the earth. Is there not already some evidence to testify to that development? Otherwise, how can anyone explain the prestige of men like Che Guevara and Ho Chi Minh and, earlier, of Gandhi?

These thoughts should be pursued further: art and ideas too are universal. Just let a poet arise who, like the Chilean Pablo Neruda, is rooted as deeply as possible in his native soil and he makes an impression that reaches the whole world, not because he is Chilean but because he is a poet. Let a scholar or a philosopher or a theologian[18] spring up in the third world, and that person will carry just as much weight as the leading figures in the contemporary science, philosophy, and theology.

The whole difficulty therefore lies in discerning the difference between cultural dependence, by which one nation's ways of thought and life are contaminated by another's, and cultural

57892

independence, the capacity to acquire and in turn to create a technique, an idea, an art of universal value, integrating within it cultural elements from its creator's own milieu. A lack of such discernment will be the surest means of keeping the third world definitively in marginal nonexistence.

Not by escaping the process of industrialization will young nations preserve their cultural riches, but by finding their own place in their own way within the process. Not by rejecting the unity into which technology draws the whole world, but by becoming integrated within it in a different way can they save their heritage. Only by so defining their cultural orginality can third-world countries free themselves from the dependence oppressing them today.[19]

## NOTES

1. According to Paul A. Samuelson, *Economics*, 9th ed. (New York: McGraw-Hill, 1973), p. 82, in 1973 individual income averaged $5,980 in the United States, $3,750 in France, $830 in Portugal, $230 in Egypt, $110 in India. These contrasts have only become more marked. "Around 1950 the average individual income of those living in third-world countries was 9 times less than those living in developed countries and the difference was 1 to 27 between Asia and the United States. In 1970 the difference between third-world and developed countries, instead of being 1 to 9, had reached 1 to 14 and, between undeveloped Asia and the United States it was 1 to 42." Paul Bairoch, *Le tiers monde dans l'impasse* (Paris: Gallimard, 1971), pp. 13–14.

2. For example, Engels' famous description of *The Condition of the Working Class in England*, trans. W.O. Henderson and W.H. Chaloner (Stanford: Stanford University Press, 1958).

3. To cite only one, we have Villermé's *Tableau de l'état physique et moral des ouvriers employés dans les manufactures de coton, de laine et de soie*, 1840. Quotations from this work can be found in *l'Union générale d'Edition*, 1971.

4. "The reality of two constituted classes is not the only, nor perhaps the principal reality capable of accounting for situations of conflict." François Perroux, *Masse et classe* (Paris: Casterman, 1972), p. 44.

5. It will be remarked that it is not a question of passing from one culture to another. Agrarian society comprises an infinite variety of almost completely heterogenous customs. An urban society has no particular culture and leaves to each civilization the possibility of retaining its original characteristics within an evolution that is inevitable.

6. *Halte à la croissance?* (Paris: Fayard, 1972), p. 174. In this book the Club of Rome raises a resounding alarm. Its anxiety arises from the cumulative effect of three factors: population, pollution, and the exhaustion of natural resources (p. 10). It has the merit of offering a solution that would make it possible to envisage an average industrial production three times greater than that reached in 1970 and a doubling of the food supply. "These technical measures include: the recycling of natural resources, the utilization of antipollution devices, an increase in the life span of all forms of capital, and the use of methods for reconstituting the soil." In addition to "a policy of stabilizing the population," . . . "Changes in the scale of priorities: the production of foodstuffs and services outweighing industrial production" (p. 268). Other experts do not share their pessimism, but no one takes lightly the questions posed. Population growth, the pollution of the planet and the destruction of the environment, the using up of natural resources, without making any reference to the potential of the great powers to annihilate all life from the surface of the earth, anguish people of conscience. For his part, Alfred Sauvy wonders, with good cause, whether theories of *zero growth* are expedient for the world of the poor, who cannot afford the luxury of stagnation. *Mythes, croyances, croissance* (Paris: Calmann-Lévy, 1973).

7. No other institute has gone so deeply into research on the phenomenon of margination as the Instituto Latina América de Desarrollo Económico y Social at Santiago, Chile. See Roger Vekemans, *Marginalidad: promoción popular e integratión en Américo Latino* (Santiago, D.E.S.A.L, 1970) and I.L.A.D.E.S., *Hacia la superación de la marginalidad* (Barcelona: Herder, 1972).

The thesis of "margination" has sometimes aroused suspicion. Many have, in fact, interpreted it as if it were an assertion that "marginated populations" could be integrated into society as a whole without making changes in the structures of the latter. But such an absurd conclusion has been expressly dismissed by those who have analyzed the phenomenon. Once this doubt has been cleared up, the concept of margination is irreplaceable in any analysis of the reality of the third world. It is bound up with ideas of dependence and liberation.

Distinguishing between urban margination (which is not limited to shantytowns) and rural margination, an attempt is made to measure the extent of the phenomenon. In Latin America alone, the number of the marginated in the cities has been estimated at 30 million persons in 1966 with an annual increase of 12 percent. The United Nations presents the figure of a billion for the whole world. "According to a United Nations estimate, a billion people live in slums." Ignacy Sachs, *La découverte du tiers monde* (Paris: Flammarion, 1971), p. 98.

8. This work will not deal directly with population problems. The accelerated increase in the number of human beings has had undeniable repercussions on the standard of living in the third world. But the subject touches questions in which personal freedom is deeply involved and demographic policies can be put into effect only while maintaining respect for the values concerned. Within the work outlined here, it would be impossible to plunge into such a complex subject.

9. In 1971, 430,000 foreign workers arrived in Germany from other Western countries (an average of 300,000 over the period 1958–1962). In France the number of foreign workers has declined: 132,000 in 1971 as against 290,000 ten years previously.

10. A statement made by Pius XI in a conversation with Father Cardijn, a future cardinal and founder of the Jeunesse Ouvrière Chrétienne (Young Christian Workers).

11. The picture is painted with unequaled poignancy in an account, based on taped conversations and written up by the sociologist Oscar Lewis, titled *The Children of Sanchez* (New York: Random House, 1961).

12. Without, however, losing sight of their negative aspects. Custom is sometimes astonishing, sometimes disconcerting, in the way it affects behavior.

13. A case in point is Gilbert Blardone, *Progrès économique dans le tiers monde* (Paris: Librairie Sociale et Economique, 1972).

14. The term is Ignacy Sachs' in *La découverte du tiers monde,* p. 22. "Europocentrism continues to dominate our thinking and, given its projections on a worldwide scale by the expansion of capitalism and the fact of colonialism, it has molded the thinking of contemporary culture, putting blinders on some and imposing a forced deculturation in others."

15. Hence the interest in research to discover the right method of development. See Léopold Sédar Senghor, *On African Socialism,* trans. Mercer Cook (New York: Praeger, 1964); and Robert Bosc, *Le tiers-monde dans la politique internationale* (Paris: Aubier, 1968), esp. pp. 88 ff.

16. Chinese acupuncture is cited as an exception, since it is based on a representation of the human body that differs from occidental medicine's. But the exception proves the rule, for acupuncture is on the way to becoming accepted by medicine in general.

17. Ignacy Sachs speaks of "the unification of cultural microworlds

which were scattered over our planet before the coming of world trade."
*La découverte du tiers monde,* p. 100.

18. Acquaintance with the best of the many Latin American "theologies of liberation" confirms the point: they integrate perfectly with the great universal currents of theology. They are not dependent upon these but participate with them in a common search and in the application of their findings to particular sociological situations.

19. In *La découverte du tiers monde,* Ignacy Sachs asks a good question: "At what point does nationalism pass beyond retrogression to become progressive?" (p. 102). He has drawn a clear line between two forms of independence. No one has emphasized more than he the existence of Europocentrism, but he has also shown the impossibility for the third world of escaping the common destiny of humanity in the years to come. "I believe it is no longer possible to elude the ascendancy of a universal system of material values concerning certain fundamental human needs in regard to health, food, housing, and education. In these basic areas general norms of consumption are imperative for all of humanity" (p. 170). "The only real advantage accruing to latecomers in the development race could be the possibility of saying no to the existing models and of making their own determination in opposition to them, in other words, of projecting new and creative types of civilization. Unfortunately, the trend today moves in exactly the opposite direction: the third world is modeling itself according to the image of industrial societies. While being fully aware of the impossibility of constructing a complete plan for an imaginary civilization, which can only originate in social praxis, I do believe an effort in theorizing is needed and should be called long-term planning" (p. 220).

# I I

# DEPENDENCE

If the third world is dependent, it is both because it has already entered into a worldwide economic society and because it has not been accepted there. Causes for its dependence lie in a migration begun but not completed. Where agrarian society remains intact there is no dependence because there is no intercourse between the two different worlds. But is there really any place on the globe where people escape the general attraction? A marginal world is by its nature dependent, for functionally its existence is directed to another world. Marginality and dependence are two complementary conceptions, two explanations, each necessary for an understanding of underdevelopment.

All those who write on the subject are justified in insisting upon the importance of the structure of relationships between dominant and dominated classes and nations as a factor in the slow economic growth of the third world and of the great and ever-increasing distance between poor and rich countries.[1] For good cause, they denounce the theories prevalent in the years 1950 to 1960 when underdevelopment was attributed to purely internal causes—failure to save, to invest, to innovate—that prevented a nation from achieving "a takeoff," the crossing of a critical threshold of growth.[2] They bring out the importance of structural factors that obstruct the development of poor classes in a particular nation and poor countries in the world community of nations.[3]

## Dependence from Within

To begin with, inequality is the cause of dependence. "Inequality and the trend towards rising inequality stand as a complex of inhibitions and obstacles to development."[4]

For a long time, Western authors were saying that inequality is a necessary condition for progress and efficiency in the economy.[5] It is certainly true that absolute equality does not stimulate people's energies. When, in an active population, each one earns just so much, whether he or she works well or ill or not at all,[6] the economy can only stagnate. But if, on one hand, inequality in income can be justified when it is due to recompense for increased production, initiative, innovation, and investment with all its risks, we do have to condemn it when it stems from or results in parasitism, when it is the source of real profits without cause or purpose. Right at this point we come up against one of the marks of developing countries.[7] The oligarchies there have extracted their riches from badly exploited lands and have more often than not squandered their revenues in lavish spending either in their own countries or abroad, without any advantage accruing to the farming regions that provide their living. The industrial oligarchies themselves have often taken their profits from excessively protected enterprises and have not been at all inclined to reinvest them, as it would have been well for them to do, in the improvement of techniques and the creation of new enterprises that would benefit their own countries. Yet it is well known that industrial capital has much better chances for making higher profits in the third world than in developed countries.[8]

To have a complete picture, we would need to take into account other forms of profit, much less likely to be acknowledged and impossible to estimate—the money made through corruption, the plague of so many third-world countries and, as it has been aptly called, a "taboo" subject.[9]

In every case then, inequality is a sign of the exploitation of person by person, of the oppression of marginal populations by oligarchies; it is absolutely not a source of growth; it is a means of monopolization. In addition, it engenders apathy and inertia in the populations it exploits. What stimulus could people possibly find in a situation of that kind?

## Dependence from Without

For the third world, entering into international exchange has meant colonization, not only because soldiers followed the traders who opened the way for them but because, even after the end of military occupation, the trade game was played with stacked cards.[10] The viewpoint of the colonizer was well expressed in Victorian England's vision that "the whole world will work for us." As a matter of fact, almost the whole world did supply agricultural products and industrial raw materials at a very low price, thanks to an abundant and exploited work force living in the worst kind of conditions, sometimes even in slavery.[11] The dependence of the third world is due, in the first place, to unequal terms of exchange. The price of raw products (with the exception of oil since the formation of a syndicate by the oil-producing countries) has been low and subject to continual fluctuations. The price of industrial products is very high.[12] This inequality exists, in the final analysis, from the fact that the developed countries, save for a few rare exceptions, find it easy to get raw materials, whether agricultural or mineral, because of the competition existing among underdeveloped countries, which must sell their products at any price, literally, because their subsistence depends on exporting them. They are absolutely dependent on the developed countries as their customers.[13]

The third world has reacted to this form of oppression by undertaking to become industrialized themselves in order not to depend upon the great metropolises to supply them with industrial commodities. This reaction has provoked another form of colonialism. An indigenous industry can come into being only with an infusion of foreign capital, an investment to fertilize the economy of a young nation. But that is not what has happened, rather, just the opposite. Quasi-automatic factories of the latest model have been established in countries where jobs should have been provided for an enormous labor force. Above all, foreign investors have made the young nations pay dearly for the services rendered them.[14] If what they have brought in were to be balanced against what they have taken out, the results would not be entirely negative, for the immense returns realized on the investments made are no proof that the underdeveloped countries have not derived some advantage from them as well.[15] Sharing, however, has been unequal, especially at the outset. And multinational companies do not hesitate to intervene, either directly or indirectly, in the politics of the countries in which they have investments by bringing their weight to bear on opinion in their home country as well as in the underdeveloped nations themselves. Under these conditions, hope could reasonably be placed in public aid. What has been done in this area should not be overlooked. However, the assistance given remains negligible, considering the potential of the wealthy nations, and is far removed from the one per cent of the gross national product proposed at the United Nations Conference on Trade and Development held in New Delhi in 1968. And it, in turn, has also led to another form of dependence.[16] Donor nations have generally put very precisely worded conditions on their gifts; they have often required that the goods made possible by the funds allocated be purchased in their own countries. Principally, they have preferred bilateral aid arrangements, thus keeping a third-world country dependent upon them, since multilateral aid would put a stop to it through entrusting the distribution of donations and credits to various international organizations.[17]

*Is Dependence the Only Factor in Underdevelopment?*

Most economists who make dependence a structural factor in underdevelopment do not, however, proceed to deny the action of other factors. Observation shows that we need to place great importance on climatic conditions. It is plainly not by mere chance that all the developed countries are to be found in temperate zones and all the developing countries in tropical or subtropical zones.[18] However that may be, the work and production techniques, together with invested savings, remain the conditions for economic growth and no nation can unload on others the effort that these demand. The experience of socialists as well as capitalist countries confirms that fact. Placing obstacles in the way of such efforts is exactly how structures of dependence restrain expansion, as privileged classes and nations do when, instead of making the economy of the young nations productive by their investments, they exploit them for their own profit; whether they squander their profits or invest them in their own country, they do not create employment, which could provide jobs for an overabundant labor force. With jobs unavailable, people can neither work nor save.[19]

It is easy to draw up a list of experts who give importance, and sometimes exclusive importance, to structural factors in this matter, and to enumerate those who stand by functional factors as the single cause. It is not at all easy to produce a going economy, regardless of the nature of its structure. Socialist countries have managed to do so only after many years and some of them have not yet succeeded. Authoritative writers today are inclined to point out the interaction of factors of two different orders in regard to dependence. Whether it is internal or external, dependence is a cause of underdevelopment—and underdevelopment, in turn, causes dependence when the true worth of a country's resources are not backed by a coherent effort of labor and investment.

## A Break in the Third World?

The spectacular rise in the price not just of oil but of many raw materials during the last months of 1973 forces us to ask ourselves whether we can make an extrapolation from the facts made available to us during the last fifteen years. Between December 1972 and December 1973 the price of copper went up by 88 percent, zinc by 268 percent, lead by 77 percent, tin by 68 percent, rubber by 150 percent, corn by 73 percent, cacao by 56 percent, sugar by 43 percent, coffee by 24 percent, wool by 25 percent, cotton by 130 percent.[20] Is this phenomenon to continue, to be lasting? The conclusions drawn by the Club of Rome [21] would seem to indicate that it will. Without wishing to draw out an argument from so recent and unexpected an instance, one could raise the question whether the third world may not be beginning to see the situation changing in their favor during the coming years. At least a part of the third world is perhaps entering into a new era and making its claim for a dominant position in the world market. Yet immense regions in Asia, particularly in India, and in Africa are increasingly experiencing their harsh dependence, being deprived of raw materials, which are now moving further than ever beyond their reach.

## A Conflict of Worldwide Dimensions

In any case, it can still be said that the typical migration of modern times, by the social constrasts it brings into being, by the exploitation of unorganized and defenseless marginated people always accompanying it, stirs up deeply felt conflict in oppressed classes and nations as they emerge from their former ways of living and enter into the logic of industrial technology. Their migration does more than cause misery; it gives birth to a series of conflicts and revolutions.

The rupture produced is not simply opposition between the classes in one country; it is most evident between dominating and dominated nations, and in that context it takes on a new nature so that, for example, national oligarchies are stigmatized, above all, as the domestic allies of foreign imperialism.

At this juncture, who could be surprised at the reactions of the young nations? Revolution in our era is first and foremost a revolution of the third world.

## NOTES

1. It is well not to forget that in absolute worth the third world situation is improving.

See Paul Bairoch, *Diagnostic de l'évolution économique du tiers monde 1900–1968* (Paris: Gauthier-Villars, 1970), p. 193: "If we limit ourselves to the period 1957–1963 and include all underdeveloped countries, we come up with a 2.4 percent rate of annual increase in gross national per capita income figured on a constant price unit." In Colombia, during the period 1950–1967 the gross national product increased 4.7 percent annually, which implies a slight rise (0.9 percent) in individual income, in spite of the country's rapid rate of population growth (3.2 percent). See Hermann Mohr, *Economica colombiana: una estructura en crisis* (Bogotá: Ediciones Tercer Mundo, 1972), p. 8. In some Latin American countries the rate of population growth is rising (reaching more that 7 percent in Colombia in 1973) as a result of the policies inspired by the Brazilian model of high profits and low salaries. See note 17 following. An amelioration in the terms of exchange in favor of certain poor countries also seems indicated. Perhaps it is not helpful to extrapolate the 1960s from this point of view. See below, p. 33.

2. The economist Walt W. Rostow is the most typical representative of this state of mind. *The Stages of Economic Growth: A Non-Communist Manifesto,* 2nd ed. (Cambridge: Harvard University Press, 1971).

3. The Second Episcopal Conference of Latin American Bishops meeting in Medellín in August and September 1968 pointed out the two forms of dependence—internal and external. See *The Church in the Present Day Transformation of Latin America in the Light of the Council,* 2 vols. (Bogotá, Gen. Secretariate, C.E.L.A.M., 1970), and ed. Louis Colonnese (Washington, D.C.: Latin American Bureau, United States Catholic Conference, 1970).

4. Gunnar Myrdal, *The Challenge of World Poverty* (New York: Pantheon, 1970, and Random House, 1971), p. 40.

5. Ibid. "Traditionally, Western economists for the most part assume, on the contrary, a conflict between economic growth and egalitarian reforms. They take it for granted that *a price has to be paid for reforms* and that often this price is prohibitive for poor countries." Myrdal cites a recent book on Pakistan, which states that "a conflict exists between the aims of growth and equality. . . . Inequalities in income contribute to the growth of the economy, which makes possible a real improvement for the lower income groups." Myrdal disagrees, saying, "contrary to the ordinary conception of a conflict between the two goals of economic growth and greater economic equality, these are often in harmony, and why greater equality in underdeveloped countries is almost a condition for more rapid growth" (p. 54).

6. Because strict rationing gives each one the necessities at low cost and there is a dearth of everything else, money no longer has any value. Such a system ends in general laziness, and no campaign against laziness suffices to put an end to it.

7. *Income Distribution in Latin America* (New York: United Nations, 1971) p. 35, offers some insight into the unequal distribution of incomes: in 1965, among a hundred people, the twenty poorest had an average income of $60, while the five richest were receiving $2,600.

8. According to Denis Bauchard, around 1955 the profit-earning capacity of capital invested in oil companies reached 30 percent outside the United States, 10 percent in the United States. He notes, however, that these profits are no longer what they used to be and the rate of income from capital invested is tending to decline. *Le jeu mondial des pétroliers* (Paris: Seuil, 1970), p. 40.

9. Gunnar Myrdal, *The Challenge of World Poverty,* p. 256: "The biased

postwar approach dominating economic research has observed a virtual taboo against ever touching the crucially important problems of the soft state and corruption."

10. André Gunder Frank has made himself the zealous defender of this thesis in relation to Latin America. *Latin America: Underdevelopment or Revolution* (New York: Monthly Review Press, 1969), p. 9: "On the contrary, underdevelopment was and is generated by the very same historical process which also generated economic development: the development of capitalism itself." His point of view is admissible to the extent that capitalism has been a big, although not an exclusive, factor in causing underdevelopment.

11. Only in 1852 was slavery abolished in New Granada (now Colombia) and later still in a number of countries in Africa and the New World.

12. See Bairoch, *Diagnostic de l'évolution économique*. A price index (the relationship between trade in raw materials and manufactured products) of 100 in 1958 moved to 91 in 1966, in contrast to 122 in 1950. The author analyzes the causes of this disparity in terms of exchange (pp. 162–69). The turmoil brought on by the rise in the cost of oil, metals, and even foodstuffs (see p. 33 in the present work) leads one to think that the situation can change in favor of certain third-world countries in the years ahead. If this turnabout proves lasting, as predictions of the exhaustion of the world's resources make us think it will, its consequences can have tremendous importance for those who will benefit by it.

13. Paul Bairoch, *Le tiers monde dans l'impasse* (Paris: Gallimard, 1971), estimates that exports from third-world to developed countries rose to more than 10 percent of their gross national product, while exports from developed to third-world countries was less than 2 percent of their gross national product at the time. And he concludes: "The difference between less than 2 percent and more that 10 percent explains many of the effects of the domination exercised by developed countries" (p. 224).

14. The profits of the *Union minière du Haut-Katanga* from 1950 to 1959 fluctuated between 2.5 and 4.5 billion Belgian francs a year, while the average budget for the Congo was 11.3 billion in 1960. Robert Cornevin, *Le Zaire* (Paris: P.U.F., 1972).

15. It has not been proven that developed countries themselves have always profited by their relation with their colonies. See Paul Bairoch, *Le tiers monde dans l'impasse,* where he says, "Paradoxically, it can even be concluded from an empirical analysis of the problem, there was no real profit on a macroeconomic scale for the countries with colonial empires. . . . Unlike physics, the economy can result in losses for both sides in an operation. . . . Profits are realized only by limited social groups and do not necessarily imply any economic profit for the nation

as a whole" (pp. 158–59). Of course, these conclusions can be questioned: the enormous profits reaped by Belgium not too long ago through the exploitation of Katanga copper, or by France through the exploitation of the Suez Canal, certainly contributed to the development of these two countries, even if other regions of their empires did not bring them like profits and even if enormous sums were swallowed up in some disastrous investments.

16. See Tibor Mende, *From Aid to Recolonization: Lessons of a Failure* (New York: Pantheon, 1973). Aid has also resulted in a state of indebtedness that contributes to maintaining dependence. Debts owed by developing countries to outside sources were estimated in 1972 and the conclusion drawn that the size of the debt was increasing considerably, going from $9 billion in 1965 to $48 billion in 1968 and would exceed $60 billion in 1970, an evolution chiefly due to loans in total aid. For these data, see Maurice Schlogel, *Les relations économiques et financières internationales* (Paris: Masson, 1972), p. 312.

17. I am of the opinion that the spectacular development of the Brazilian economy in recent years does not weaken these conclusions about the damaging effects of internal and external dependence. Without a comprehensive study of what would doubtless have to be called the Brazilian miracle (after the Swedish miracle—see Jean Parent, *Le modèle suédois* [Paris: Calmann-Lévy, 1970]; and the Japanese miracle—see Hubert Brachier, *Le miracle économique japonais* [Paris: Calmann-Lévy, 1970], it is difficult to form a definitive opinion. The most knowledgeable hesitate to give an interpretation of a phenomenon so unforeseen. At first sight it appears to contradict the whole new orientation of economists just referred to; its stake rests on inequality as a fundamental element in development and has no fear of either internal or external dependence. People of influence who hold this view figure that an increase in the income of less advantaged social categories will inevitably follow an increase in the income of the wealthy. And it is true that, even if social inequities do increase considerably, the standard of living of wage earners, for example, does tend to improve. Looking at it from another angle, large-scale investment of national and international capital establishes solid economic growth. Brazil thinks that, if its development continues at the same rate for ten years (about 10 percent annually), it will be able, as Japan has done, and with greater reason—the almost unlimited area at its disposal—to deal with the great powers as their equal. This new mastery is already arousing anxiety in the nearest neighbors. It should be acknowledged that this unexpected growth of a completely classic kind has taken place in contradiction to all those who

have asserted that capitalist methods cannot achieve purely material growth in the third world. No doubt it is too soon to draw conclusions. The success of Brazilian capitalism in the strictly economic sphere depends, in my opinion, on one condition—the creation of a national market as an absolute requirement for sustaining its expansion. This means distributing the revenue being created and, above all, having it reach the most disinherited regions of Brazil, the famous Northeast, where the misery and exploitation of workers are still shocking. The works of Celso Furtado, who has worked for the development of this region, continue to be of value. See, in particular, his *Les États-Unis et le sous-développement de l'Amérique latine* (Paris: Calmann-Lévy, 1970), pp. 163 ff. Obviously, this does not take into account more recent expansion. Some helpful information can be found in *The Economist* 18 (September 2, 1972) 244.

18. Gunnar Myrdal, *The Challenge of World Poverty*, pp. 33–34.

19. Paul Bairoch, *Le tiers monde dans l'impasse*, asks a good question when he inquires why economic growth in the third world cannot operate according to the same models that have led to growth in Western countries.

20. *Le Monde*, December 25, 1973.

21. See note 6, Chapter 1.

# III

# LIBERATION

Most of the growing discussion about liberation is apt to limit it to a single model, a simplification that fails to take history into account. In reality, the revolutionary process observable in the world unfolds in a dialectical form. What can be seen is not one revolution and one liberation but successive revolutions and liberations mutually linked together. More than any other entity, the third world witnesses to this complexity.

The word "revolution," like the word "liberation," is being used so much these days that we need to begin by going back to its original meaning.

Some pages in history do treat of revolution in the strict sense; radical, complete, universal, irreversible mutations in human mental and social structures. A revolution is a radical change, although it manifests continuity as well. The foreign policy of the French Revolution was not very different from the kings'; nor does the foreign policy of the Russian Soviet differ much from the czars'. But nobody today thinks like Charles V or Louis XIV. And few people still reason like the Liberal Democrats of the nineteenth century. Revolution is all-embracing, modifying every aspect of existence—economic, social, political, cultural, and religious. It is global: no geographical or ideological frontier can prevent the diffusion of a new idea. Finally and perhaps of first importance, revolution is irreversible: no "restoration," unless it be merely apparent and provisional, is going to follow it. Must violence be considered as an essential characteristic of revolution? That seems uncertain. Great Britain has preserved the monarchy and is probably more democratic than republican France. The process of socialization seems more advanced in some Nordic countries, where it was achieved peacefully, than in Soviet Russia.

In this narrow sense, revolutions are rare. Just two that seem deserving the title have been observed in the last two centuries. Perhaps a third is now making its appearance.

During one historical moment, beginning with the end of the eighteenth century, a series of events took place in America, in Europe, and, more recently, in Africa and Asia, which were all connected with the same revolution. Doubtless today people are apt to minimize the victories these won, for a new wave has rolled in to cover the first. Yet they will see that these still have drama and timeliness. Many modern demands spring directly from them. Their dates are familiar: 1775–1783, the war for independence in the United States; 1789, the storming of the Bastille; beginning in 1810, the wars for liberation in Latin America, bloodier than the Napoleonic wars and supported by republican ideology. Simon Bolivar, the liberator, had lived in Paris during the years of the revolution. Finally, since World War II, colonial countries in Asia and Africa have won their independence. A world has come to an end. A new world has been born.

A century after the revolution began in 1775, a second one flamed up. It too is radical, universal, and irreversible. In one form or another it inevitably reaches every country without exception. It is more difficult to recognize than the revolution that preceded it because it is still in process, still incomplete. The 1848 days in France, with their fallout over Europe, the 1871 Paris Commune, were its warning signals and forerunners. In any case, Russia in 1917, the countries of eastern Europe after World War II, China in 1949, Cuba in 1959, all moved into socialist revolution. Elsewhere the process of socialization unfolded less spectacularly but was no less a revolutionary change.

Are there, at the present time, signs of a third revolution? Are there new ideas, which do not have their source in either the first or second revolution but tend, nevertheless, to transform the structures of our thinking and our society today? It would be difficult to deny it, and still more difficult to define just what those ideas are. If conflicts exist that are not reducible to clashes between classes or nations, then we do have something new making its appearance right now.

At all events, it is impossible to consider historical processes as contradictory as a democratic revolution, a social revolution and, perhaps, a "cultural" revolution as one and the same revolution, a single, unique liberation. Yet the revolution of the third world is being formed by being involved in the same dialectical process.

## The Origin of Contemporary Revolutions

The unity in plurality marking successive revolutions of the contemporary era exists because all of them have a common origin, the industrial mutation. It is impossible, however, to apply to each revolution a single schematic explanation.

It is no accident that democratic ideas initially germinated in countries where industrial development first took place—in England,[1] then in France. Democracy is contemporary with the industrial era. Well before it triumphed, its first signs could be observed in the market towns, the *bourgs*, where artisans and merchants, "bourgeois" in the strict sense, formed free enclaves in a feudal world.

Eighteenth-century France was a place of slow development. Everybody had a confused impression that the old structures, corporative and authoritarian, were giving way under the pressure of new techniques. The Physiocrats, as conservative as they were in their monarchical convictions and even in their economic ideas—the land remained for them the essential source of wealth—put forward revolutionary principles in demanding the suppression of the corporative structures that were paralyzing the economy. Their ideas cannot be separated from the revolutionary movement: liberty in 1789 meant political liberty but it meant economic liberty as well. Turgot made the first move of the revolution in 1776 by suppressing the corporations. But the *Ancien Régime* was still too strong to permit a transformation that would so completely call it into question. Necker served as its instrument by reestablishing the corporations. The new political economy had to await the decree of Allarde, March 2–17, 1791, and the law of Le Chapelier, June 14–17, 1791, for its triumph. In the French Revolution and, more generally, in the birth of democracy, the concurrence of the economic situation with the new political ideas cannot be denied. It matters little that people at the time were not fully conscious of it. A new day had already dawned and liberty was a condition of it.

However, it would be presumptuous to trace the whole revolution and all Enlightenment philosophy to one single origin alone The first revolution had other aspects besides the economic. For it, the political was not a superstructure, it was the driving force. Nor was it a social class that provided the lever for the revolution but an "estate," the commoners, the bourgeoisie, who only much later became a social class when the working proletariat appeared on the scene. Democracy is a contemporary of the industrial era, but is a condition rather than a consequence of it.

Socialism, on the contrary, originated with the beginning of industrial development. Paradoxically, it seemed to gain a foothold only in countries with a feudal structure, Czarist Russia, eastern Europe, China, and Cuba. But the paradox is only apparent. The socialist revolution in those countries was so violent because the accumulated energies of the first and second revolutions exploded at the same time. Elsewhere it was effected more peacefully and progressively in a socializing process no less revolutionary.

New ideas, linked with new situations, came to light. To the extent that they are not those of either the socialist or the democratic revolution, they cannot be entirely dissociated from the mutation of the industrial era. Not by chance has the current contestation had to do with the "systems" and "bureaucracies" generated by industrial development, whether in planned economies or in economies based on supply and demand. A "society of consumerism" and the collectivist monolith seem equally "repressive" to the new generations. What has given them both birth if not the necessities of a monopolistic and centralized industrial society?

Admittedly, a global ferment is at work, particularly in the third world. Nobody would dream of maintaining that it is entirely due to contradictions in the economic structure. Neither the conflict between the generations nor most of the other recent confrontations have their source there. Neither the economic structure alone nor the political structure alone caused these eruptions. What is at work is something broader, something that has to do with the human makeup itself, with the relationship of human beings with their physical and social environment. Historical materalism, with its exclusive insistence on the forces and relations of production, offers an explanation of only one moment of contemporary history, its socialist phase.

Perhaps the recognition that the revolutions of our time revealed their first signs in the Reformation of the sixteenth century would give us a fuller understanding of their complexity. That last great religious controversy divided the Christian world well before the great secularist currents developed into Enlightenment philosophy, dialectical materialism, and the most recent controversies of our day. Admittedly, this heritage could provide a supplementary proof for the materialistic interpretation of history. Max Weber's theses on the role of Protestantism in the development of capitalism and, therefore, of industrial society, are familiar. They have often been considered as the antithesis of Marxist theory because they point to a religious factor as a critical element in historical evolution. But they also let it be understood that economic development has been conditioned by a modification in religious consciousness, a view not too far from the Marxist analysis. The historical mutation set off by development is more than a screen on which successive revolutionary ideologies are projected. The consciousness that gave them birth was not restricted to mere awareness of development and its inherent contradictions. Liberal democracy corresponded with an early stage of development when new energies, creative of new techniques, had to be allowed to express themselves. Socialization in both planned and market economies correlated with a more advanced phase of development, when it proved necessary to coordinate productive energies that had become anarchic and a cause of confrontation between social classes. And when the controls of monopoly and centralization themselves apparently became alienating, new ideas of a cultural revolution flared up.

To acknowledge that fact is not to fall into a rigidly materialistic interpretation of history. It means simply reporting how people, as they move forward in their ineluctable search for greater humanization, try to overcome the successive obstacles that the development of an industrial society has placed in their way and how they attempt to control the really formidable forces unleashed by scientific and technological discoveries. What could be less materalistic than the conviction that human beings are to triumph over the many contradictions that occur in the creative process, which they cannot accept because they are inhuman and not a definitive source of freedom? Is it by chance that the sciences and the methods of the sciences themselves, and all the revolutions issuing from their progress, were born in a Christian world, which made them possible because it freed them from the shackles of cosmological religions and because it has an essential faith in human beings in all their dimensions?

The third-world revolution, because three great revolutions meet and merge in it, bears within it the hope of humanity's final triumph in the historical mutation in which it is caught up.

## The First Revolution

The socialist revolution sometimes makes us lose sight of the importance of what the first revolution won. In reality, its timeliness is obvious, as the great socialists are the first to acknowledge.[2] When writing of the triumphs of the first revolution, it is customary to designate them, with a nuance of contempt, as "formal liberties" in contrast to the "real liberties" of the second revolution. But no matter whether or not socialists call them formal, these liberties seem particularly precious in the eyes of our contemporaries, as we are aware if we think about the powerful protests leveled at governments that attempt to limit them. They have become the immediate *givens* of contemporary consciousness. We have simply lost sight of the fact that they are new.

Let it suffice to recall, even summarily, the content of the famous "declaration of the rights of man," so characteristic of the first revolution.

Power belongs by right to no person. It is delegation by the people and is essentially provisional and revocable. The will of the "nation," a new concept issuing from the Revolution, is freely expressed by universal suffrage. It is true that as the revolution initiated it, franchised suffrage was limited to taxpayers, and therefore, to the well-to-do.

The days of 1848 would be needed to establish universal suffrage. Even then, only half of the human family were franchised.

Only in the twentieth century did women win the right to vote. But that delay only served to make the importance and timeliness of the new ideas that much more evident.

Every individual enjoys freedom of opinion, of speech, of religion. Parties have the right to establish themselves and can aspire to power by obtaining a majority in free elections. Under these conditions the right to overturn the government is a fundamental right. Power is to be exercised according to constitutional laws determined by the nation.

No adult person can exercise power over another adult person: a principle that put an end to a complex web of personal statutes that constituted the feudal world and its servitudes. Every modern feminist challenge is covered in that assertion.

An individual can be condemned only after a public trial and under laws that are not retroactive. The home is inviolable. Torture is abolished.[3]

The right of every nation to self-determination is recognized: the third world was born of that new awareness.

These principles have changed the world. It is true that they often remain a dead letter. But their violation provokes conscientious protest and that is new. The socialist world, even when it proclaims "the dictatorship of the proletariat," respects them or at least their form. The rite of elections is still celebrated, the majority is still appealed to, public trials continue to unroll. Nor are fascist dictatorships, whether military or populist, any more able to abstract from these principles. "Formal liberties" they are perhaps, if that means that they do not define everything encompassed in freedom, but not if it means that humankind in general considers them nothing but a form. On the contrary, people attribute to them a value that seems to grow as they are increasingly belittled.

These liberties were new. The *Ancien Régime* had had a presentiment of them but they were in no way acknowledged. To give one example, everybody took for granted the torture of criminals before the revolution; no one questioned it. Torture goes on today but it brings a protest from conscientious people all over the world and in a number of countries it has been altogether abolished. That we can call revolution.

There is no question of proving the first revolution a complete success. Its failures have been flagrant. It may be that democracy is a highly artificial state; historically, it has never lasted for long. In any case, it is a state much to be desired,[4] judging by the violent movements stirred up by the abolition of democratic liberties. But are people who enjoy them or who want to enjoy them sufficiently conscious of the first condition of any democracy: that each individual and each group must be capable of abiding by norms for the common good and of not abusing their liberties? If not, democracy turns into anarchy. The liberties of democracy are a great good and they have to be merited.

If a name must be given to the first revolution perhaps it could be called *libertarian-humanitarian*. Its achievements are articulated around the idea of liberty. Even today the word "liberty" still retains the political connotation conferred upon it by the first revolution. No more revolutionary idea exists than the assertion that, in opposition to all discrimination and the arbitrary will of princes and governments, both things and human beings have natures wherein norms for existence are found inscribed.

Yet man is an individual. His liberties are individual liberties. A new revolution is at hand.

## Capitalism

Starting from its own legitimate principles, every revolution engenders its opposite.

Nothing is more contrary to the principal ideas of the first revolution than capitalism. Nothing is more logical than socialism when viewed in the perspectives thrown open by Enlightenment philosophy. Very often, the prophets of democracy have had a presentiment of it. All we need do is to recall the famous condemnation of private property penned by Jean-Jacques Rousseau in a work of his youth.[5]

Every revolution is apt to be taken over by the social form in which it is worked out, and so it gives rise to its own contradiction. The people made the revolution but "the people" were the bourgeoisie, and the bourgeoisie, during the early years of the industrial era, became a class. With that, a new conflict broke out and a new revolution was proclaimed. Here we have the reason why capitalism, no matter how much it contradicts the principles of the first revolution, is also its fruit.

We need to analyze the dialectical process at work here. It consists not in logical abstraction but in concrete reality.

At this point, nothing seems more legitimate than the affirmation of human nature in opposition to the arbitrary action of governments. The notion of a natural and therefore universal law binding all alike belongs to the conceptual matrix of the revolution. But wait—and watch that idea turn against itself. When the proletariat workers arrive on the scene, any attempt to make social laws was blocked for a long time, by defining them as categorizing or "classifying." The first social law in France had to await the year 1848. And what did the law legislate? It prohibited factories from employing children under eight years of age and from having children less than twelve work more than eight hours a day! A law had become necessary for that. Yet it met with long resistance; to some minds it seemed to contradict a fundamental principle of the revolution

As the law is general, the republic is one and indivisible—another principle of the revolution. Only the nation and the people who comprise it exist. Any association of more than twenty persons is forbidden by penal code. No professional group, whether permanent or temporary, was to be tolerated. In promulgating this prohibition, the men of the revolution had in mind destroying the aristocratic and clerical "estates," reducing society to a single "estate." They also thought that they would do away with the absurd way in which the feudal lords, great and small, had carved up the country among themselves. Finally, they had a hazy notion that the corporations and their excessive regulations were obstructing new production techniques and so they put up a fight against them. Their really productive thoughts became pernicious when they were erected as a barrier against worker associations by which men sought to defend their "alleged common interests."[6] France had to mark time until the law of May 25, 1864 authorized associations and the law of March 21, 1884 granted the right to form trade unions. In general, the very idea of a regional or social structure was violently attacked beforehand. Nothing is more tragic than the delayed response that history makes to an idea.

Against the abuse of power and the accumulated wealth of monarchs and feudal lords, monasteries and clergy, and corporation heads, the revolution also proclaimed economic liberty. The newly conceived political economy of the Physiocrats in France and of Adam Smith in England urged it to take that direction. The right of property was an inviolable revolutionary principle that led to a re-partition of the land and a redistribution of the wealth of the "former" aristocracy and clergy. Yet on the basis of that principle and in flagrant contradiction to it, individuals were installed as absolute monarchs over their property. Any intervention by the public powers was condemned. Within that prohibition lay the seeds of great social and economic crises to come. In this case, as in others, the inertia of a principle, no matter how legitimate it was to begin with, converts it into an obstacle to progress.

Capitalism arose wholly from inertia of this kind. It achieved unquestionable miracles: we owe it our industrial development, but it brought in its train an unbearable hell, the misery of the proletarian workers and great economic crises and disasters. Private property that is not needed for the work or subsistence of the individual, that consists in savings or profits from production set up as "capital" is real oppression and disruption, since it admits of no other law than the rule of profit and recognizes no bonds either with the work which gives it its fruitfulness or with society in general. It is a reality that invades the social organism like cancer and serves as a source from which the socialist revolution stems.

*The Second Revolution*

As the first revolution rose up against the feudal world, the second undertook to do battle against capitalism.

Its conquests, too, are new and the modern mind attributes great value to them, no longer giving primacy to political but to economic or "real"—that is, material—liberties. What is proclaimed is the right of the individual and his family to live—to have food, clothing, and housing, which means the right to remunerative employment, to have access to the good things of a new world: education, information, culture, sport, leisure. And, beyond that, the right to means with which to meet adversity: sickness, disability, old age. But what socialism holds as first and foremost is that individuals enjoy these rights *as equals.* Socialism puts greater emphasis on equality than on freedom. To preserve equality, it will not hesitate to centralize and unify at the risk of destroying liberties. It may be defined as *egalitarian-unitarian:* egalitarian because what matters most is that all have equal opportunities in all domains: unitarian because of a double imperative of (1) high productivity—so that the new liberties be truly "real"—and (2) social leveling that results in an overall reinforcement of centralized power.

The idea of a highly productive society in which all share in a common condition, a society, therefore, in which property is no longer a source of privilege and power, is also a part of the conceptual matrix of socialism.

*A higher standard of living.* Every socialist system aspires to it. Nothing is less socialist than romanticizing poverty. The proletariat of the world will not be rescued from their misery without an enormous effort at production. If property is attacked, it is in proportion to the part it plays in keeping production from becoming an application of the collectivist rationale.

*A society without privileges.* Socialism prescribes a society in which a few people will no longer have means for solving their problems that are not available to everybody else; it decrees, as one of its fundamental stands, an interdependent society, in which one man has as much worth as another.

Some inequality will continue to exist. Efficiency cannot be had without it. Marx himself makes a distinction between "simple labor" and "multiple or skilled labor," thus giving a scientific basis for unequal wages. We have to be realistic. Men are motivated to work efficiently by receiving a fitting recompense. Nevertheless, inequality is not an end but a means. Society must always strive to prevent inequalities from leading to lasting inequities, a source of collective enmities. Privilege is systematized inequality grounded in a structure that makes possible every kind of reasonless gain as well as accumulation and monopolization. In both its political and economic aspects it must disappear. Property makes sense to the extent that it is a source of freedom and gives some autonomy to persons in a society. It makes no sense if it becomes a source of privilege. The abolition of privilege takes place inevitably with the establishment of some kind of unitarian society. All can then be equally protected against the great threats to existence: sickness and old age. All can have equal access to schools and universities and to all the good things that economic development makes available.

In other human areas it is the same. Society is seeking for collective security, to protect all against the risks of life and to give special help in the struggle to those who find themselves most deprived.

A number of examples demonstrate that such a transformation can be carried out well in different systems and with respect for personal liberties, such as choosing one's doctor or adopting inspiring educational ideals. But those who already have privileges are apt to do everything that they can to prevent it. In the name of principles which they believe are grounded in nature, they put their full strength into holding onto what they have and are—to keep from falling down into the common condition of other human beings. Their fear, their panic in the face of losing what they possess deprives them of any consciousness of what they could have in common with others in a new human solidarity. Certainly, every unitarian organization does involve danger and needs more collaboration from those who have, to a high degree, a feeling for personal liberties.

*A society without private powers.* That means a society in which property is not a source of power. Power belongs to the public. There is no reason why a person who owns capital should carry more weight in ordinary decisions than the person in the street. Capital adds nothing to one's ability to discern the common good.

Presupposed then is the destruction of that "social prepotency"[7] which the propertied arrogate to themselves in both the national and the international spheres, and the leveling of classes so that economically powerful people can no longer interfere directly in government decisions. Modern means of communication have made available to them a whole arsenal for influencing public opinion. Conscience has already condemned national oligarchies and economic imperialism. As realities, however, they continue to exist and hold on all the more tenaciously when their existence goes unrecognized and unacknowledged. People and organizations are not subjectively but objectively imperialist.

To control and obliterate the powers that accompany privileges and so prevent their influence from expanding against all logic is not easy to do. Before a whole world of power, whether open or hidden, is brought down, it will keep on resisting with every means at its disposal, and it has many. Yet it is weak too because it has no defense against conscience.

Putting an end to private privileges and powers can be effected in different systems but presupposes putting economic control into the hands of authorities at the national and multinational level, an action with risks that do not diminish its urgency.

It also presupposes that in decision making at this level there must be present people who have no reserves, who have nothing to offer except their daily work to make a living, simple wage earners and, even more important, beyond them the great mass of the marginated. Against the pressures exerted by the favored classes, their interests must receive sufficient consideration. Unless these social categories have some kind of access to power, it is hardly possible that the struggle against the privileges and powers produced by wealth will be carried on with vigor enough to end them.

What the socialist revolution demands seems to be: a high standard of living, everybody sharing in a common condition, suppression of all forms of private power, planning, and participation in power by the most disadvantaged social categories. As these are met they lead to a unitarian organization of society and to the takeover of the economy by the public powers. To the exact extent to which the socialist revolution succeeds in doing that, it generates a new threat.

## "The System"

"The system" is an expression that crops up in countries called capitalist in which the process of socialization has not been imposed at a single stroke but is developing gradually without suppressing either private enterprise or the commodity market. In some cases, for example, in the countries of northern Europe, the leveling of material conditions has been sufficiently effected and private power has really been brought under control. In other places, on the contrary, the process of socialization, even while straining to raise the standard of living, allows enormous social contrasts and great private power to continue.

It is noteworthy, however, that even in the second instance, in the United States, for example, what is denounced is not exactly capitalism but a society of consumerism, a broader and entirely new idea. Protesting or, more exactly, contesting, is not aimed exclusively at privileges and monopolies; it strikes at something larger, at a "system" in which the criteria for an economic rationale and for high consumption dominate the whole of existence, even to the point of invading the most intimate recesses of private life.

Herbert Marcuse, among others,[8] has expressed the sudden awareness of this phenomenon.[9] It would indeed be rash to see it as just a traditional socialist or Marxist denunciation. As a matter of fact, the new "protesters" keep their distance from Marxism. In their criticism of capitalism new objections are put forward which concern not only capitalism as such but more generally the technocratic and bureaucratic organization of social existence within which people no longer live but have their living done for them, so that they have no possibility either of expressing themselves or of putting their mark on their own existence. Indeed, they cannot even find a refuge into which to retreat from the damage done to their social and physical environment by a triumphant industrial technology.

What demonstrates the unquestionable originality of this new attack is that it strikes at collectivism as much as at capitalism. In rationalized and monopolistic capitalist systems contestation takes the form of criticizing consumer societies. In socialist economies, the attack is aimed at the ruling bureaucracy, at "the Plan" in the economic sector and at "the Party" in the political. Basically both strikes are directed at the same thing. In each case, and for the young particularly, with their burning thirst for freedom, the world seems suffocating. The students who demonstrated in Paris during the memorable months of May and June 1968 were attacking the American type of capitalism as well as communism of the Soviet variety, a society of consumerism as well as a managed society.

*Consumer society.* Although capitalism today retains the same principles, it reveals little of what Marx and Engels denounced in nineteenth-century England, France, and Germany. It has allowed itself to be taken over by the very ideas that it then opposed; it has become centralized and socialized. In this new form it has also become the object of a new protest.

Present-day capitalism is concentrated. In a sense, it has accepted the lesson of socialism. Planning is a necessity.

But in capitalism, planning does not work in the same way as in collectivist economies. It is being carried out, but by industrial conglomerates. To face the technical, commercial, and financial problems which they must meet, their directors have formed enterprises into clusters linked together by personal bonds, frequently by reciprocal use of capital, and by agreements that amount to trusts in embryo. They aim at unity in profit making and in direction. Everything has been said about the considerable power that all this concentrates in a few hands and the danger that it represents to national and international life. But let us not forget the economic basis on which these fiefdoms were built. An isolated enterprise specializing in the manufacture of one product is unable to procure the information needed to make an estimate of the market and to reach canny decisions, and so it is too vulnerable. A group or cluster of enterprises can take risks, since it can compensate for failures in producing one line of commodities by successes in others. It can avail itself of the expensive means required by today's economy and technology. Through publicity it can mobilize broad public demands for its products. It achieves, privately, the planning that the public powers are not prepared to do or have no intention of undertaking. On the international plane, there is no public planning because no authority exists that could impose it; until now multinational corporations are the only form of economic organization. Concentration is not then an obedient response to the moves of interested manipulators, as is often said. It came about through necessity and, for that reason, European governments, for example, favor it for the time being, while trying to reduce its negative effects. Actually, in an industrial society it is the only means of meeting in a coherent way the problems posed by the technology of advanced production. Coordinated action can only be assured, enormous risks assumed, and vast amounts of information gathered by organizations of great power and great complexity. On the whole, capitalist "trusts" are small in comparison to socialist "trusts," each of which encompasses an entire branch of production in a subcontinent.

Present-day capitalism is, on the other hand, *socialized*. [10] The spread between income and wealth tends to diminish for various reasons: the twin action of progressive taxation on income (in cases where it is really working) and of pressure groups, especially the unions; competition (which often reduces profit margins in developed countries by pricing products reasonably). When prices are lowered, the profit margin goes down too. Financial losses and even bankruptcy may result—one way of cutting down incomes and fortunes and shortening the distance between the unequal capital holdings of different people. [11] Nationalization and expropriation are ultimate weapons that blot out whole sectors of an oligarchy. And the relative development of public investment removes from the private domain increasing portions of the economy.

Nonetheless, some profit taking continues that has no relationship whatever to any service rendered. Just as concentration has not been good for small businesses, so socialization has not always put an end to social contrasts; far from it. [12] Yet, from now on, privileges arise from a different source. Invested capital, with its attendant risks, is no longer the spring that usually yields considerable surplus value. Business is no longer the privileged place where surplus value is engendered. Nowadays income from invested capital comprises only a minimal part of national revenue.

When people work with their own capital, as is largely the case in agriculture, the crafts and trades, in small and average industries, and in the liberal professions, their incomes are not, save in exceptional cases, very high and are often lower than current salaries, especially when "social security"—which is not available to all—is taken into account. The wage differential is generally much greater in free than in planned economies and continues to be a permanent wellspring of inequalities. But the most questionable profits are still those which come from lucrative financial operations through the shrewd management of portfolios. For the big operators, the game is played almost without risk, whereas small investors lack the necessary information and leisure to perform well. Nothing good or useful is done for society and some fortunes are made by arbitrage, movements of capital that destroy the monetary equilibrium. Here we have extortion by a regime with revenues and fortunes kept free for speculative investments. Inequality is maintained by means of these lasting resources, all the more dangerous as they are difficult to reach.

Although socialized, capitalism today is still a locus for privileges. Being concentrated, it also creates power in private hands. Both of these factors have been the object of recent protests, chiefly in the third world. There profits on investments are higher than anywhere else. Multinational corporations, protected by their mother countries, exercise pressures that are increasingly resented by peoples who are throwing off the yoke of colonialism in every form.[13]

*Managed society.* If the new form of capitalism, consumer society, is called to account because it reduces the areas for individual and group freedom and initiative, the managed societies that are being built up in socialist countries through rigid planning are also taken to task and with equal violence by protesters. They comprise a part of a system within which centralization has been pushed so immeasurably further than in capitalist countries that it implies dictatorship. It also calls for a form of domination over satellite countries. Just as the French Revolution proclaimed the nation one and indivisible, at one stroke achieving the unification begun by great feudal lords and monarchs, so has the socialist revolution organized the economy into a single, indivisible entity, thus bringing to term the work undertaken by private economic powers.

In both cases, the result is the same. All decisions about production and consumption are imposed by authorities beyond the reach of any individual. Could the people have access to those high levels they would sow anarchy there. Both consumer and managed societies are the fruit of pursuing a single rationale to its extreme logical consequences.

Of all socialist ideas, "the Plan" has been the most indispensable. To be found as early as 1848 in *The Communist Manifesto,* it contains the seed for the whole system.

Through planning and organizing, the socialist process, whether reformist or revolutionary, has built up a world in which "economic" logic reigns supreme and determines existence. The Marxist analysis, centered on the development of the forces of production and new relations in production, gives the edifice a particularly rigid armature. Everywhere the same consequences of the primacy of the economy are in evidence. The socialized or socialist world is constructed like an immense and rigorously disciplined factory. Like the managed society, capitalist consumer society is fashioned in line with the logic of industry.

Is the recent contestation that challenges both societies capable of creating another world? Is it leading to another revolution?

*The Third Revolution*

During the last ten years signs of revolt have been multiplying everywhere. In the universities, the family, civil society, and the Church, crises have shaken what before seemed most stable.

It is easy to point out the heterogeneous character of these manifestations. The cultural revolution in China is, from many points of view, the antithesis of rebellion in the West. In the third world, Latin America, black Africa, the Arab world, and Asia are not at the same stage of evolution. In addition, national differences on each of these continents are considerable. But was not the world of the eighteenth and nineteenth centuries even more heterogeneous? Yet first Enlightenment philosophy and then socialist ideology spread without any respect for frontiers. Is there no relationship between these earlier manifestations and the revolts which have been breaking out everywhere during the last ten years? Are these not signs of a third revolution?

All eras have experienced upheavals. That being so, it is tempting to conclude that what is happening is nothing new. Nevertheless, it seems justifiable to conclude that the world today has entered into a period just as decisive as the two preceding revolutions.

The most evident aspects of the recent contestation are negative. Those participating in it know best what they *do not* want.

The target is "repression" as exercised by the system in power and in any form that tends to reduce the area in which people act freely: it is the violence of power, "institutionalized violence."[14] The power category against which opposition is directed is, above all, technocracy, "the technostructure," to use a term suggested by Galbraith.[15] The expert and the technician, because they unconsciously serve the established order, are open to question. The scholars are, too, to the extent that they pride themselves on their knowledge as a privilege. People are rising up against repression wherever it shows up and in whatever system, capitalist or socialist. They are also setting themselves against prepotency, too much power in cadres within enterprises, parental authority in a family, the unequal status of women, the hierarchy of the Church. Even God has become an object of contestation, and "theologies" are erected on the notion of the death of God.[16] It might well be asked whether the "cultural revolution" is not, after all, a revolt against the father figure,[17] whatever its avatars may be, the fountainhead of all social prohibitions that keep people from living their own lives. In any case, any analysis based on the consideration of "production reports" is not abolished by the protesters but just completely passed over. Neither the fetishism of commodities nor of wealth matters any more; what does matter is the fetishism of the institution and the structure as such. Nothing in Marxism would lead anybody to anticipate such a shift in critque.

Contemporary contestation separates into several currents.

Some preach violence but no longer from a traditional Marxist view, for communism condemns violence that is only an anarchical explosion with no real possibility of overturning the established order and substituting another actual structure in its place. Others, on the other hand, believe in nonviolence, in active nonviolence that experiences no hesitation in having recourse to illegal but unarmed demonstrations, exposing themselves to injury and reprisals, in this way putting pressure on those in power to modify or even reverse their decisions. Lastly, a third group, who have no political pretensions, simply seek to set up a world apart, where human relationships can be completely free. The young are not simply looking for an escape through drugs and free love, they want to be left to live in a world of their own and are astonished at the aggressive way in which society has reacted to such an innocent attempt.

Yet, can a new society be built upon a contestation as radical as this?

As long as the cultural revolution is limited to protest, it negates itself by succeeding. To protest, to oppose, demands "a system," "an order," to be attacked. Contestation feeds on what it destroys. The day when it achieves its objective it no longer has any reason to exist. When that happens, it is inclined to preach permanent revolution, thinking that revolution will never really succeed and perhaps unconsciously wanting it to fail so that it can continue to survive. Its vision of society is radically pessimistic. It makes no pretense of founding a new society: it is, then, not a revolution but simply a revolt.[18] In Edgar Morin's words, it remains a faceless revolution.[19]

However, this purely anarchical stance is far from accounting for all the new trends. In the face of the increasing difficulties met by liberal as well as socialist democracies in establishing a free world, signs of a new image of society are becoming perceptible.

What is new is, first of all, the pursuit of a qualitative rather than a quantitative change in life: the fundamental dynamisms of social life that people want to attain. Among active minorities, a strong desire has emerged to choose a lifestyle far removed from all conformism, in the sincerity and spontaneity of "a commune," where all are free to be themselves. At the very core of

Marxism new accents are detectable. Appeal is made for inner transformation, for sincerity and conviction. There is no question of eliminating an adversary; he is to be converted. "Those who have committed errors must, above all, be educated and reeducated." "It is strictly forbidden to extract a confession under duress and then make it authentic."[20] Egoism becomes the enemy, a capital sin, and sacrifice for the people's cause, a cardinal virtue.

Something else that is new is the attempt to face and break up massive power, not by denying the necessity for power (at least in those instances where contestation does not descend into pure anarchy) but by bringing together the power of the masses and performing the difficult task of elaborating the complex structures through which confrontation can be translated into dialogue. In this regard, it is significant that in China[21] students, intellectuals, and the upper echelons of employees are obliged to return to basics in order to learn, in a long symbiosis with peasants and workers, who the people are and what aspirations they have. In Cuba, too, students and employees must work in the fields on Sunday. Sometimes we hear talk of establishing "labor power" or "peasant power" or "student power," that is, "popular power" in a sense that no longer has to do with the democratic or socialist revolutions. Beyond these expressions, debatable because they seem to have in mind creating other parallel powers, some new realities emerge—worker-management, farming community, autonomous university. These experiments are certainly still rejected by official Marxism. But is not the Chinese "commune" an attempt to restore power to the masses? Contestation, insofar as it is not satisfied with just destroying, is a quest for community: nothing is less collectivistic or individualistic than to essay that. The elaboration of a new world is founded on the affirmation of people as responsible beings, who work out their own destiny; it includes a plan for basic communities, without which that affirmation would be meaningless. The new liberty is not pure spontaneity put into a formula; nor is it created by a mass situation in which every individual is lost in anonymity. It consists in a more radical freedom that calls for an organic and flexible structure wherein roles differ but do not form a hierarchy.

What is novel, then, is the idea of a revolution that is never to be finished, that has to be taken up again and again and again, not a revolution in which new structures constantly replace the old, in a kind of unending cataclysm, but one in which the human spirit keeps communicating to structures the meaning of their relationships to the whole scheme of things and tries to do this through a new dynamism in the group. The paradox of the third revolution lies, perhaps, in that, unlike the two preceding revolutions, it is not done once and for all. New contradictions keep on cropping up to endanger it. With a stroke of the pen, personal statutes can be abolished and replaced by universal suffrage, and economic privileges can be wiped out by expropriation. No one can, at one fell swoop and for all time, invent a new relationship between power and the body of the people or a new rapport between the institution and the individual.

Pushing schematizing to the extreme, it could perhaps be said that if the first revolution had liberty in view; and the second, equality; the third seeks for the brotherhood that the first two failed to produce.[22]

## The Movement of May–June, 1968 in France

Was it brotherhood that students and workers were looking and longing for in the historic days of May and June 1968 when they rose up against "the system" and paraded effigies of Mao and Che Guevara through the streets? Their movement formed no part of third-world revolution but the third world played a role in their movement, unquestionably fed, as it was, by new ideas. "The stake in the struggle is not just the appropriation of profit but control of the power to decide, to influence, to manipulate."[23] "Their undertaking was anti-authoritarian and pro freedom, pro community, and pro spontaneity."[24] The May movement was "a new form of class struggle . . . a conflict not of a directly economic character."[25]

There was aspiration for a new pedagogy, a new education. "What took place touches our concepts of society in all its forms. Fundamentally, it concerns the pedagogical relationship as it bears on educational institutions, on families, and, more broadly, on the rapport between group staff and members, boards of directors and those whom they direct, governments and governed. In other words, it has to do with every situation in which relationship *with others,* such as pupils, children, is effected within the scope of a *common* language, but where, however, those partners who hold *particular* meanings are assigned positions of power."[26] To "reinstate" the use of certain terms such as *class struggle* and *resistance* ought not to be done as it would be "misleading and plainly inadequate in the new situation."[27]

The May movement was deployed on the same terrain as the Chinese cultural revolution[28] but contradicted it on some fundamental points. In the Marxist context there is nothing like the sexual liberation pursued by Western youth.[29] The austere life, the discipline demanded and, above all, the blind obedience to orders from on high, which remain the norm even for the Red Guards, would not find acceptance in the Western youth movements.[30] In the new Chinese revolutionary committees the young in no way fill top roles; they must prove themselves before having access to functions reserved for adults. A great distance still separates the Chinese revolution and the anarchical eruptions of Western youth. In the former, severe disturbances do occur and much confusion results from factions so rife that it is sometimes impossible to tell friends from enemies. Yet, even at that, all remains under the control and undisputed authority of a great leader.

Between the two views—the one of the Chinese cultural revolution, the other of Western contestations—some identity is detectable. In both cases, the commune is considered the basis for the new society. For that reason, the third revolution has a new way of defining freedom and man in his social environment. The new definitions are not the same as those given by the first and second revolutions. Just as the socialist revolution was already explicit in some statements of the democratic revolution and implicit in some of its principles (as Jean Jaurès would have put it. "Socialism is logical democracy"), so it can be claimed that the cultural revolution is Marxist because it is implicit in Marxism or by appealing from current Marxism to "original" Marxism, or from a Marxism of history to a Marxism of faith. But in the writings of Marxists and of Marx himself not one word is to be found in defense of men's freedom in face of the rigid economic and political apparatus built up as a logical consequence of Marxist doctrine. Just as the socialist revolution was needed to break down capitalist preconceptions of the scheme of things, a post-socialist revolution is needed to create some new quality, some new structure, that will allow people to express themselves in another way than by losing themselves in an anonymous collectivity.

The third revolution poses two questions. The first relates to the Western contestation. "If, as a conscientious demand, it fails to organize, to insert itself, as a strategy, in the network of national forces in order to effectively change the system, it will not reform, it will not revolutionize, it will dwindle away in going off to other countries or choosing exile at home, taking refuge in vagabondage or in ineffectual ideological resistance."[31] The second question relates to the Chinese cultural revolution. Will it really be able to break out of the absolute dictatorship in which it continues to operate?

*Revolution in the Third World*

To find an answer to this twofold question, many turn to the third world. Does not the future of humanity lie in the forces of liberation at work there? Is not hope for the world to be found in those who have no hope?[32]

If such an expectation does, in fact, exist, it can only find realization through long-drawn-out, enormous, and creative effort, for neither the Western nor the socialist world can supply the young nations with all the elements for the kind of model that human aspirations seem to be calling for.

Springing up in the context of a world divided into two solid blocs, the capitalist bloc under the undisputed hegemony of the United States and the socialist bloc in equally strict dependence on the U.S.S.R., the third world is having no easy time of it finding its place in a world where these two dominant giants are now under violent attack. The entrance of China into the concert of nations, its conflict with the U.S.S.R., the appearance of new great powers, Europe, Japan and soon, perhaps, India and Brazil, have created an entirely new situation.

Even before the recent multiplication of "blocs," diversity among third world countries was extreme. It makes no sense to put together into "one world" Latin America, freed from colonialism a hundred and fifty years ago, deeply stamped by democratic ideas, and already relatively well on its way in the process of industrialization, with Africa, just emerging out of a colonial era and shaken by political struggles caused by tribal as often as by ideological reasons, and with Asia, still more diverse, with each "subregion" asking to be considered by itself—all this, without counting the still developing countries in southern Europe.

In the face of the great industrial powers, the only bond among third-world countries is their poverty, caused by the degree of their economic underdevelopment and their division into minute political entities. Does this make the third world a place of predilection for a third revolution? Is the third world prepared for a revolution in the exact meaning of the term, that is, is it ready for a historic change, a radical, complete, general, and irreversible mutation in mental and social structures, a revolution that would not be in line with preceding models and would avoid both the anarchy of Western contestation and the dictatorship of the Chinese cultural revolution?[33]

Of the three continents, Latin America would seem to be most nearly ready for such a discovery. The crisis there is more violent than anywhere else, perhaps because the three revolutionary currents are merging there. In a number of ways, the personal character of dependent relationships is still at a feudal stage. The relation of the peasant tenant to the owner of the great estate remains one of near servitude. But where industry has developed, capitalism, national and international, reigns supreme. And already signs of a reaction against technocracy and bureaucracy are making themselves felt. Thus, fighting on three fronts at the same time, against the remnants of a feudal world, against capitalism, and against "the system," the Latin American continent could be closer than any other to a "liberaton " that would serve as a reference point for humanity.

On one condition, however, that it is able to break free from contestation for its own sake and avoid becoming a monolith of uniformity and conformity, so that it can conceive and bring to birth both the quality and the structure of that liberty that must be characteristic of the new society that is a-borning.

No single analysis is going to provide us with an answer. That will take reflection and wisdom, which science alone cannot provide.

## NOTES

1. In the seventeenth century, with Cromwell, the rebellion of Parliament against the monarchy showed the first signs of revolution in Great Britain and the advent of that liberal ideology which has made England what it is.

2. The importance of the revolution won by the bourgeoisie against the feudal world is in no way minimized by Marx and Engels in *The Communist Manifesto*.

3. For a study of these laws as defined in France, see Georges Burdeau, *Les libertés publiques* (Paris: Librairie Générale de Droit et Jurisprudence, 1972).

4. The oft-quoted saying of Churchill has it that democracy is the worst kind of political system—with the exception of all the others.

5. "A Discourse upon the Origin and Foundation of the Inequality among Mankind," *French and English Philosophers: Descartes, Rousseau, Voltaire, Hobbes* (New York: Harvard Classics, P.F. Collier, 1910), pp. 216–217: "Let us unite . . . to secure the weak from oppression, restrain the ambitious and secure to every man the possession of what belongs to him.

"Much fewer words of this kind were sufficient to draw in a parcel of rustics whom it was an easy matter to impose upon. . . .

"Such was, or must have been had man been left to himself, the origin of society and its laws, which increased the fetters of the weak and the strength of the rich; irretrievably destroyed natural liberty; changed an artful usurpation into an irrevocable title; and for the benefit of a few ambitious individuals subjected the rest of humankind to perpetual labour, servitude, and misery." See Michel Launay, *Jean-Jacques Rousseau, écrivain politique* (Cannes: C.E.L., 1971), which brings out the originality of Rousseau's ideas. The outcome of fifteen years of teaching, this book offers us a new image of the political writer by situating him in relation to his whole literary output and his personal history. In his article on political economy in the *Encyclopédie,* Rousseau has a statement that expresses an entirely different view from the one above: "Certainly the right of private property is the most sacred of all a citizen's rights, and, in some ways, more important than freedom itself" (p. 220). All the ambiguity of the first revolution can be found in these two contradictory assertions. Launay's work contains a complete, up-to-date bibliography on Rousseau's works.

6. This is the statement of the penal code (article 29). See also art. 291, 414, 415.

7. Pope Pius XI's words are: "The war against private property has also abated more and more. In such a way that nowadays it is not really the possession of the means of production which is attacked but that type of social rulership, which in violation of all justice, has been seized and usurped by the owners of wealth." *Quadragesimo Anno,* no. 114, *Five Great Encyclicals* (New York: Paulist Press, 1939), p. 156.

8. John Kenneth Galbraith, for example, in his work *The New Industrial State,* 2nd rev. ed. (Boston: Houghton Mifflin, 1971).

9. Chiefly in his (Herbert Marcuse's) book *One Dimensional Man* (Boston: Beacon Press, 1964).

10. On this subject see Georges Lefranc, *Le socialisme réformiste* (Paris: P.U.F., 1971), in which he studies socialist ventures in western Europe during the last half century.

11. In some cases, in Sweden, for example, the leveling process has been pushed too far. Nowadays to speak of "capitalism" without making any distinctions has no meaning.

12. John Kenneth Galbraith reminds us of "the continuing scandal of great deprivation amidst the great wealth of the United States" and thinks that "increased production is not the final test of social achievement, the solvent for all social ills." *The Affluent Society,* 2nd ed. (Boston: Houghton Mifflin, 1969), p. xxvi.

13. Salvador Allende, president of Chile, made himself the spokesman for the third world in his address to the United Nations, December 4, 1972. Previously, at the meeting of the United Nations Conference on Trade and Development in Santiago, Chile, Philippe de Seynes, United Nations assistant secretary general, remarked that exchanging views as to the best way of making another start on helping development would have meaning only when the exact role of the multinational corporations was frankly studied. *Le Monde,* December 6, 1972.

14. This expression, adopted by the bishops of Latin America meeting at Medellín, Colombia, in 1968 had already been used by Herbert Mar-

cuse, *Five Lectures: Psychoanalysis, Politics and Utopia* (Boston: Beacon Press, 1970), p. 89.

15. Galbraith, *New Industrial State*, p.59.

16. Anglican Bishop John A.T. Robinson made the kick-off in this theological game with a work that popularized the ideas of the Protestant theologians Paul Tillich and Dietrich Bonhoeffer. See *Honest to God* (Philadelphia: Westminister, 1963).

17. How can we help recalling Christ's words, "You must call no one on earth your father" (Matt. 23:9)?

18. This is the thesis of Jacques Ellul in his *De la révolution aux révoltes* (Paris: Calmann-Lévy, 1972).

19. Edgar Morin, *Mai 1968: la brèche* (Paris: Fayard, 1968), pp.63 ff.

20. *Report to the Ninth Congress of the Chinese Communist Party*, by Lin Piao (Peking: Foreign Language Press, 1969), pp. 54, 56.

21. Ibid., p. 57.

22. This is the view of Robert Bosc, *Le tiers-monde dans la politique internationale* (Paris: Aubier, 1968), pp. 16 ff. The constitution *Gaudium et spes* suggests this rapprochement by speaking of "the values of human dignity, brotherhood and freedom" (no. 39,) *The Documents of Vatican II*, ed. Walter Abbott and Joseph Gallagher (New York: Guild Press, 1966), p. 237.

23. Alain Touraine, *Le communisme utopique*, 2nd ed. (Paris: Seuil, 1972), p. 11.

24. Ibid., p. 12.

25. Ibid., p. 15. In an epilogue to the second edition, Touraine makes some distinctions regarding these evaluations and returns to a more classical stand: "The worker movement is still the most important protest force." But he continues to hold to the essence of his analysis: "In the May movement new themes were introduced and new players appeared on the scene."

26. Michel de Certeau, *La prise de parole* (Paris: Desclée de Brouwer, 1968). p. 48.

27. Ibid., p. 74

28. This subject will be treated in more detail in Chapter 11, pp. 189 ff.

29. In China, men are strongly urged not to marry before thirty, women not before twenty-five. If contraceptives are being used, it is only within marriage; premarital relations are considered a disgrace.

30. Jacques Ellul bring this out clearly. The Red Guards obey both when they attack "revisionists" and when they receive the order to back off: their placards then disappear as if by magic. *De la révolution aux révoltes* (Paris: Calmann-Levy, 1972), pp. 175 ff.

31. De Certeau, *La prise de parole*, p. 36.

32. The saying of Walter Benjamin with which Herbert Marcuse closes his *One Dimensional Man* is well known: "It is only for the sake of those without hope that hope is given to us" (Boston: Beacon Press, 1964), p. 257.

33. Virgil Gheorgiu brings out how the third world is refusing to allow itself to be absorbed into "a factory society." "America has created a twentieth-century technological society modeled on Ford and General Motors factories. All civilized people, all citizens of that sort of civilization, are social counters, replaceable and interchangeable. With citizens of that kind, the social machine runs at full speed. However, in its expansion over the planet, America comes up against uncivilized people, human beings who are persons, that is, who are not a part of a whole but are each a whole in themselves. These uncivilized people have remained just as they were when they came from the hands of God, each one unique and irreplaceable. They are a danger to a social machine that can accept only uniform counters." Are not his reflections equally valid for a collectivist society? See *L'oeil américain* (Paris: Plon, 1972), p. 25.

# PART TWO

# A READING FROM THE GOSPEL

## The Political Dimension of the Faith

Although it may be difficult to establish any scientific proof to that effect, many reasons suggest that the revolutions of our era are linked to the shock created in the world by the proclamation of the gospel. The faith has a political dimension. It is not surprising then that political theologies are flourishing nowadays, theologies of liberation, or revolution, and even of violence. Regrettably, the sociological foundation on which these are based is sometimes insufficient, since they lack satisfactory analyses of the realities about which they want to theologize. It is also to be regretted that, for want of proper theological reflection, they are often identified with prevalent ideologies. Yet their significance cannot be denied. Through them, we have been made conscious of the importance of the political field in human existence and the need for the Church to be involved there.

Before looking into the strong points of a Christian community of thought in this area and the perspectives for action thus opened up, which will be the subject of Part Four, we need to establish the relationship between the Church and the world on the political plane. How did Christ and those who followed him bear themselves in the midst of the revolutions of their times? What relationship has salvation, the object of faith, with liberation, the object of these revolutions?

# IV

# JESUS AND THE POLITICS
# OF HIS TIME

Underlying the current debates in political theology is a certain representation of Jesus' role in the political struggles of his epoch and region. It seems best to meet this in a straightforward way. Of course the Christian community is not Christ and, furthermore, the situation in Palestine in the time of Tiberius is not the same as in the twentieth-century world. Yet Jesus did live and speak in a time of political troubles, a fact that is not without importance for the question posed here. Thanks to recent studies,[1] it is now possible to come closer to the reality of those distant days. It has been found that the environment in which Jesus lived and preached makes us think of many aspects of our own. Peace reigned in Palestine and in the Roman world. There were no wars but there did exist reactions, some clandestine and some violent, of an oppressed people who resisted their integration into the empire. In Galilee particularly, resistance against Roman occupation had been organized. What position, then, was Jesus to take in the midst of upheavals that awakened people's dreams of Palestinian movements?

Now for some dates. Tiberius reigned from A.D. 14 to 37. The most probable date of Jesus' birth lies between the years 7 and 5 B.C. Herod died in the year 4 and the division of his kingdom followed. Herod Antipas ruled over Galilee and Perea from the years 4 to 39. Caiaphas was high priest from the years 18 to 36. Beginning in the year 6, a Roman procurator presided in Jerusalem, Palestine being at that time under a protectorate regime. Pontius Pilate, a hard man, was procurator from 26 to 36, when his career came to an abrupt end.

According to most hypotheses, the baptism of Jesus would have taken place about January in 28 and his death in April in 30.

His public life is thought to have lasted little more than two years, two years that would change the course of history and the face of the earth.

It was a tragic time for Palestine, ending in the siege of Jerusalem and the destruction of the temple in the year 70, "the disastrous abomination, of which the prophet Daniel spoke, set up in the Holy Place" (Matt. 24:15). The whole country deeply resented the humiliation of the Roman conquest, the oppression that followed, and its material expression in the tribute to Caesar. The tribute, a tax, was a sign of submission: Roman citizens did not pay it.

Revolt smoldered and at times flared up. In confronting the occupying power, the country was divided into two opposing political factions. The Herodians and Sadducees represented the dominant class and accepted Caesar's yoke. The high priests took the same position, allying themselves with those in power. The Pharisees, devoted to the Law, did not submit to the Roman yoke. They were "the pure," the resisters.

Attempts were made, especially in Galilee, to organize a secret underground resistance force. It seems that these terrorists were called Zealots and were also known as "Galileans." Luke (13:1) alludes to "the Galileans whose blood Pilate had mingled with that of their sacrifices." Shortly before Jesus, Judas "the Galilean" had been arrested and crucified. He had his head-quarters at Sepporis, above five kilometers north of Nazareth, called for sedition, and advocated refusing to pay tribute to Caesar. His movement was both political and religious: all actions done to please the masters of this world were to be condemned, since there is but one God. So Judas the Galilean took his stand on the great Exodus proclamation which Jesus would later invoke when repulsing a political temptation.

It is not impossible that Jesus had among his disciples men of the underground, Simon the Zealot in particular. Perhaps Barabbas and "the two others" crucified with Jesus were terrorists. However, that is nothing more than a hypothesis.

Along with political factions, purely religious movements also existed. At the monastery of Qumran, and doubtless elsewhere, lived the Essenes, gathered together in communities of poverty and celibacy. The figure of John the Baptist stands out: in him are brought together the Saints of the Last Days in view of the final kingdom of the Promise.

In this context, this distinct local situation, Jesus appears. Many things that happen in his life are understandable only in relation to these events. What position is Jesus going to take? Among many others, three particular incidents stand out.

*1. The Temptation in the Desert (Matt. 4:1–11)* Here we are certainly in the presence of an early account.[2] It would be difficult to conceive that it was invented by the early Christian communities.

Jesus is faced with a choice. At that moment in his life, a double expectation of his people is brought to bear upon him: that he be the Messiah, a political leader, a role sustained and promoted in clandestine movements, and that he be the suffering servant, an ideal cherished and fostered in the prophecy of Isaiah and a subject of constant meditation in the Jewish religious communities. Messianism had taken on a very temporal guise among the people in general and a very spiritual form among the few, like old Simeon and the prophetess Anna, both capable of recognizing the coming of salvation in the weakness of a baby. There was nothing political in the epiphany that made Simeon exclaim, "My eyes have seen . . ." (Luke 2:30).

Then the temptation supervenes, a threefold temptation. Three times Jesus is tempted to place his divine mission and power at the service of a wordly enterprise. Three times he is called Israel's one and only, Satan addressing him as "Son of God." His triple temptation is in fact the same temptation that his people had once experienced in the desert and his answers explicitly refer to the great revelations of Sinai.

After forty days of fasting, Jesus is hungry. Satan suggests to him, "If you are the Son of God, tell these stones to turn into loaves." Jesus answers, "Man does not live on bread alone but on every word that comes from the mouth of God."

The second temptation is more insidious. Carried up to the top of the temple, Jesus is enticed to throw himself down. Nothing will happen to him because he is the one about whom it is said, "He will put you in his angels' charge, and they will support you on their hands in case you hurt your foot against a stone." And Jesus replies, "You must not put the Lord your God to the test." To tempt God is to test him, to demand a sign from him, to know "if it is true," to put conditions on the love of one who loves without conditions, all those implications of which the people who put God to the proof in the desert were well aware.

The third temptation is the one with most relevance to the present subject. This time Jesus is on a very high mountain and the devil shows him all the kingdoms of the world and their glory and says to him, "I will give you all these if you fall at my feet and worship me." And Jesus answers, "Be off, Satan, for scripture says, 'You must worship the Lord your God, and serve him alone.' "

Judas the Galilean incited people to resist and revolt against Rome. You cannot adore Caesar, he would explain, for you must worship the one true God. The temptation that Jesus explicitly rejects is not to head a sedition, nor is it the temptation of the Herodians, to ally himself with the occupying power. Instead, it is the temptation to go the way of the satanic condition: to be worshiped, to attain a glory like Caesar's, to become, like him, the deified master of the universe, "the Son of God" indeed but in a perverted way. The suggestion against which Jesus directly addresses himself is that, clothed in the full power of his divinity, he do what he is able to do, overcome the world and make himself adored instead of being the humiliated and suffering servant foretold by Isaiah. A diabolic counterfeit, indeed, for it would presuppose that he prostrate himself before Satan and exchange his authentic divinity for a demoniac divinity. The answer given by Jesus would be devoid of meaning if the political temptation had not taken this form.

At that moment the destiny of humanity is at stake. In the crowning conflict with the tempter, Jesus chooses to adore God, that is, to remain the servant, the son, willing no kingship except that which has already been conferred upon him. Did he not make that choice, humankind would remain subject to the powers of darkness: concupiscence of the eyes, the "glory" of the kingdoms proposed by Satan, the pride of life, the spirit of domination, all the different forms of the will to power. All are vanquished and give way to one Kingdom, won by a servant's feat of poverty, humiliation, and suffering. Because Jesus turns away from the worship that princes of this world exact, he is truly adorable and his renunciation brings him into the very heart of human society. His dramatic confrontation with the powerful will end by destroying a whole political mythology and bringing Jesus to his death.

Perhaps Satan let Jesus foresee that he would conquer kingdoms by becoming a guerrilla chief, a political leader of his people. On the whole what we need to retain from the temptation episode is Jesus' involvement in "the political" in a death struggle with the "Sovereignties and the Powers" (Col. 2:15), and with a mythology of power.[3]

2. *The Coin of Tribute (Mark 12:13–17).*    Even more specifically related to the subject with which we are concerned is the episode of the denarius.

According to Mark, first some Pharisees and Herodians interrogate Jesus, and then some opponents and collaborators together. Luke has left out the Pharisees, perhaps to make the scene more believable.

"Is it permissible to pay taxes to Caesar or not?" Here is a question to be dreaded. Whatever Jesus answers, he is done for. If he says Yes, the people will disavow him. If he says No, he gives the Herodians and the high priests the weapon they are looking for: he is a seditious man whom Pilate will not fail to condemn.

Jesus responds with an action: he has a denarius brought to him.

It is difficult for us today to imagine the gravity of the scene. The likeness of the emperor had an awesome significance. It was not to be profaned. Those who failed to show respect to it were treated as criminals. On the face of the coin was a representation of Tiberius, crowned with laurel, the symbol of divinity. On the reverse side, Livia, the widow of Augustus and the mother of the emperor, was represented. If the denarius brought to Jesus carried a Latin inscription, it read, "Tiberius Caesar, Supreme Pontiff Augustus, and son of the Divine Augustus." If in Greek, the inscription was even more explicit, "Emperor Tiberius, Adorable Son of the Adorable God." It was a provocative medal.

Jesus' response has full significance only in a context that accepts power as divine and worship as its due.

What he answers is, first, an act of rebellion. By saying "give back to God what is God's," an evident allusion to the first commandment, "I am Yahweh your God. . . . You shall have no gods except me" (Exod. 20:1–3), Jesus refuses Caesar what Caesar exacts. A choice of civilization, of a culture, with tremendous import. Future martyrs will bear the same testimony. And they will always arise when power refuses to recognize something above it by which it is judged, when power pretends to derive its title from no other source beyond itself and makes itself the equal of divinity.

But what Jesus replies is also a refusal to identify himself with rebellion. "Give back to Caesar what belongs to Caesar." In other words, you accept his money, his order, and his peace, so pay his tribute. Tradition has retained only this aspect of Jesus' statement. It was a part of his truth. Power is not illegitimate. We need to remark that Jesus is not siding with Caesar and is not, therefore, condemning political resistance. He is simply saying, you accept a regime when you make use of its money.

Jesus' answer gives his enemies ample means to destroy him. They will lie when they state before Pilate, "We found this man inciting our people to revolt, opposing payment of the tribute to Caesar" (Luke 23:2). But they could well say, "He is inflaming the people with his teaching"—for the precept to adore God alone was subversive.

The mission of Jesus has political import, for it calls power into question, all power that attempts to divinize, to absolutize itself. Yet his mission is not a political project, as his adversaries took it to be.

*3. Pilate's Interrogation of Jesus (John 18:33–38).* The Gospel according to John was recorded around the end of the first century, much later than the three Synoptics. People no longer knew who the Herodians, the Sadducees, and the Pharisees were: John usually speaks of "the Jews." But the Gospel remains astonishing in the precise information that it gives. And the dialogue with Pilate bears the mark of this exactness: it makes complete sense only in function of its political context, forgotten by the time it was written down.

Pilate has just come out of the Praetorium, which the Jews did not want to enter in order to avoid incurring defilement that would prevent them from eating the Passover meal. He has held a hasty exchange with them. "What charge do you bring against this man?" "If he were not a criminal, we should not be handing him over to you." "Take him yourselves, and judge him by your law." "We are not allowed to put a man to death."

Pilate understands full well that Jesus is being accused of sedition. When he has Jesus brought before him he goes straight to the point: "Are you the king of the Jews?"

As he did in the case of paying tribute to Caesar, Jesus gives a twofold response. The parallel between the two is significant.

He first states, "Mine is not a kingdom of this world." And he offers proof of that. I have no armies and no people under arms. My kingdom has no use for the means of force and repression used, and abused, by the kings of this world. It consists in giving testimony to the truth and, if people listen to my voice, they come to me freely, brought only by the power of truth. Pilate's only response is, "Truth? What is that?" It is conceivable that his question has to do with everything that Jesus had answered and that he might be asking, what are you saying about testimony to the truth and your strange royalty?

Pilate is convinced that Jesus is not the head of any sedition, of any *guerrilla* movement. Three times he says to the Jews, "I find no case against him."

But Jesus has also asserted, "Yes, I am a king." To be a king is to be a son of God. The Jews immediately undertake to remind Pilate, "We have a Law and according to that Law he ought to die, because he claimed to be the Son of God." (John 19:7). In Pilate's eyes this is a sacrilegious statement, like "Give back to God what belongs to God."

This is why, when the Jews persist, Pilate abandons Jesus. Certainly, in his eyes, Jesus is not a rebel, another Judas the Galilean. But he has said that he is a king and even if his kingdom has no armed forces, he has denied Caesar's divine filiation. When the Jews cry, "Anyone who makes himself king is defying Caesar," they hit a vulnerable spot. Yet Pilate still tries to defend himself, "Do you want me to crucify your king?" But they are intractable, "Crucify him!" And resort to servility, "We have no king except Caesar." Then Pilate abandons Jesus to them. What comes to light in these three episodes in no way expresses a lack of involvement on Jesus' part. Whether alone with his conscience or in confrontation with his adversaries or in Pilate's presence, Jesus stands up against power that pretends to deny its relative nature and claims to be absolute. In truth, what Jesus does at this moment marks the end of a world. The end of the pagan world, which aureoled power with a religious nimbus. It was also the end of the Jewish world, of the time which identified the divine covenant with earthly domination. Both the pagan and the Jewish temptations keep on coming to life over and over again.

Jesus takes a position that precludes neutrality. He is in contest with the powerful, an age-old struggle that will come to an end only with the end of time. But there is no longer any cause for confusion about the nature of Jesus' calling: it is to no political enterprise that he invites his own.

In the position that Jesus takes we can rightly see that, historically, politics and faith achieve their true essences.[4] And let it be added, they enter upon their true relationship. More than any party program, Jesus' message has political import and can lead a man to his death; but it proposes no ideology, no strategy, and is not a political message. In this difference the whole mystery of the Church in its relation to the world is expressed.

## NOTES

1. See in particular: Oscar Cullmann, *Jésus et les révolutionnaires de son temps* (Neuchâtel: Delachaux et Niestlé, 1970); E. Stauffer, *Le Christ et les Césars* (Paris: Alsatia, 1956); Charles H. Dodd, *The Founder of Christianity* (New York: Macmillan, 1970); J. Guillet, "Jesus et la politique," *Recherches de science religieuse*, no. 4 (1972); Martin Hengel, *Victory over*

*Violence: Jesus and the Revolutionists,* trans. David E. Green (Philadelphia: Fortress, 1973). It is certainly difficult to conclude from Jesus' attitude in the face of the political happenings of his time just how we should act in our own. In a sense, as "an agitator" he is a man neither of his time nor of his place, an anachronism. Hence his timeliness now; he questions people today as he did yesterday and will tomorrow. Without wishing to draw a strict parallel, it is possible, nevertheless, thanks to recent research, to indicate a perspective that can be of help to the Church today in discerning what path to pursue in the circumstances in which it finds itself.

2. The fact that Satan is personalized signifies that evil is unmasked and the temptation overcome.

3. In a secularized world, the triple temptation to take food, to work miracles, and to make use of power assume different forms but remain essentially the same.

4. René Coste, "La figure politique de Jésus," *La Croix*, August 5, 1971. See too his *Les dimensions politiques de la foi* (Paris: Editions Ouvrières, 1972).

# V

# THE GREAT
# BIBLICAL CONTESTATIONS

At times today there is a tendency to give more importance to the Old Testament than to the New because it has a more recognizable political dimension.[1] This is a reaction against an interpretation of the gospel that has been prevalent for a long time, that is, that what was new about faith in Jesus was a conversion from a vision bound up in this world to a vision that reached beyond the world, beyond time, a change from a political to a nonpolitical conception. In reality, authentic Christianity, like messianism, has never dissociated the here from the hereafter, or earthly promises from an outlook on eternity. Each of them has proclaimed a relationship at once present and to come that transforms every human view and prospect. If Christ has founded a new covenant, it is not because he continues the temporal blessings of the old covenant into infinity, it is because he fulfills its promises. And he achieves this for time and for eternity. In this matter, no difference exists between the Old Testament and the New.

The difference is to be found in something else: that the gospel is proclaimed not to a single people descended from Abraham, Isaac, and Jacob but to all peoples, without distinction of race. It should be recognized that universalism was already present in the great prophecies; Israel never lost sight of the universal dimension of its vocation. In proportion as it drew near to the new times, the Jewish faith was offered to neophytes who had no racial bonds with the Hebrews. So it was that the one God who had made a covenant with Israel gradually came to be presented as the God who, through an elect people, makes a covenant with all humanity.

The truth remains that Jesus severed all links with Jewish particularism and nationalism. In this sense, his message is disengaged from the political aims proper to the Hebrews, one race among many, one people among many. For that reason, the political dimension of revelation can be seen in the right perspective. Like the prophets, Jesus initiates a conflict with the powers of this world and announces the liberation of the oppressed. But the way in which he does so is new. The conflict that he starts and the liberation that he proclaims are no longer identified with the struggle for deliverance being carried on by just one people among the many peoples of the world. Jesus would even foretell the destruction of the temple and the dispersion of Israel. Because they refused to be what they were called to be, a people with a universal mission, the Jewish nation was to see that mission taken away from them and confided for the future to a new "nation" without any political or racial particularity. Peter himself would have to fight a hard inner battle to make up his mind to accept this mutation in the history of salvation.

When freed from links that still bound the prophetic message to the destiny of a nation, the political import of the gospel message takes on its true dimensions. All the evangelical contestations are already to be found in the prophets: they announce a new society. But the prophetic "political" views gain incomparable clarity and strength in the gospel from the fact that they are no longer tied to any particular "politics" whatsoever.

## Eros

The Bible first gives us an image of contestation and liberation in the primary social relation of man and woman. As the foundation of all society, it manifests all the characteristics of any interhuman relationship. To study it is, therefore, particularly important; and the women's movement makes it, moreover, especially timely.

In this relationship, human beings experience both the most intimate opening of the self to the other and, consequently, liberty. God created them "man and woman," "male and female," says Genesis in a conjoint formula all the more surprising as it is linked in the text with another declaration that "God created man in the image of himself . . . male and female he created them" (Gen. 1:27). In the second and Yahwist account, the reality of the "two in one" is symbolically expressed—the creation of Eve from Adam. Let us read the account as telling us that God desired to give Adam a companion like himself and did so not by fashioning her from Adam's rib but by drawing her out of his side (Gen. 2:21).[2]

In the story we are given no revelation of any historical primacy and still less of any ontological primacy of man over woman.[3] There is no first and no second sex. What is expressed in this passage is their reciprocity in being. It could have been just as well expressed by a reversal of the myth, by having man taken from the side of woman. In either way, an explanation is given of the movement of tenderness that irresistibly attracts man to woman and woman to man so that they form a radical unity. "This at last is bone from my bone, and flesh from my flesh!" Adam cries out.

Originally, the impulse was not to possess, to appropriate, but to reciprocate, to reach out to one another, to be realized in and through each other, a real freedom with mutual pledge for life. It is noteworthy that Genesis expresses the indissolubility of the bond by starting with the command given to the man and not with the precept imposed on the woman, which flows from it. "This is why a man leaves his father and mother and joins himself to his wife, and they become one body" (Gen. 2:24). This unity in fullness, in which two beings are not absorbed but, on the contrary, are completed, is specifically a divine likeness. It signifies God's marriage with humanity; it is a symbolism that gives to the Bible myth[4] of the creation of man and woman all its power, as Paul would make completely clear (Eph. 5:32). By comparing the divine covenant with the marriage contract, the prophets had first given expression to this great mystery (see Ezek. 16 and 23; Hos. 2, for examples).

But see how this gift, one of God's best, changes into servitude, its opposite, when man transforms into depredation and possession what was openhanded unconstraint. If eros is the earliest form of relationship of the one to the other, it is also the primary locus for iniquity, which closes off one human being from another. When that happens, the rule of the stronger and the enslavement of the weaker follows. "Your yearning shall be for your husband," says the Lord, "yet he will lord it over you" (Gen. 3:16).[5]

The alienation involved is possible only because man finds in woman and woman in man an object to possess, a something to be taken—to the extent that the relation of man to woman is also a relation of person to nature. Man must reach a relationship with woman through nature, but this necessity can also destroy the relation, for it opens the way to servitude.

Without wishing to look to the biblical account for some sort of historical primacy of one form of iniquity over another, we cannot help but see that man and woman, according to Genesis, came to know in this primary relationship their earliest experience of sin. A whole series of considerations leads us to that conclusion. In all cosmological religions, the serpent is the symbol of male virility and is the most naked of animals. The most immediate consequence of the sin of Adam and Eve was that they were ashamed of their nakedness (Gen. 3:7).[6]

It is not surprising that man and woman had in this primitive relationship an experience of fundamental iniquity. They were invited to share a gift and through that sharing to bear a divine likeness. Their freely given love was really the sign and presence of the divine friendship. But the insinuation of the serpent perverted it. "No! You will not die! God knows in fact that on the day you eat it your eyes will be opened and you will be like gods, knowing good and evil" (Gen 3:5); you will be capable of deciding to your own liking what is good and what is evil. In their mutual relationship, thus diverted from its symbolic meaning, man and woman experienced an alienating and enslaving license instead of knowing a liberty that would serve to unite them and give them heightened personhood. Woman will be the victim of this ancient iniquity. If eros is possession, every man tends to consider a woman as something to be possessed, and every woman, to offer herself as such an object. Then we no longer have the myth in its authentic meaning but mystification instead. The bitter fruit of the perversion is loneliness, anguish, unhappiness, and enslavement at the very core of the relationship and radical deprivation instead of the fullness of knowledge that the serpent had held out hopes for. Nothing is more striking than the nostalgia for love in the heart of a world that experiences eros so often and so cheaply.[7]

To free all the energy contained in eros, to give love meaning, and to really know each other, a man and a woman must henceforth pass through death, a death to all that stands for depredation, enslavement, and iniquity in their relationship so that they may be reborn to all that is meant by gift, by liberty, by mutuality. Of course, there is no question of doing away with the bodily bond, which human beings experience as an elementary and vital need. But it is a question of reaching, through this need, a relationship of freedom. To give a comparison, an infant has not experienced his own humanity as long as his mother is only a breast filled with milk to him, for then he is still limited to the realm of necessity. He begins to be what he is, a human being, only when he enters into a relationship with his mother by being touched, looked at, smiled upon, spoken to. In a comparable way, a man and a woman who are content with possessing one another are limited by that necessity. They have to relax their hold, to let go, if they are to reach that liberty in love that lies at the very core of their union. They must die, in a way, to all that threatens their love if they are to come to know its reality. For love to be a new gift, a complete gift, all must be given in a sort of death that knows how to relinquish what is most needed so that it may hold onto what is most precious.

The "continence" so intimated, if authentic, is not repression but freedom. It will be manifested by "times" of continence, as Paul suggests (1 Cor. 7:5), each couple discovering the rhythm best fitted for their relationship to develop daily in mutual giving, communion, and freedom. The same continence will lead others to conceive of the man-relationship differently, to the point of giving up the very gift which bodily union signifies, not because they consider it of little worth and still less because they think it in some way tainted by sin, but on the contrary, to give back to it its signification as gift. "There are eunuchs who have made themselves that way for the sake of the kingdom of heaven," according to the trenchant words of the gospel (Matt. 19:12). Their gift of celibacy presupposes not the elimination of the man-woman relationship, but another form of it, for the words of Genesis have value for all: "It is not good that the man should be alone." Manliness and womanliness must find expression in meetings of a different kind, in which men and women both find themselves involved. The gift of celibacy, to which all are not called, has meaning socially only within a community in which different situations are articulated. At a deeper level, it restores authenticity to the relationship between man and woman.

It is possible for us to understand how Jesus stood in relation to this mystery, a part of the life of every man and woman. No one can doubt that he freely chose celibacy. Yet more fully than anyone else, he lived the mystery contained in the primary relationship.[8] Very probably, John was mindful of the Genesis account when he gave so much importance to the centurion's lance thrust which opened up Jesus' breast (John 19:34). Like Adam, Jesus is the man whose side has been opened. Like Adam, in a movement of tenderness, he draws all humanity to himself as his bride.[9] He himself had said beforehand, "And when I am lifted up from the earth, I shall draw all men to myself" (John 12:32). The whole mystery of marriage is implied in that love of incomparable fruitfulness. Later, Paul is to teach that the union of man and woman is the symbol of the union of Christ and the Church. Truly, this is a great sacrament for it signifies the love of one who, by stripping himself of everything, gave to love its meaning of mutual self-giving.

The relationship of man and woman in marriage can regain its primitive signification of liberty only through a dialectic of death and life. A new experience was necessary—continence—not as a negation of love and fruitfulness but, on the contrary, as the fullness of love and fruitfulness. So lived, continence strengthens the foundation of marriage in its mystery, continually inviting it to that self-denial which restores its form of mutual self-giving and freedom. Then, and then only, is to be found the eradication of the long enslavement of woman by man implicated in the negation of the meaning of their relationship.

In every social relationship, we shall find the same logic: the meaning of mutuality, the mystery of iniquity, the dialectic of life and death.

*Power*

Strictly speaking, the end of politics is to win and wield power. Politics consists in all those activities with this end in view, whether in conformity with the established order or in conflict with it. In the latter case, it is revolution. Except when it falls into ineffective idealism, politics never loses sight of its aim—to get hold of and use power.

Every analysis of relations within the city of man begins, therefore, with some reflection on power. Since the gospel message announces a new relation, does it also modify the structure of the city of man?

Historically, Christianity has confronted the mythology of power in a long and bloody struggle. Christians, and Jesus himself, have given outstanding witness and known martyrdom in the combat. The refusal to accord worship to the Caesars throughout subsequent history has not been fanaticism. What made such adoration suspect was nothing more or less than the essence of faith in Christ, the only Son of God. The religious aspects of this age-old struggle are well known by everybody; its political implications are often forgotten.

Citizenship is not a primary relation, like the relationship between man and woman. It comes into existence only as political society slowly breaks away from patriarchal society in a complex process in which economic exchange plays an important part. Christian faith interprets it too in terms of reciprocity, openness, and freedom. To the extent that, in order to become a reality, this relation presupposes a structure, faith recognizes power as an ontological necessity that does not issue from the mystery of iniquity but expresses and mediatizes a person as a political being. It proves useful to choose from among the citizens persons whose specific function is to promote the general good.

Such a conception is implicit in what Jesus says to Pilate, "You would have no power over me if it had not been given you from above" (John 19:11). At that really crucial moment in his life, Jesus undergoes the experience that many martyrs after him were to know—the coercive power of those who hold the right to life and death in their hand. Every person, when this happens for the first time, cannot fail to feel a kind of anguish in the face of an abstract reality created by people themselves, which is capable of crushing one. Jesus experiences that drama in its harshest form; yet he does not deny the necessity for power. He simply states that no people, of their own right, have any title to exercise power and must account to God for every power entrusted to them.

To gain a better understanding of Jesus' words to Pilate, we need to compare them with the response he made in regard to paying Caesar's tax. With a denarius before him, Jesus first denies Caesar's divinity, a sacrilegious statement that radically desacralizes and laicizes power as not a divine but a human institution. People have fashioned it not in a divine but in a purely human undertaking in accordance with cultural models that can, in time, be modified. This fundamental affirmation provokes a question, which leads to another statement: if the institution of power is a human work, whose work is it? And the answer is—it belongs to society itself. Jesus' statement, by definitely putting aside the myth of divine generation, also rejects the idea that a person or persons in society can hold on to power as if it were their property. Power comes to them through the people as a whole. Taking the sacred character away from power means taking away its possession by and identification with particular people as well. Power as an institution is of human construction and can be built only by the whole people.

When Jesus says that power comes from above, he does not mean to revive the idea of power as a divine right. He means, on the contrary, to refer it to the supreme power which both founds and judges it. He is affirming not the divine but the human nature of power: that is the meaning of his testimony. He is not saying that the prince is engendered by God, he is not saying, "If it had not been given to you *by God*," but that above and beyond the "justice" of the prince is a higher justice to which every man can appeal. He is not saying that power is divine but just the opposite, that it comes from a source which transcends it absolutely and that it is, consequently, something essentially human.

Just as the Bible, by referring the relation of man and woman to the covenant between man and God, does not divinize this relationship but gives it back its true dimension and, consequently, humanizes it by restoring its meaning of freedom, so, likewise, by referring power to God, Jesus gives it back its human reality and its meaning of relatedness. Power is not the negation but the condition of liberty. Its whole purpose is to serve freedom.

To refer power to a supreme authority is, therefore, to demystify it. The theology prevalent in the East, Egyptian or Syro-Babylonian, and that doubtless also infected the Roman world at the time of Augustus, made of the king (or the Caesar) the son of God. In early Egyptian thought this was conceived in so completely a physical sense that Pharaohs married their own sisters to keep the divine race from becoming attenuated. But being the son of God because a king or Caesar was also accepted in a figurative sense. This popular understanding is important, since Jesus, in the same dramatic dialogue with Pilate, declared himself a king, that is, a son of God: the two expressions were equivalent and were linked together in the account of the Passion (cf. John 19:7, 21).[10]

The incompatibility between the old mythology of power and Christian faith shows up immediately and completely: a fight for freedom in which men without weapons and with no other force than their own testimony and their own blood, dethrone the formidable caricature of power to which John alludes in the Book of Revelation when he speaks of the Beast and the Dragon.

In Jewish thought, the king was also a son of God but was so through election and not by generation, a major difference. David, the son of Jesse, forgotten by his father when he presented his sons to Samuel, was taken from the pasture, from among the sheep. Nothing distinguished him as the one to receive the kingly anointing. Could there be any more striking reminder of the completely human origin of the one who was to hold power? Here we are given a preparation for the revelation of a new era.

Faith in Christ, the only Son of God, definitively destroys the whole mythology of power. In civilizations which have received the graft of Christianity, power can no longer be proposed as having a divine nature. Wherever Christianity has succeeded in reaching, whether directly or indirectly, the final forms of theocracy fade away little by little in an inevitable process in which power, by being desacralized and laicized, becomes separated from any cult of personages and is democratized.

When a religious mythology of the king as the son of God gives way to a profane, secularized mythology of a monarch, a leader, or a state as omnipotent in judgment and decision, Christians continue to stand up to give the same witness. Power comes from above and we can always appeal from its judgments to an ultimate authority, something quite different from a superpower, for it is a relation, that is, a reciprocity which gives power its meaning—which is to further people's freedom through mutual giving.

This reference establishes the relationship between the person and society. The person is anterior to society in the sense that society, like the power that integrates and represents it, is completely at the service of the persons within the community; at the same time, the general interest comes before the interest of the individual, for the person is defined by relationship with other persons and cannot be called free outside of that relationship.

These ideas are new, characteristic of the new times, and were almost unknown in the pagan world and barely roughed out in the Jewish. It will take time for them to be accepted. And power has an innate tendency to throw them off, to free itself of them. If the establishment of power brings with it the necessity of *setting apart* people whose specific function is to serve the general good, it is inevitable that it tends to become sacralized (the sacred is what is *set apart*). With power, then, comes a perennial temptation, the mystery of iniquity manifesting itself in its distinctly political form.

Just as in the relationship between man and woman alienation is possible because human beings can find in it an object to possess, a relation to nature, so power, too becomes a source of iniquity because it is related to force.

In a sense, it is legitimate that strength be the source of right and that power be confided to the strongest. "Saul has killed his thousands, and David his tens of thousands" (1 Sam. 18:7). Human cities are built, armed and defended with weapons against enemies within and without. A city is ready to fall when those who live in it can think of no reason to die for it. No community is possible without some force to promote and protect it. This is a vital physical necessity. But that need is replaced by unjust domination the day when a man lays hands on force as if it were booty taken to impose upon the citizenry what is of his making, not theirs.

To overcome temptation and reverse that tendency so that power may be true to its nature, even more is needed than the example of a political leader capable of understanding and using power from a fresh viewpoint. What is needed is the witness of a person capable of winning power and capable of renouncing it completely for the freedom of the kingdom. Jesus is truly king, that is, the Son of God, but his sovereignty is not domination. It is expressed in the subjection of humiliation, arrest, torture, and death. It is a complete reversal of the meaning of royalty.

Believers came to discover in Jesus a new kind of kingship. With the centurion others too were to say, "In truth this was a son of God" (Matt. 27:54), summing up in that testimony the whole of faith, all that Christians have seen, heard, and touched (1 John 1:1) of him who came to them as the Word of Life. Yet we should not lose sight of the political dimension of revelation. We must not forget that the revelation of Jesus as the only Son of God definitively destroys the claim of any power to be taken as divine, as absolute.

Christ has no hesitation in claiming to be a king. While ascribing to himself the fullness of kingship, he completely changes its meaning. It no longer signifies any kind of domination but complete renunciation: not just because it gives up the use of arms—Jesus is not going to send others to death, he is not going to defend himself with weapons (John 18:36); not just because he renounces constraint of any kind—he is heard if we want to listen (John 18:37); but even more because his kingship must go through the darkness of humiliation and death, and can only be actualized in the mystery of the resurrection. His kingliness can lay full claim to divine sonship at the very moment when Jesus makes a definitive denial that divine sonship belongs to any other royalty. "I put you on oath by the living God to tell us if you are the Christ, the Son of God." "The words are your own

Moreover, I tell you that from this time onward you will see the Son of Man seated at the right hand of the Power and coming on the clouds of Heaven" (Matt. 26: 64–65). When Pilate puts the same question to him, he replies, "It is you who have said it. Yes I am a king" (John 18:37). Before the Jewish high priest and before the Roman procurator Jesus gives exactly the same testimony, not glorifying himself but putting his signature on his own death warrant. It is God who will ratify his sovereign lordship.

We have some understanding of the cost of the self-denial, the *kenosis*, that made Christ victorious over temptation. Satan offered Jesus ownership of the kingdoms on earth. More than anyone else, Jesus could aspire to that. But to gain access to that empire, he would have to accept the satanic condition, to make himself, like Caesar, "the adorable son of the adorable god" and to receive a demoniac adoration in direct contradiction to the adoration of God alone. We know too that this temptation was not proposed to Jesus just in the desert but followed him throughout his life. Every time the crowd wanted to make him king, every time the apostles wanted to turn him aside from the mission that was taking him to his death, Jesus had to repulse the temptation again. "Get behind me, Satan! You are an obstacle in my path, because the way you think is not God's way but man's" (Matt. 16:23).

In the songs of the humbled servant in Second Isaiah, particularly in chapters fifty and fifty-three, a king is foretold who will realize his divine relationship in an authentic way through humiliation (cf. Matt. 12:18). The Greek word *pais* with which the Septuagint translates the word "servant" means "child" as well. In these pages, which are among the most mysterious and most messianic in the Old Testament, we already encounter the radical inversion that replaces the pagan mythology of power with the mystery of the servant of God, of the Son of God, of a king persecuted unto death, an ignominious death, to atone for what is most alienating in abuse of power.

Just as the experience of celibacy by some is needed to restore authenticity to the relationship between man and woman, so obedience unto death, even death on a cross (Phil. 2:8), was needed to restore to power its original character as a human reality at the service of liberty, to demythologize it by referring it to a divine authority of freedom and relation. Like celibacy, the radical renunciation of every form of power in society is a choice open to only a few. Then it is not a theoretical teaching, but a living witness, an invitation to all those who hold power in the city of man to use it only in the service of liberty.

By choosing the last place, by accepting access to kingship only through death, and death on a cross, Christ has pointed out a way for all people in power. "Anyone who wants to be great among you must be your servant, and anyone who wants to be first among you must be your slave" (Matt. 20:27). At the same time he is also telling us that individual freedom cannot be regarded as a refuge for willfulness but is a responsibility and, therefore, also a relationship. His testimony has opened the way to democracy, contesting all forms of monarchy, of oligarchy, and of anarchy—all adversaries of democracy; it is also a protest against power that is exercised in the name of the people when it claims, in one way or another, to be absolute.

Like Christ, the community of his disciples renounce power, an essential principle for the secularization and autonomy of civil society. Their renunciation is also a negation of absolute power and provides the basis for a new society.

## Wealth

Political society and economic society are contemporaneous and inseparable. To contest wealth is to contest power and represents the two faces of the same biblical contestation. In revealing himself as "the Son of God," Jesus presents himself as both the humiliated servant and the deprived poor man. Just as no one can adore God and Caesar, no one can serve God and mammon. The whole faith of Israel in the One and Only is expressed here and brought to its fullness in the preaching of the new era.

Insofar as wealth is a relation, man is its source. In primitive communities, where each one fulfilled a function and received the necessities, this relation remained obvious. Work retained its meaning; people had charge of the land, the plants, the animals (Gen. 1:26). Private property did not exist: each worked with the means and according to the methods at the disposal of the community and made use of the portion determined by custom. In their relation to nature, people "humanized" nature by molding it to meet their needs and the earth "naturalized" them by accepting their mastery. The relation of one human being to another through work existed from the beginning not just because work implies complementarity of roles[11] but because the fruit of each one's work is put at the service of all.

The Bible first brings us into the presence of a nomadic people with a patriarchal subsistence economy. When did trade take form in that primitive society? Probably at the time of its integration into Egypt's more economically advanced civilization.

It is said that giving came before exchange. That is true, but a gift calls for reciprocity, that is, a proportion between the gift and the recipient that suggests an incipient form of exchange. Episodic exchange is not yet trade because at that point, the instrument of trade, money or silver, has not yet been created. Once that is done, economic society is born.

Tremendous progress then takes place. Trade completely transforms the rapport of people with nature. The social division of work and the development of production forces result. For a long time, however, primitive production and exchange and the character of the relationship between persons all continue. Trade implies dialogue. Originally, it was always accompanied by bargaining. Buyer and seller met face to face in a subtle negotiation in which cunning played a part in determining the price. While becoming depersonalized by degrees (in modern society, selling at a fixed price dates back at least a century), trade relations became extended and provided the basis for a political society that continued to expand. At certain epochs in its existence, under the reign of Solomon and of Jeroboam II, for example, the kingdom of Israel consisted in an economically and politically developed society.

In the increasing domination of humankind over nature and in growing social relationships, the Bible sees neither progressive nor regressive evolution. It perceives a gradual becoming in which Israel is accompanied by the one God who has made a covenant with it. "Sacred history" is penetrated by a hope that is incarnated in successive visions of "the promised land" flowing with milk and honey, then of economic prosperity and political power, and finally, of the restoration of an independent people. Before being a human expectation, it is a hope for a new relationship with God. "You shall be my people and I will be your God" (Ezek. 36:28). That is why Israel's hope is not extinguished by any of the tragedies that mark its history. Nothing in the Bible lends itself to substituting for this genuine hope an expectation of some kind of temporal progress. In this perspective, history is gathered up in each moment of becoming and the final hope is realized then and there. If there is "an appointed time" (Gal. 4:4), it has its roots chiefly not in temporal progress but in an increasingly intimate encounter with God.

Jesus will bring this hope to fulfillment. Not even the destruction of the temple and the dispersion of the people will extinguish it. Henceforth all humanity, without distinction of race or nation, is called. A mutation of that kind was doubtless conditioned by a certain breaking up of tight political and economic communities. Yet the hope proper to the new times is not an expectation for a development in production forces or the growth of the economic society. It is something entirely different, makes no change in the nature of things but is a waiting for Christ's return, an anticipation of mankind's ascent to the One and Only or of the coming of the Creator to his creation, which technological progress neither gainsays nor guarantees.

Only the Bible opens up to us a world in which there is no conflict between people and nature or between people and their fellow creatures because there is no conflict between people and God; and so it makes it possible for us to understand that nature has been created to be a friend to people and people to be friends to their fellow men by being God's friends. Unfaithfulness to God is what brings about at each passing moment the enmity of nature for humanity and of one person for another, not as a punishment from God but as the immanent consequence of a free decision.

Just as the relationship between man and woman gives way to iniquity and enslavement because it is also a relation of people to nature, because within it there is something that people can grasp for themselves, so the economic relation gives way to plunder because it too is a relation of people to nature. The product of work is something good, wealth. It can be accumulated and it can be hoarded.

Human beings accumulate and hoard. Animals know only how to capture and kill in order to eat. Once their hunger is appeased, they take their rest and allow weaker animals to help themselves from their kill. Human beings, with their capacity to reason, can keep some distance from nature by dominating it and, in regard to their fellow human beings, by entering into real relationships with them. This magnificent privilege is perverted by the itch to accumulate and monopolize. A twofold conflict follows with its source in a more primitive hostility brought into the world when man and woman gave up the even more magnificent gift of God's friendship to become rivals of God.

This is the meaning of the myth of the expulsion of Adam and Eve from their earthly paradise. Because they no longer saw their history as a covenant and made themselves rivals of God, nature became their enemy (Gen. 3:17); people rob each other of the fruit of their work [12] and henceforth iniquity reigns and cuts human beings off from each other. [13]

Christ's thought is much more developed but its meaning is identical. It is presented in his usual direct way. "No servant can be the slave of two masters: he will either hate the first and love the second, or treat the first with respect and the second with scorn. You cannot be the slave both of God and of money" (Luke 16:13).

What is given us here is a prophetic, that is, a revelatory view: wealth rises up before people and wins their adoration—as if it were spun out of itself and not fashioned by and for them. Now wealth is a relative thing, having its origin and end in human beings. As a work of the community it is to be shared.

Luke's whole sixteenth chapter is almost entirely given to presenting the theme of money. Its most telling verses are set between two great parables portraying the salvation of the rich (the parable of the unfaithful servant) and their condemnation (the parable of the rich man and Lazarus). They announce a new economic society by denouncing the old.

It seems surprising that the doctrine presented in Luke (16:10–12) has gone almost unremarked, since it coincides with some of the most recent intuitions of our modern age. It is true that the closely packed quality of Jesus' words in this passage does not make the signification of his words immediately evident.

The text is linked with the parable of the unfaithful steward. Whereas in the parable, the sharp practice of the steward is given as a model to the children of light (Be as sharp as he! Make yourselves friends by distributing to the poor the wealth that does not belong to you.), the idea of faithfulness is what is brought out. "The man who can be trusted in little things can be trusted in great; the man who is dishonest in little things will be dishonest in great" (Luke 16:10). The doctrine is clear: only the one recognized as faithful in the stewardship of those little things that comprise earthly goods when they exceed real necessities will receive the stewardship of divine riches.[14] Two ideas are implied: that riches count for little and accumulating them is idle; and that we are to be faithful in the stewardship of wealth in this world and faithfulness consists (as the whole context of the chapter makes plain) in sharing and not in accumulating it.

The verse that follows introduces a new idea, "If you cannot be trusted with money, that tainted thing, who will trust you with genuine riches?" Riches are called tainted either because they have been taken from those who created them or because they are not distributed, which is already iniquitous. Furthermore, riches are not genuine, they add nothing to the person but, rather, impoverish him by cutting him off from his fellowmen and separating him from himself.

The final intuition sounds the most modern. "And if you cannot be trusted with what is not yours, who will give you what is your very own?" Wealth is not people themselves; if they attach themselves to wealth, they are alienated by it. Only the gifts of God really belong to them; they alone make a person a person.

People are alienated by holding onto what they do not need. They are then not in command of what they have made; it is their ruler. The Marxist theory of the fetishism of commodities proves itself capable of offering more precise economic analyses of a particular historical situation but it will reach no more penetrating intuition. It is held back by its inability to recognize the ultimate origin of servitude: that people, having refused to adore the one and adorable God, have made riches their god.

In the same chapter, the Gospel develops at length the doctrine on hoarding wealth in the two great parallel parables of the unfaithful steward and Lazarus the poor man. For the rich, salvation lies in distributing their riches; and their downfall, in keeping them for themselves. The two parables express both the irony and the drama of the situations presented.

Make friends with the riches which do not belong to you by distributing them to the poor, so that the poor may receive you into everlasting dwellings when you have nothing left: this is the meaning of the parable of the unfaithful steward (Luke 16:6). The poor are at home in God's house. And the rich are going to enter that homeland of the poor only if the poor "naturalize" them, as Bossuet put it so well. [15]

The immeasurable distance stretching out between Lazarus and the rich man is impossible to cross on earth: people do not pass over from the world of the poor to the world of the wealthy. In eternity it will be just as impossible to cross, but there the roles played will be reversed: that is the meaning of the parable that closes the sixteenth chapter of Luke. [16]

Obviously, these texts could be interpreted in a purely individualistic way. In that case, they would simply deal with the duties of the rich to the poor and the rights of the poor in regard to the rich. An interpretation of that kind would be a partial reading, not false but incomplete, inspired by the ideology prevalent in the nineteenth century. The Gospel goes much further, not content with determining an ethics for the individual, it defines a new society in which the rupture between rich and poor will be healed and, with the sharing of goods, friendship will rule.

The Gospel conception is not simply the idea of a classless society in which each one receives what is due for work. Instead, it is the idea of a society with no poor and no rich, with each one receiving according to need. A critique of capitalism as an historical epoch evidently still remains to be done, but a foundation for it has now been laid. Does not the injustice of riches, according to the strong expression of the Gospel, consist in a few accumulating what the shared labor of many has produced so that those who have done the work are deprived of their due (Isa. 65:21–22)?

The point at which the Gospel completely outstrips socialist doctrine is where it takes up accumulation as such, not confining itself to riches that result in social divisions but including riches accumulated without limit, so that they become a crushing burden on people and on society. The twelfth chapter of Luke features this teaching in a well-known pericope about the rich man with a bumper crop who is preoccupied with the problem and joy of storing it all when suddenly, out of the blue, his life is demanded of him. Beginning at that point, Jesus developed his teaching about worrying: "I am telling you not to worry about your life and what you are to eat, nor about your body and how you are to clothe it" (Matt. 6:25). These words already ring with what might be called postsocialist accents, with a challenge to a society of consumerism. If human society does not employ technology in serving people, society itself will become the slave of technology. A mad rhythm is created when new needs are escalated so that new products can be created in order to satisfy the new needs.

Jesus does not tell us not to work. He does say that, when we are provided with what we need, further material production no longer makes sense. A certain abundance in having can mean a certain loss in being, not only for the individual but for society as well.

And again, the Gospel goes to the root of the matter: to refuse to adore and put our hope in the one true God is the source of the slavery imposed upon us by a logic no longer grounded on human beings but on things.

Whence will arise the good news of a society in which justice will prevail? When will it be proclaimed to the poor? And the glad tidings too of a society in which being will have more value than having? Who is going to pluck the passion to possess out of people's hearts?

In the economic relation, just as in political and conjugal relations, freedom will not follow from teaching doctrine; it can come only from a life witness. This is what evangelical poverty is all about.

The words that invite us to renunciation in the domain of wealth as well as of power and eros (the conjugal relationship) are not spoken to everybody and are not heard by all those to whom they are addressed. "Go and sell what you own and give to the poor, and you will have treasure in heaven; then come, follow me" (Matt. 19:21).

Before he proposed the renunciation inaugurating the new age, Jesus lived it himself: "The Son of Man has nowhere to lay his head" (Luke 9:58). He is a poor man. In the parable of Lazarus and the rich man, Lazarus is the one who rises from the dead (Luke 16:27–31). In the last judgment, the Son of Man who separates the sheep from the goats is the hungry, the thirsty, the sick, the oppressed. The poor person is to be our judge.

The poverty that kept Jesus out of human affairs so that he could give himself to the one work of the Kingdom made him the Worker, the source of everything good. "My Father goes on working and so do I" (John 5:17).

No one who fails to share can be a disciple of Jesus. Only a small number are called to despoil themselves of their possessions. But all, even if they remain bound to possessions, "should live as if they had nothing of their own" (1 Cor. 7:30). One way leads to happiness: "How happy are you who are poor" (Luke 6:20); and one way, to unhappiness: "But alas for you who are rich" (Luke 6:24). No persons can enter into the Kingdom who do not practice justice, who do not distribute to the poor whatever they have over and above their own real needs. And no one can do that who does not have at heart the meaning of poverty. Matthew's "How happy are the poor *in spirit*" (5:3), is not to be misunderstood and taken to apply to those who, while remaining rich, believe that they are interiorly detached—at no cost—from riches. The poor *in spirit* are those who share, not through constraint, but by the power of the Spirit. When Jesus spoke of eunuchs, he also made a distinction between those who were forced to be so and those who freely became eunuchs for the sake of the Kingdom.

It is not surprising that, according to the testimony of Acts

(4:32), the early Christians of Jerusalem held all their goods in common and continued to testify to the resurrection of the Lord Jesus with great power (4:33), that is, the coming of the risen and living Poor One. The Christian community can be a sign of salvation only to the extent to which it continues to give this testimony. "None of their members was ever in want, as all those who owned lands or houses would sell them, and bring the money from them, to present it to the apostles; it was then distributed to any members who might be in need" (4:34–35).

In this testimony lies the seed of a new economic society. The Church has meaning only if, through its communion, it transmits to its faithful the light and strength to build such a society.

## NOTES

1. Chiefly in the account of the exodus from Egypt when taken out of the whole context of the divine interventions with which it is marked.

2. It is true that the Hebrew word does mean "rib." But it is conceivable that in Hebrew the expression does not have the same specific anatomical meaning as it does in English.

3. It is possible that St. Paul's commentary in 1 Cor. 2:8 and Tim. 2:13 was inspired by the ideas of his time. It is noteworthy that in his ethic regarding the conjugal relationship, the Apostle always situates man and woman in a completely reciprocal relationship (1 Cor. 7:4).

4. To what extent can this expression be used? See the distinctions drawn by Pierre Gibert, *Mythes et légendes dans la Bible* (Edition du Sénevé, 1972), pp. 27 ff.

5. "The woman and the man are not cursed (it is unthinking to speak of their malediction!)." Gerhard von Rad, *Genesis, a Commentary,* rev. ed. (Philadelphia: Westminster, 1973). p. 90.

6. In the perception of their nudity they surely had as well an apprehension of their complete insufficiency as human beings who believed that they could attain the fullness of divinity. Their eyes were indeed opened but on a reality quite different from what they had anticipated.

7. Teilhard de Chardin writes: "Love is the most universal, the most tremendous and the most mysterious of the cosmic forces." And he adds, "Let us look very coolly, as biologists and engineers, at the lurid

atmosphere of our great towns at evening. There and everywhere else as well, the earth is continually dissipating its marvelous power. This is pure loss. Earth is burning away, wasted in the empty air. How much energy do you think the spirit of the earth loses in a single night?" *Human Energy,* trans. J.M. Cohen (New York: Harcourt Brace, 1969), p. 32.

8. John the Baptist presents Jesus as the bridegroom. "The bride is only for the bridegroom; and yet the bridegroom's friend, who stands there and listens, is glad when he hears the bridegroom's voice." Jesus too presents himself as the bridegroom in several situations: Matt. 9:15; 22:1–14; 25:1–12. See too Revelation 21:2; 21:9; 22:17; and esp. 2 Cor. 11:2.

9. Joseph Ratzinger, commenting on this expression of Jesus, writes: "This expression is meant to explain the meaning of Jesus' death on the cross . . . The crucifixion seems like an opening out to others by which the scattered human monads are drawn within the embrace of Jesus Christ . . . Christ, as the man to come, is not a man for himself, but essentially a man for others; the man to come is such precisely as the man open to all." *Foi chrétienne hier et aujourd' hui* (Tours: Mame, 1969), p. 163.

10. Ibid., p. 144. The expression "son of God" stems from the kingship theology of the Old Testament.

11. We are familiar with the exact way in which primitive societies, in Africa, for example, define the function of each one of its members.

12. Isaiah 62:8 makes the precise proclamation that what workers produce will be given back to them: "Never again shall I give your corn to feed your enemies. Never again will foreigners drink your wine that you have laboured for. But those who gather the harvest will eat it and praise Yahweh. Those who gathered the grapes will drink in the courts of my sanctuary."

13. For the teaching of the prophets on this fundamental theme, permit me to refer to my *La doctrine sociale de l'Eglise,* 2nd ed. (Paris: P.U.F., 1966), ch. 1.

14. For an explanation of the form of this verse, see André Feuillet, "Les riches intendants du Christ," *Recherches de science religieuse* 35 (January 1947).

15. Bossuet, *Sermon sur l'éminente dignité des pauvres,* Septauagésima, 1659. For the meaning of this parable, confirmed by the entire great Christian tradition and discussed by some exegetes, see Pierre Bigo, "La richesse comme intendance dans l'Evangile," *Nouvelle revue théologique* 87 (March 1965) 267–71.

16. See Bigo, *La doctrine sociale de l'Eglise,* ch. 2.

# VI

# WHAT LIBERATION?

*One God*

The great evangelical summons all come down to the essential: "Listen, Israel: Yahweh our God is the one Yahweh (Deut. 6:4); "You must worship the Lord your God, and serve him alone" (Matt. 4:10). Expressed here is the whole faith of Israel and of the Church: the most intimate revelation of God and man.

A comparison between the theology of the Bible and the theogonies of Egypt, Assyria, and Bablyon is striking. The same trait characterizes all of the latter: the area of human relations is continually being altered by the sacred character attributed, not only to natural forces, but also to the powerful of the world. The gods invade it, kings claim divine sonship and riches as a blessing from the gods. On the other hand, divinity itself is encroached upon by conflicts, tragedies, murders, the same crimes that mark and mar human relations; the gods are sexually active, they carry out political deals, they are not without evil and introduce it into the world.

That Israel should be able to escape this religious ambiance seems beyond belief; yet no alteration of the human by the divine or of the divine by the human is observable in its faith. The prophets guard the faith jealously; they do battle without mercy against the cult of the baals although it was sometimes authorized by the kings themselves, as happened, for example, during the closing years of Solomon's reign. What proud pagan Rome could not prevent, the influence of oriental theogonies and the divinization of Caesar, a small, humiliated, and enslaved people fought off by fierce resistance.

Israel did not transfer into the world of the divine the conflicts and dramas that belonged to the world of human beings. Sexuality, the city of man, work—all were of a "creatural" order,[1] a revelation that Jesus was to bring to completion.

Two truths are implied here. According to Christian faith, the human does not contaminate the divine, the uncreated does not encroach upon the created: in this way, existence is defined as a field for freedom. Yet, according to the same faith, God became man and man shares in the divinity; in that way existence is defined as a field for symbolism.

No other monotheism has affirmed at the same time and with such force this double character. Here the salvation that revelation alone can bring to the world has its source, bringing liberation from all idolatries and the oppressions stemming from them together with the communion of men in a single love.

*A field for freedom.* The entire absence of any contamination of the divine sphere by the human and their complete interpenetration indicate, first of all, the radical demystification of existence and, in the degree to which ideology is a secular substitute for mythology, its radical "disideologization." All existence, familial, political, economic, constitutes a field for freedom. God the preeminently free being, forms a union with another free being, putting into that person's hands a world to transform and society to build, a human work that needs no unreal religious justifications.[2]

In this space thus opened up to them, people enter into a relationship with nature and take on its governance. The exact sciences and technology give them increasing power over the universe of things. If they are to rule, they need to be freed from cosmogonic religions that populate nature with mysterious and intangible forces and offer only incantation as a means to humanize them.

The worship of the one God completely liberates human beings from fetishism. Provided that science and technology are not transformed into absolutes, they contain nothing that faith cannot assume. Everything they have to offer invites a Christian, more than anyone else, to give them meaning and import.

In order to survive, people have to dominate nature, to humanize it is some way by adapting it to their needs. At the same time, they do not lose sight of another need, just as elementary, to give harmonious forms to the things they make, the clothes they wear, the house they live in. In ancient cultures, the artisan was naturally an artist as well. For humanity, art is a form of relation to nature as basic as work. It took the aberrations of a budding industrial technology to dissociate one from the other; and only after a long slow process are technology and art coming to be reconciled. Yet efforts to do so are indeed maladroit compared to the creations of civilizations dubbed primitive.

Through work and art, in action and in contemplation, a human being enters into relationships with fellow creatures. The product of labor, like the product of art, is a social work; its creation is itself cooperation and its sharing brings people together in communion. In a very broad sense, it can be said that every relation between human beings begins with their relation to nature because nature is the source of work.

The sciences called "human" have as their end the discovery of the laws of intersubjective relations in all their aspects. But the social sciences, although they aim at objectivity, cannot be called exact sciences in the same sense as the natural sciences, because the organization of life in common at all levels has to do with persons. People enter into relationship with things and dominate them. They enter into relationship with other people and seek a reciprocity that excludes domination and is truly free.[3] Freedom must be studied according to methods that are proper to it. Right from the start, it implies a mystery that belongs to faith as much as to science; each cannot fail to recognize the competence of the other in a domain where the whole human being is constantly involved.

Life is all of this, a field of freedom open to people through adoration of the one God. The idea of creation, according to the Bible, does not go so far as complete secularization; it does, nevertheless, establish a foundation for it by clearing up any blurring of the lines between creation and Creator. The still earlier idea of an alliance between Israel and its God does not change but provides a foundation for a vision of a secularized world. When the day came that the people wanted a king, the priests did not oppose their will (1 Sam. 8:22). God, because he is God, leaves people free to work out their social organizations.[4]

*A symbolic field.* Faith in creation and in the covenant, just because they completely desacralize the world, make it the very place in which to meet the one God, to come upon the One who is absolutely not the world, the place of his Incarnation. A laicized world is the other, and just as essential, face of reality. Only a secularized world can establish an authentic relation with God, for only it can be conceived as symbolic.[5] And only a world that lives its relationship with God in this way and lives its existence as a symbolic field, can be totally desacralized.

If people lived only at the level of necessity, like the animals, their relationship to things and to others would pose no problem. But it is proper to rational human beings to go beyond the limits of time and space. Through nature, through their fellow human beings, they seek an opening to the other which is for always and everywhere. Although psychology and sociology cannot follow this truth to its end, they do introduce and suggest it. Human beings have something absolutely above and beyond the animal, evidencing even in their prenatal existence a whole group of reactions not explicable simply by their need to organize their individual and social life on earth, as the animal does, but betraying their desire to reach, through this very need, a relationship of an altogether different nature.

Failure to realize this desire threatens people even in their very will to survive. Human work lacks meaning if it is no more than finite. "The more I think about it," wrote Teilhard de Chardin, "the more clearly I see that I would be psychologically incapable of making the least effort if I were unable to believe in the absolute value of something in that effort. Prove to me that one day nothing will remain of my work, because there will be not only a death of the individual and a death for the earth, but a death, too, of the Universe—prove that and you break the mainspring of all my activity."[6] The world circumscribed by time and space is irremediably finite; it has no future. Humankind, not just the individual monad, but the world is condemned to die.[7] Among the certainties to which science leads us is the conclusion that the world is going to die. Will the appearance of reason within in the cosmogenesis put an end to the powerful creative dynamism to which nature testifies?

Human beings are made to open themselves to the other in unlimited and mutual self-giving. In that way alone loneliness, anguish and fear, enmity and hate come to an end. "Everything becomes one by becoming self."[8] "Union differentiates."[9] The other whom people cannot find completely either in nature or in their fellow man, both as finite as they are, is God. In Jesus, God is committed to humankind from all eternity.

In worshiping the one God, people do not get down on their knees before something they have made with their own hands or mind. Quite the opposite. They situate the absolute just where it is, at the term of conscious relationship, which is existence itself. In this sense God is the one adorable being. Only in this way is God presented to us in faith. The refusal to adore God, and God alone, leads a person to adore what is finite. As a conscious and rational being, capable of thinking about life, the individual is made for adoration because the individual is made for the infinite. When the person turns to adoring the finite, perversions begin.

The Judeo-Christian idea of creation and covenant, unique among all the religious ideas of antiquity (polytheism and Greek philosophy had only a presentiment of it), represent an entirely different notion from the absorption of persons by divinity and their domination by divine disposition. It means just the opposite, a communion offered to be freely accepted in a real reciprocal relationship, a divine communion that gives meaning and reality to every human community.

All the ancient servitudes of a universe closed in upon itself broke open at the lightning-like revelation of *the one who is*, the living and only source of life. The fear that human beings then experience is not due to the threat of tyranny but to being poised on the threshold of freedom that seems too great, too beautiful, too joyful to be known. In the great biblical theophanies, this reality erupts in consciousness together with a feeling of truth and completeness. Time seems to stop, history to be summarized, the whole universe made present in that place and at that moment. At the Transfiguration (Matt. 17:4), three men attained an instant of freedom—as if the walls of their prison had crumbled, as if the seal on heaven had at last been broken.

That, all that, is what faith means by life as a symbolic field; not to sacralize existence, that is, to attribute an infinite character to what is finite, but to perceive through the finite an infinite relationship of communion. Relationship to nature and relationship to other people is for human beings the figure, the sensible and efficacious sign, of an entirely different relationship in which, nevertheless, they find meaning and reality.

Love expresses itself spontaneously in words like "always" and "forever." A fantastic dream? No, rather a mysterious reality. But how can people hope if nothing but history is to go on forever? In every authentic human relationship and particularly in the relation of man and woman, when two beings reveal themselves to each other, there is a human moment that touches on the absolute. How are we to explain it? Perhaps this is the fleeting instant when the lines of life intersect in space and time, a moment that is absolute only because it prefigures the everlasting meeting with the absolute.

## The Mystery of Iniquity: Fetishisms

The area separating figure from reality is the place for history and also a locus for temptation and iniquity.

At the moment when the first man and woman broke the alliance that God had offered them, they became conscious of everything encompassed by that relationship and of their indigence without it. Literally, their eyes were opened. They discovered that they were naked and had their first acquaintance with shame and fear.

They believed that their first act of freedom would make them capable of determing good and evil by eating the fruit of the tree of knowledge (Gen. 3:5). What did happen was a break in symbolic unity. "You will be like gods" the serpent said to the woman—and so two human beings attempted what every temptation invites us to do, to live their lives in the world as if it were the whole of reality, the absolute. They denied their existence as "symbolic." They denied themselves as related to God, the very source of life. A mystery of iniquity and, for the prophet, a matter for astonishment that people should prefer broken cisterns to the source of living water (Jer. 2:13).

The rupture that occurred changed the relationship of human beings with nature: "Accursed be the soil because of you" (Gen. 3:17). And the relationship of man and woman: "Your yearning shall be for your husband, yet he will lord it over you" (Gen. 3:16). Finally, the break empties existence of its reality; it introduces death: "For dust you are and to dust you shall return"(Gen. 3:19). Seeking for the infinite in the finite, the divine in the human, human beings make idols for themselves. When they give up adoring God they continue to adore, for they are made for the absolute and end by prostrating themselves before forces that have no claim to adoration.

In this basic perversion lies the source of every form of alienation, of slavery, enmity, and discrimination, in brief, of all iniquity. All the relations of people with nature and with one another are altered when they break the radical alliance which God offers them and which constitutes them in existence, that is, in relationship and in liberty.

Paul, in particular, has shown its tragic consequences in the proliferation of evil powers within the universe. His epistles are full of this vision. The world is not evil but the iniquity of man has introduced hidden forces into it. "For it is not against human enemies that we have to struggle, but against the Sovereignties and Powers who originate the darkness in this world, the spiritual army of evil in the heavens" (Eph. 6:12), "the elemental principles of this world" (Gal. 4:3).

These malign forces are the false gods who invade the cosmic universe; they are also the demons who pervert social life: infamous mammon, power when made "the adorable son of the adorable God," eros when deified. All of them come from the heart of human beings, for it is from there that all maleficent powers arise (Matt. 15:19). All life, economic, political, and sexual is upset. The field for freedom becomes a place of servitude.

When people make humankind their own god, they are no longer themselves; they are themselves only so long as they hold onto what gives them meaning: sharing in the very life of the one God as that is offered to them by God.

## The Liberation of Christ

*The savior.* Man has turned away but God has not yet said the last word. God is going to follow but never force the unfaithful one. To draw near the one who has repulsed him, God must now choose, from among the rebellious human race, a being of a kind and character to reestablish the structure of existence and over-come temptation for all time, a being in whom people and God could be seen again, could be heard and touched, a being for whom God would again be the one and only God and who could be God's only Son.

Faith tells us that Jesus is that person. But when he appeared, "his own people did not accept him" (John 1:11). All the forces of iniquity formed a league against him. In order to remedy the self-sufficiency of humankind, the Son of Man must know the insufficiency of poverty, powerlessness, servitude, and death, that *kenosis* about which Paul speaks (Phil. 2:7). [10] What was the immanent consequence of the first iniquity became its healing: through the poverty of one man others can have abundance; through his servitude, they can know freedom; through his death, they can be reborn to life. Taking up life in a symbolic form, Jesus revealed its truth to humankind, gave them access to freedom, that is, to relationship in all its aspects and dimensions through a dialectic of death and life.

In so doing, Jesus grounded existence in its sacramental and paschal reality. In the case of marriage, faith recognizes it as a sacrament in the formal sense. The conjugal and family relation-ship is a sensible and efficacious sign of God's union with humankind. But all relationships, including those of political and economic society, are sacrament in an authentic sense, for they all have the same ultimate meaning.

So the visible world is a sacrament, and a sacrament to be celebrated. That is what the liturgy means, especially the Eucharistic liturgy: to signify the relationship of human beings to God at the very heart of their relationship with the world and with other human beings. [11]

For this deliverance to be perpetuated throughout the ages God had to choose not only a person born of God but a people "reborn" of him, a people not indentified with all humankind, although it would have meaning only in reference to the whole human race. Thereafter a proper history of salvation is discernible within history but does not coincide with it, even though it gives history its ultimate significance. It is a long history of germination with Jesus as its fruit, and of maturation with Jesus as its seed and it is made up of witnessings and martyrdoms, of revelations and dark nights.

Without the "mystery of iniquity," every person would have been a Christ and the whole human race would have been the Church. Once iniquity was consummated, Christ and the community of his disciples are necessary to restore its symbolic structure to existence and, by that very fact, its structure of liberty and relation.

Christ and his Church are often spoken of as sacraments, as they are. [12] But Christ and the Church are sacraments, efficacious signs of salvation, only because the world itself has been created in a symbolic form and that form is restored by Christ.

In giving human beings faith, God began by placing complete confidence in them. But humankind was to prove undeserving of so much credit. From then on, God could put his faith in people only through one person, Christ, and through all those who, in Christ, give God their faith. The very structure of the Church is determined by this condition. The Church receives its light and life not from itself but from the Spirit; like Christ, it does nothing of itself (John 5:19; 8:28). What the Spirit wills is not discovered by finding the common factor in what its membership wants and so arriving at "a common will" and accepting that as the will of the Spirit. What the Spirit wills is reached by a laborious discernment neither by numbers nor by an elite but of the Spirit. This is what gives the Church a structure different from all other existing social structures.

*Salvation.* In this fundamental relationship with the source of all life, every relationship broken off by humankind's will is in turn resumed. Because the one and only God is again adored, humanity is again made free. Woman is no longer the slave of man, the subject is no longer the bond servant of those in power, the poor are no longer oppressed by the rich. But this threefold liberation is possible only because Jesus freely chose to renounce being a husband, exercising power, and owning possessions. Of itself, this relinquishment has healed the effects of the appropriation by which humanity, being separated from its source, attempted to be itself the source of its own pleasure, power, and possessions. A completely virile man gives up ever possessing a woman in the flesh and offers himself as a spouse in a way that gives a new relationship to every marriage. A man, better endowed to rule than any other, renounces all power in the city of man and proposes himself as a king with all the power of the Son of God in order to serve and to win back royalty to its role of service. A man, more capable than any other of owning and using wealth, renounces all possessions so that, by becoming a poor man among the poor he opens up his riches to everybody[13] and restores to ownership its meaning of sharing.

God's image has been altered by the initiative of human beings. By making themselves God's rival, they have set up God as their rival. See how the primitive image is rediscovered without shame or fear: by making themselves true children, human beings regain God in his truth. And this alliance establishes a new relationship between man and woman, between governing and governed, between haves and have-nots—a real relationship that implies new ways and new structures.

The law of love and charity inscribed in human hearts (Rom. 5:5) is fulfilled only if it is expressed in a personal and collective conversion of consciences and conduct. To pardon offenses and love enemies is a manifestation of that law and the chief characteristic of the new times. And it is not only the norm for conduct in conjugal, political, and economic society but its fundamental law. God pardons humankind, which has offended him, and makes people friends instead of enemies; from then on human beings too can make an enemy into a friend. Only a man capable of pardoning adversaries who submitted him to ignominious torment could preach the pardon needed for human beings to love one another and form and maintain a stable society.

Love, so preached and so lived, necessarily involves death,

through a hatred of self that refuses to cling to life if it means using force to do so. It means a lasting death to self through which man attains to life, to liberty, and to truth in every relationship and in all phases of existence.

That, all that, is what Jesus has brought to the world of the poor and the oppressed—their liberation.[14] Had Jesus organized a political enterprise, taken on the leadership of a guerrilla movement, he would not have changed people's consciences and the structures of society. And humanity would have been definitively delivered over to the servitude of false adorations. Being invested with divine power, Jesus could only properly fulfill his mission by making it sacred. His divine mission led him to his death more directly than any political enterprise could have, for it challenged the very forces of iniquity. By fulfilling it, Jesus has taken his place at the very core of history and inaugurated a new era. The pagan and Jewish world, with their mythologies, are overthrown. They will always keep on reviving but their decline is inscribed in history, on condition that the disciples of Jesus remain united in their faith in him in order to continue his work down through the centuries. Their combats, their martyrdoms, like his own, are not political, but, just like his, they have tremendous political import.

Among the disciples, some are not given any other mission than Christ's own. These are a small number, invited to follow Jesus in renouncing sexual fulfillment, power, and possessions. Others, on the contrary, remain in marriage, in political and economic activities. Both groups, each in its own way, work to transform the structure of familial, political, and economic society, the first group in a more radical manner, the second in a more involved way, all living according to the law of love learned from the Lord.

Nothing is more needful than the presence of both for the Kingdom to be truly realized. The Church encompasses all in both groups. What characterizes it is that in the world and throughout history, Christ's work of liberation is accomplished by both, one by following the great liberating renouncements, the other by remaining in the very core of familial, political, and economic society.

Salvation is worked out in the very heart of relationships which make up life, the only life given people to live. Just that, and all that, is the liberation announced by Jesus Christ to the poor and oppressed.[15]

## NOTES

1. The expression is Gerhard von Rad's. "An imperceptible process of profound demythization was effected by which faith in Yahweh assimilated cultic ideas and usages derived from entirely different milieus . . . But Israel did not participate in the 'divinization' of sex. Yahweh stood absolutely beyond and above the polarity of sex and this meant that Israel never considered sex as a sacred mystery. It was excluded from the cult because it belonged to the creatural order." Trans. by Lyons but see also *Old Testament Theology*, trans. D. M. G. Stalker, 2 vols. (New York: Harper and Row, 1965), Vol., 1 pp.27–28.

2. The "theologies of liberation" and "political theologies," that have appeared in recent years, chiefly in Latin America, are so numerous that it is impossible to enumerate them. In *Ecclesiastica Xaveriana*, no. 22, (1972), there is a bibliographical study by Roger Vekemans entitled "Anticedentes para el estudio de la Teologia de la Liberación." I.L.A.D.E.S., Bogotá, has drawn up a mimeographed list of articles and works on the question which includes more than a thousand titles: *Iglesia y liberación, desarrollo y revolución*. A second list is in preparation. Hugo Assmann, *Opresión-liberación: desafio a los cristianos* (Montevideo: Tierra Nueva, 1971); Joseph Comblin, *Théologie de la révolution* (Paris: Editions Universitaires, 1970); Gustavo Gutiérrez, *A Theology of Liberation: History, Politics and Salvation*, trans. and ed. John Eagleson and Caritas Inda (Maryknoll, N.Y.: Orbis Books, 1973).

3. According to the definition of liberty which faith suggests and which contrasts with contemporary conceptions: an opening to the other in reciprocity.

4. The great theologians of secularization are well known, Dietrich Bonhoeffer and Fredrich Gogarten, and their thinking has been diffused by Harvey Cox in *The Secular City* (New York: Macmillan, 1966). These theologians have shown, and not without cause, that people have turned from the world beyond to fix their whole attention on this world and time and, by doing so, have acted in a logically Christian way. Have they not, however, been inclined to forget the other face of reality—the

symbolic area? In any case, the importance given to symbol in recent anthropology no longer allows us to be satisfied with so negative a theology.

5. Today the human sciences all emphasize the value of symbol. The symbol can be said to be the meaning attributed to a thing by convention. The flag is a symbol of a country. There is no reason why some colors rather than others must be chosen. "Symbolic" designates an artificial, a conventional association by which a thing comes to signify a relation. Because of this, a nuance of unreality clings to the word as it is currently used. But symbol also designates—and this is the sense which the human sciences attach to it today—a sensible relation that has meaning only by another that is announced and prefigured. The kiss is a symbol of love. In a sense, existence is symbolic, not unreal but quite the opposite, so real that actuality projects itself toward a plenitude alone capable of fulfilling it.

6. "My Universe" (March 25, 1924), in *Science and Christ*, trans. René Hague (New York: Harper and Row, 1968), pp. 42–43. Teilhard expresses the same idea a number of times, for example: "An animal may rush headlong down a blind alley or towards a precipice. Man will never take a step in a direction he knows to be blocked. . . . By the nature of the work, and correlatively, by the requirement [*exigence*] of the worker, a total death, an unscalable wall, on which conciousness would crash and then forever disappear, are thus 'incompossible' with the mechanism of the activity of reflection (which would immediately break its mainspring)." *The Phenomenon of Man* (New York: Harper and Row, 1959), pp. 229–30.

7. Teilhard de Chardin, "The Mass on the World," in *Hymn of the Universe* (New York: Harper and Row, 1965), p. 31.

8. Teilhard de Chardin, "My Universe, " p. 74.

9. Teilhard de Chardin, *The Phenomenon of Man*, p. 262. For a study of Teilhard de Chardin, see the works of his associates who have followed his thought from its origins: Henri du Lubac, *The Religion of Teilhard de Chardin*, trans. René Hague (Garden City, N.Y.: Doubleday, 1967) and *Teilhard et notre temps* (Paris: Aubier, 1971); René d'Ouince, *Un Prophète en procès* (Paris: Aubier, 1970); Emile Rideau, *La pensée du P. Teilhard de Chardin* (Paris: Seuil, 1965) and *Teilhard, oui ou non?* (Paris: Fayard, 1967).

10. Emile Rideau, *La Révélation* (Paris: Fayard, 1972), brings out clearly "the *inversion* by which God is made known in his truth, the disclosure that he makes of his hidden identity" (p. 91).

11. Teilhard de Chardin's poem *Hymn of the Universe* brings out beautifully this meaning of the Eucharistic liturgy.

12. This theme is developed in depth by Edward H. Schillebeeckx, *Christ: The Sacrament of the Encounter with God* (New York: Sheed and Ward, 1963).

13. Remember how generous the Lord Jesus was: "he was rich but he became poor for your sake to make you rich out of his poverty" (2 Cor. 8:9).

14. Much confusion would be avoided if people would only read the entire text in which Jesus presents himself as the one who brings the good news to the poor. " . . . the blind see again, the lame walk, lepers are cleansed, and the deaf hear, the dead are raised to life, the Good News is proclaimed to the poor" (Luke 7:22; cf. Matt. 11:5). In the gospel the oppressed are not just those whom society oppresses but those whom life bears down upon: Jesus spent his time healing the sick and afflicted. He never dissociated the "political" aspects of his mission from all the others and, at one stroke, shows us in what sense we can speak of his political role and in what sense we cannot. Like Jesus, the prophets have never separated the poor from all the others bruised by life. "He has sent me to bring good news to the poor, to bind up hearts that are broken; to proclaim liberty to captives, freedom to those in prison" (Isa. 61:1). Neither the Old Testament nor the New lends itself to a purely political interpretation. Both move within a cosmic perspective that encompasses a social perspective but is not limited to it. They never lose sight of an eschatological horizon: it is finally in a combat between life and death that liberation is completed.

15. All that and only that is the "social doctrine of the Church." André Manaranche in his thought-provoking book, *Y-a-t-il une éthique sociale chrétienne?* (Paris: Seuil, 1969), p. 246, concludes that in Christ "all is revealed and nothing is known. For the faith says everything, and so very little. . . . That, without a doubt, is the point of departure for a Christian social ethic." In fact, the faith does say little, but that little is much. In presenting himself to us as bridegroom and king and the source of true riches, Christ has changed the fundamentals of social existence. All that the human conscience today owes to Christ in its search for a new relationship within the family, and civil and economic society—even after we subtract sociological contributions that have another origin—is incalculable. No historical study or research can demonstrate it. The fruitfulness of the gospel remains in part a mystery. But the person who has faith in the Spirit cannot deny the extraordinary eruption made in history by the resurrection of Jesus Christ, even if the new times are not yet completely free of the old.

# VII

# THE CHURCH:
# ITS FIDELITY
# ITS TEMPTATION

*The Time of the Church*

To reveal the one adorable God, and so to deliver the world from the fetishes crushing it, to lead it to freedom, to lay the basis for a new relationship among people is the mission of Jesus. Through it, he inaugurates the new times; and he can accomplish it only if it is continued by a community of disciples nurtured together in the same faith. The Church's mission is the same as Jesus' and it is overwhelming: to reveal the one true God; to struggle until the end of time against idols that never stop reappearing; to combat the powers of darkness enslaving people; to bring deliverance to the world of the oppressed poor and to their oppressors by bringing oppression to an end; to bring to completion throughout the long, long stretch of history the new era inaugurated by the resurrection of Jesus.

A truly unheard-of transformation, scarcely suspected by the pagan world and barely introduced by the Jewish. Jesus divides history. Beginning with him, there is a before and an after.

Many seem to think that from the resurrection of Christ until the end of time, nothing is to happen in the coming of the Kingdom, with the disciples of Christ keeping their faith in his return and passively waiting for it, untouched by the disasters that befall peoples and nations. Scripture gives no authorization for such an interpretation. The Word has come into the world to transform it. "You give breath, fresh life begins, you keep renewing the world" (Ps. 104:30).

Until the end of time the powers of iniquity will surely be at work and, in a sense, all that has been done will always have to be done again and again. Christian faith is not faith in progress. Christian hope is hope that is both tragic and invincible. In the midst of cataclysms and calamities— our words cannot translate the force of Jesus' predictions (Matt. 24)—a kind of forerunner of spring nevertheless speaks of the rising of the sap into the barren trees. A seed has been entrusted to the earth and the earth is working out its salvation.

Christ's return is the slow germination and maturation of a new world. In this way will the Lord return. But no one will need to look for Christ here or there. The Lord will be like a lightning flash at night setting earth and sky alight from east to west (Matt. 24:26–27). Christ's return will not be an event belonging more to the close of history than to other times; it will fill the whole of history from end to end, happening for every moment everywhere, for it is nothing less than the overwhelming outpouring of the Spirit all throughout history. No instant of time, no foothold in space is cut off from sharing in the coming of the Kingdom.

Looking at it from another aspect, nothing indicates that we may reduce Christ's return to a simple interior event. It means the end of the pagan and Jewish worlds and the birth of a new society, in which man and woman, citizen and fellow citizen, worker and fellow worker discover one another in a new relationship. Such a work cannot be accomplished in a moment. As the parables of Jesus lead us to foresee, its slow fermentation will go on and on through the centuries to come.

If such is indeed the mission of the Church, then to it as to Christ the dramatic question is put: What have you to say about oppression? What are you doing to liberate the peoples of the world?

## The Temptation of the Church

Jesus and his first disciples, particularly John and Paul, have all spoken of the lot awaiting a people chosen to carry out a mission of that kind. They are to be a sign of contradiction among the peoples of the earth. The powers of this world, vested in all their prestige, will not forgive them for daring to challenge them.

The flashing pages in which Jesus foretells, in the disciples' hearing, what will happen to them promises something less than an idyllic future. John the Baptist had already announced Jesus as one who would baptize "with the Holy Spirit and fire" (Matt. 3:11). Violence and hatred on the part of those near and dear to them await the disciples. They will be dragged before tribunals. Those who condemn them will believe that they are honoring God by doing so—a mysterious saying that gives a glimpse of the zealous opposition to come.

Against the disciples demoniac forces will rise up, marked with all the prestige of power and glory—and of fervor and purity as well. They will bring down to the ground some of the stars of heaven (Rev. 12:4), those most marked by the Spirit. Mankind's eternal demons—money, power, the flesh—bent on being adored, will ravage the Church itself, seeking to devour those who stand up against them and hold them at bay.

In the enduring struggle, the Church's temptation, the same that Jesus had, is unrelenting too: to place at the service of powers and principalities the power of the Spirit that has been imparted to it; in reality, to serve them and adore them in a demoniac counterfeit of worship, returning, in fine, to the ancient theogonies which made riches, power, and sex sacred by introducing them into the sphere of the divine. It all comes down to a refusal to adore the one true God. The temptation without end is, as it has ever been, to "be as gods."

For the Church, sacralizing the profane world is the major obstacle to its liberating role. Instead of destroying the unclean idols, the Church consecrates them. When it has done that, it no longer speaks to the rich of their iniquitous culpability in appropriating for their own use what had been produced by work in common and intended to meet the needs of all. The Church no longer braves the established powers when they exact adoration from their subjects or impose themselves upon their subjects as authorities from which there is no appeal. The Church is silent before the tyranny of technological growth, letting it seem as if bread were indeed the only human nourishment.

What of the community that Christ founded to be the light of the world, the salt of the earth, a city on a mountain living communion in such a way that the human community might find it a witness of help in structuring and consolidating itself?[1] Today does it not, rather, present a spectacle of collusion with riches and power? Does it not incur the threats addressed by the prophets and by Christ himself to those who prostitute themselves with baals and worship mammon? Has it not yielded to the temptation in the desert by bowing down before worldly prestige, more preoccupied with its own development than with confronting the obvious iniquities of power and opulence?

It must be admitted that, down through the centuries and still today, the Christian community has, in large part, succumbed to the temptation. The Church is not identified with Christ and only with Christ. Perhaps in the past, theology has tended to be too ready at assimilating. In recent years it has accented differences. Not only in each of its members, whatever position they occupy in the Church, but also as a collectivity, the people of God is a sinful people. Yet it possesses Christ's promises, "And know that I am with you always; yes, to the end of time" (Matt. 28:20). Members of Christ's Body, if they are sincere, do not feel themselves better than others. They know only that, without the light and strength drawn from their faith, however little they have wanted to live by it, they would not be what they have become. To that, and only that, they bear witness. The Church is a sinner, picked up from the streets and, even though a leper, embraced (Ezek. 16). It is made the "scorn of mankind, jest of the people" (Ps. 22:7). It carries the flame, but in "earthenware jars" (2 Cor. 4:7). It asks public pardon of God and men. For it, which has received the mission to witness to the truth, silence is the gravest fault. And it does not always speak; it does not always testify. Confronted by the powerful, it seeks alliances and resorts to compromises.

Historical reasons give a partial explanation for this. After the long and bloody age of martyrs, the Church became the "official" religion in the Roman world at the time of Constantine. Thereafter it was burdened with the full weight of feudal structures, becoming the capstone of medieval society and the *Ancien Régime*. Protected by the secular arm, defended by a "civilization," it launched into equivocal undertakings of a political character—the crusades, the wars of religion. Historical misconceptions of tremendous import. Inhibiting political and cultural ties with a particular order and civilization. By the very fact that it came to be one institution among others in the Western world, it accepted as part of itself a mass of "baptized" who came to it more because of tradition and convention than because of conviction and conversion.

With the beginning of the great modern revolutions, the scandal has taken new forms. During the epoch of triumphant liberalism, the Church, in spite of some inept protestations against the new ideas, partly alligned itself with the bourgeoisie, its adversary at first and then its ally. The people then drew back from the Church. The strong voice of Leo XIII stigmatized the burgeoning industrial societies with the shameful state of the proletariat and proclaimed the right of working people to form trade unions, but that voice was raised only belatedly.

Nevertheless, circumstances only partly explain this obtuseness; internal and external forces will always be at work to turn the Church aside from its testimony and its mission. Those who are its harshest critics cannot forget that, if it were too severe in choosing its members, they would not belong to it.

It is no less true that when the Church loses sight of its essential mission, it allows itself to be again invaded by mythologies and sacralizing ideologies; and amazing adulterations take form with it. The heavy yoke of a religion of prohibitions and taboos is then substituted for commandments issuing from the single precept of love. Faith, a source of life, becomes an obstacle to life. And the Christian world, instead of being a world of freedom as it is called to be, becomes a place for collective murders and slavery, the accounts of which are among the darkest pages of human history. They are all the more monstrous when an attempt is made to justify them in the name of faith and in spite of the prophets, whose voices no one has ever been able to still.

*The temptation of the zealous.* The temptation to ally oneself with the established powers is the temptation of the high priests. But there is another and more subtle one, the temptations of the zealous, the temptation to be allied with those committed to toppling the people in power in order to take their place. Jesus came to grips with this temptation; he had to in order to protect his followers from it. He did not allow himself to be confused with the Zealots, and Pilate made no mistake about that—he knew that Jesus was not one of them. Judas the Galilean invoked the great commandment to adore the one true God in order to mobilize the people against the Romans, a political enterprise. As such, it had its reasons. Jesus never condemned it but he never justified it for religious reasons. Those who have received a divine mission cannot put it at the service of a political cause without running the risk of sacralizing what is profane, of deifying what is human.

It needs to be said that many in the Church undergo this identical, inverse temptation. Those in power are not the only ones who impose their yoke on the masses; it is also done by those who mobilize the masses, not for the divine work confided to the apostles but for human enterprises, for reasons akin to the Galilean's. By wanting to yoke the Church to the revolution, these people, like Judas the Galilean, invoke high principles and, without meaning to, cause the same kind of confusion. By investing a human enterprise with all the prestige of the divine, they yield to the temptation to bend down before worldly powers and make idols of them. In this way, they contribute to building up new absolutisms, new servitudes. By sacralizing the world, they destroy the field of freedom and reinstate false gods. Today ideologies, rather than mythologies, are substituted for theologies. They may be more occult but have the same result.

Historically, each of the great revolutionary ideologies has been a source of temptation for the Church's fervent members. In opposition to the popes' condemnation of modern ideas at the beginning of the nineteenth century, some wanted to identify the coming of the Kingdom with the revolution. Rightly recognizing in it ideas of a Christian origin, they thought that it incarnated Christianity. A century and a half later it is easy to recognize the threat that they represented—a Catholic liberalism! Such an undertaking could only fail, and who now could be other than glad that it did?

Evidently it is as difficult for the revelation of the one true God to find its way through the thicket of revolutionary ideologies as it is to keep to its course among established powers. Both claim dominion; neither intends to submit to the one Kingdom but, on the contrary, to try to bring to their knees those who witness to it.

The temptation to collusion is the same, whether it occurs in a conservative or a progressive form, whether it compromises with a powerful established order or courts the favor of rising revolutionary forces. The Church's authorities are apt to give in to the first form, the Church's enthusiasts and those attracted by prestige are more likely to succumb to the second.

## The Church's Fidelity

The Christian community is afflicted with opacity but blessed with transparency too. And for anyone not unmindful of human fraility, the latter is perhaps, if not more spectacular, at least more astonishing.

To realize this to the full, we would need to enter into the secret depths of human hearts. And it so happens that in regard to what has become familiar to the Christian community, those outside it are more sensitive than the faithful. The Christian community has been and is today a place for the opening up and maturation of initiatives which come to grips with the powers of our century and give the world's poor a chance. Beginning with the early Christian community at Jerusalem, people like Francis of Assisi, Vincent de Paul, Charles de Foucauld, and many others have not been content to preach the gospel with words but have proclaimed it in truth. Certainly their undertakings sometimes met with institutional resistance within the Church. Yet that institution, in spite of its ponderousness, has often helped in their conception and realization. In Francis's case, when he stripped himself of everything, had he not already found a bishop's mantle with which to cover himself? Since Leo XIII, the popes have not lagged behind but have often been in the vanguard of the Christian community's struggle. Witnesses outside the Church recognize that fact. The words of the Communist Rappoport are unforgettable, "We don't despise your encyclicals. What we do despise is the way you disregarded them."[2] Oftentimes the clear-sightedness of pastors has run up against the blindness and inertia of the bulk of Christians. But here again, is it a mistake to say that the picture is not as dark as it is generally painted? Christians are accused of being particularly passive in the purely political sphere; yet even there, believers do think through and carry out actions inspired by their faith, without in any way confusing these with the mission proper to the ecclesial community to which they belong. A world de-Christianized for several generations has lost a sense of many Christian values. But at least where Christianity has escaped the assaults of aggressive irreligion, where people have kept the faith, anyone with eyes to see discovers, along with "practices" and "superstitions" that have become the subject of so much scorn, a receptivity to the gospel, a sense of sharing and forgiving, a readiness to serve others—which are definitely "political" virtues and keep the ferment of renewal alive. And some testify to the truth daily and unto martyrdom. In the midst of a world where injustice and the will to power triumph, a "little remnant" of Christians who live their faith, confront the powerful of this world, and are the bearers of a new society, is an enduring miracle. To perceive them, are especially keen eyes or exceptional circumstances needed?

*The Church's poor.*    The Church's extraordinary power of regeneration—evident to anyone who looks at it attentively—wells up from an inexhaustible source, the world of "the poor." As it was with the people of Israel during the period of their great trials so it is today: the poor preserve intact the ability to distinguish between true and false adoration. They are just in the sense that they actualize what is right because they participate in the common human condition and do not seek to reserve for themselves a situation apart from the community. They are just, too, in the sense that they are justified by being continually relegated to the margin of society by the powerful. They are also humble because, even when humiliated, even when overwhelmed by trouble, they do not abandon fearing God, in whom they continue to hope. And God's hope is in them.

In recent times, Yahweh's poor have a still more marked significance and role. From the moment of the Incarnation, the Magnificat of Mary, the mother of Jesus, makes this manifest.[3]

All the beatitudes speak of the blessing of the humble[4]—the gentle, the merciful, the pure of heart (that is, those not tainted with injustice), those who work for peace, those who hunger and thirst for justice, as well as those who suffer persecution for it. All these find in the fire of the Spirit the energy to keep on being poor.

The whole expectation of the Church rests in them. When Paul celebrates charity, *agape,* in his letter to the Corinthians, he does not hesitate to place it above all the charisms, and even beyond faith and hope. "Love is always patient and kind; it is never jealous; love is never boastful or conceited; it is never rude or selfish; it does not take offence, and is not resentful. . . . Love does not come to an end. . . . there are three things that last, faith, hope and love; and the greatest of these is love" (1 Cor. 13:4–5,7,13). The poor are those who hold others dear; should the Church lack self-denying charity, the charisms themselves would lose their wellspring.

Evangelical poverty is defined by two inseparable dimensions, one social, one spiritual, for the struggle against riches takes place in the human heart. It consists in participation in the common lot by sharing things and in an interior attitude as well. It is at the same time visible and invisible; for that reason, it forms no class and eludes sociological investigation.

The race of the poor will never die out in the Christian community, a fact that promises the Church lasting life. Thanks to them, the faith will not fade away. They will save it. On this point, Jesus is categorical. Not to the intelligent, not to the wise, but to them, "the little ones," mysteries are revealed (Matt. 11:25). They are told the good news (Matt. 11:5). Everybody who teaches or preaches in the Church, clerics and lay people alike, every magisterium and every prophecy can express the truth only if they interpret the wisdom of the poor. The actual grace received by pastors to enable them to teach is precisely this faithful interpretation.

Because of the poor, the power of the Spirit is not extinguished in the Church. Stripped of prestige as they are, the poor hold onto it. As Peter said to the paralytic, "I have neither silver nor gold, but I will give what I have: in the name of Jesus Christ, the Nazarene, walk!" and immediately the man stood upright (Acts 3:6). All who hold power in the Church, whether in a formal or an informal way, cannot forget that the source of spiritual power rests not in their prestige but in the poverty of those who possess no prestige.

By the poor God is worshiped in spirit and in truth. All the Church's liturgy has as its end the celebration of the mystery of the world and its deliverance from false adoration. The Church must look to the poor for that. Without them it becomes lost in vain ritualism. They are with the Church to preserve its character of simplicity, to keep it from ostentation and, above all, to prevent it from making distinctions between different classes of people (James 2:1) and so alienating or wounding them. The liturgical community is an anticipation of the new society; within it at least the poor are held in honor and feel at home.

In a word, the poor perpetuate the mystery of Christ, the poor man, in the Church. Through them the Spirit is immanent in the Church, working to make it a lasting structure; for the Spirit is essentially free, breathing where it will (John 3:8), not giving itself to people of property. The poor alone are to receive it, for they have nothing of their own and believe themselves to be nothing. Neither the masses nor the elite but the poor hold fast the Spirit in the Church. By very definition they do not set themselves apart from others; nor do they seek to take the place of needed institutions.

If temptation exists in the Church, it is in the degree to which ministries and charisms lose sight of their bond with the world of the poor, and the bulk of the faithful forget the mystery of renunciation that constitutes the Church. With that vision lost, the Church no longer fulfills its liberating mission. And if the Church is found faithful to its mission, it is because it always has the little remnant of the poor; through them faith and charity are continually renewed.

Doubtless close scrutiny is needed to discover lives led in secret devotion to the service of others with Christ as their light and strength. But they are present and are, I dare say it, the Church's salvation. In them the church continues to be a sign, a light on a lampstand, a city on a mountain.[5]

The picture has shadows but it has lights too. In the face of so many merciless indictments of the Church, we reach the point of asking ourselves whether the view of it may not have been distorted from the start by a misunderstanding. As it was with Jesus, could it not be the same with the Church—that it is asked to fulfill a mission that does not belong to it? Could it not be that people demand that the Church rally to some political project of their choice, whether it be to bolster up the existing order or to support a revolution, just as in Christ's time, people would have had him either authorize submission to the *pax romana* or take upon himself the leadership of a rebellion? Contentions multiply. But are they justified? Is it not significant that these accusations issue from opposing political positions? As far as reproaches are concerned, each person has his or her own different reasons for lodging a reproach depending on political stance. In order to make judgments on solid grounds as to what the Christian community is saying and doing in order to denounce evil and uphold the good, we need to recall that there was also a trial in which Jesus as the accused incurred the same condemnation and the same capital punishment. Surely a great distance lies between the one to whom no one could impute sin and the sinful people who are his disciples. But to the extent to which the contestation directed at the Church begins from the same preconception regarding its nature and role, that is no more justified. If the Church is criticized because it does not want to become involved in an area that is not its own, then it, like Jesus before his detractors and judges, finds itself obliged to explain with difficulty what kingdom it seeks to bring about and with what arms it will fight for that.

What is the Church's position in the political field? What is the relationship between the political project of liberation and the work of salvation? There is no more urgent or difficult question being debated today.

## NOTES

1. *Gaudium et spes*, no. 42, *Documents of Vatican II*, ed. Walter Abbott and Joseph Gallagher (New York: Guild Press, 1966), p. 241.
2. Quoted in the Collective Pastoral Letter of the Bishops of the

United States, January 21, 1968 (Washington, D.C.: United States Catholic Conference, 1968).

3. "He has looked upon his lowly handmaid . . . he has routed the proud of heart. He has pulled down princes from their thrones and exalted the lowly. The hungry he has filled with good things, the rich sent empty away" (Luke 1:47–53). A Protestant theologian, Asmussen, has no hesitation in saying that Jesus had had, in the person of his mother, a living model of evangelical poverty. To that it can be added that the apostles, after the death of Jesus, also found her such a model. See A. Asmussen, *Maria, die Mutter Gottes* (Stuttgart, 1950).

4. See Edward Schillebeeckx, *Mary, Mother of the Redemption,* trans. N. D. Smith (New York: Sheed and Ward, 1964), pp. 28–32.

5. See Georges Bernanos: "I say that the poor will save the world, and they will save it without meaning to. They will save it in spite of themselves, they will ask for nothing in return except to know the worth of the service which they will have rendered. *Les enfants humiliés* (Paris: Gallimard, 1949), p. 249.

# VIII

# THE CHURCH AND POLITICS

The Church is a source of liberation to the extent that it keeps up the worship of the true God in the world, delivering the world from all forms of idolatry, whether religious or profane, and from those servitudes that stem from them. The Church stands up against oppression to the degree to which it does not hesitate to challenge that oppression with churchly weapons. It enters into political combat in a sense, for to take part against racial or social discrimination inevitably means entering the political field, but it does not make use of political means, as it has no intention of establishing a regime or of putting into effect a particular policy or of employing weapons of power—coercion, pressure, and material force—but only of taking up the arms of the Spirit.

For the Church to renounce the struggle would mean allowing the fetishisms of wealth and power to invade the world; to engage in the struggle with political weapons would result in raising up new idolatries, new absolutisms, by placing at the service of limited undertakings the energy of adoration.

Here is where all the debates about the Church and politics, the Church and liberation have their source. And the confusion that reigns often stems from the fact that people have lost sight of one or the other of the two components involved: on the one hand, the more the Christian community sees the political as a symbolic field, the more deeply it becomes involved in it; on the other hand, as it continues to discover the political as a field for freedom, it recognizes its increasing autonomy. The whole debate centers on this paradox.[1]

## The Christian Community, Foremost
## in the Struggles for Liberation

In the matter of liberation, although it may begin with the personal options of individual Christians, it does not end there. The faithful have a quickened sense of the value of the political, of the necessity for becoming engaged in the struggles for liberation and involved with the ideologies and strategies these necessitate. They feel a special challenge to adopt these options. Despite the fact that action is often partisan and has unavoidable defects, it is needed. Christians must not forget what Péguy said about the Kantians, "They have no dirt on their hands, but then they have no hands." They do not demand that their brothers in the faith line up behind their own choices, for they are aware of the uncertainties and risks attached to them. But in working in the service of the city of man they really do advance the Kingdom in the measure to which, within their commitment, they keep in view the properly political conditions necessary for success and the sacramental significance of the commitment in all its implications. To reconcile the sharp conflict arising from the twofold aim of political effectiveness and human authenticity is no easy task. To help each of its members reach a conscientious discernment in choosing from among the options is precisely the role for a common search within the Christian community. Once that is done, there is a Christian presence, there is fullness of meaning; then it is true to say that a particular action, even a particular rebellion, reaches both a political and an ethical level.

This sudden awareness is, up to a certain point, new among Christians. A small minority in the Church have always had it. Now many are beginning to experience it. However, it is not something essentially new. Today the Christian community is alive not only to the obligations of its individual members to engage in political action but also to the collective options demanded of them and the impossibility of taking a neutral position as a group. Here we come up against a serious situation. The universal Church is the Christian community gathered together in the Eucharist, and the tendency is to keep every political question and involvement at a distance from the sanctuary. Now, on the contrary, the presence of "the politcal" in the Christian assembly is perceived as a necessity, a necessity not because of some title to act as a substitute for the political and still less in the name of some civil function it has as an ecclesial institution, but because of what is most authentic in the faith—the affirmation of the sacramental and paschal character of existence.

The point is that today the liberation of the oppressed seems to be and is in fact a most urgent form of salvation itself. The liberation of the oppressed obliges us not only to give them individual assistance in the religious and spiritual aspects of their lives but in their political, economic, and cultural features as well. It is not enough to say that doing so is a condition for salvation; it is the very coming of the Kingdom in its temporal form. Oppression is the gravest "sin," if we restore to the word "sin" its biblical meaning of iniquity; and collective forms of oppression are even more serious than individual ones.

This represents at once the prophetic and evangelical conceptions; both are "political" in the sense that they denounce and destroy a former structure of relation and announce and establish a new structure. To uncover the meaning of iniquity, we must leave behind an atemporal and individualistic reading of the Bible; then it will become evident.

In a world in which relationships are continually expanding and multiplying, *metanoia,* conversion, is not limited to individual consciences and behavior; it increasingly extends to collective consciences and conduct; it means, in other words, a conversion of social structures insofar as they are a reflection of human consciences and express a line of conduct. A political structure that incorporates slavery or racial discrimination is sin itself, for it is, of itself, iniquity. In such a system it would do no good to try to establish a human relationship with another without having in mind at the same time transforming the relationship itself.

According to the Bible, every one of us will be judged by whether or not we gave bread to the hungry (those who have experienced hunger know the value of bread); water to the thirsty (water is something rare in desert country); freed the captive (so many are unjustly detained, even in countries most enamored of democracy). Today to give bread means to defeat hunger in the world, an impossibility without organizing the economic community that includes rich people and poor people—something that implies that everybody must become conscious of and conscientious about the dimensions and urgency of world hunger. To care for the sick means to set up public health organizations and to keep working to improve them. To free prisoners from their chains means to reform the penal system and to help the delinquent to regain their place in society. In sum, all this means challenging the structures of society. On these grounds we people of today are judged and saved or lost. The collective as such does not sin, is not saved. "Two will be in one bed: one will be taken, the other left" (Luke 17:34): salvation is still a personal matter. As individuals we are lost or saved according to whether or not, with the means at our disposal, we have done our part in changing the collective conscience and in transforming the structure of the group.

Under these conditions, the Christian community as a whole cannot be either silent or static in the face of oppression. It is involved, and involved as a whole. It denounces the disorder that can be hidden under the accepted order of things or masked by the new face of revolution; it proclaims a new society and does its share in building it up. Its activity is not something besides the Kingdom. It is the Kingdom itself coming to pass. It is not a function foreign to the mission assumed by the Christian assembly but its proper function. In exercising it, the group enters of necessity into the political field. In the celebration of the Eucharist the political has its appointed place, along with all the other aspects of life and is there offered for the ends of freedom.

*The Christian Community Increasingly*
*Aware of the Autonomy of the Political Field*

The modern conscience has demanded "the autonomy of the temporal" and Vatican Council II has conceded it.[2]

Politics has its own laws, which are not derived either from the gospel or from ethics, and can be the subject of a positive science. There are two distinct competencies, the one of science, the other of faith; two experiences: empirical discovery together with the laws that it brings to light, and the whole of existence and the meaning waiting to be uncovered there.

Liberation in the political sense of the term presupposes putting into effect ideologies and strategies that can be diverse even if inspired by faith. Of course, what pluralism is legitimate in the Church is not without importance, for the conception of human relationships that originates in the gospel ultimately indicates the range of possible options—but the Church does not suppress plurality.

*Faith and ideology.* An essential difference exists between faith and ideology.[3] Both lay claim to universality; both, too, appeal to the whole range of human dynamisms that spring up in beings of flesh and spirit. Their difference is due to the fact that an ideology is conditioned by the interests and values of a specific group in a definite historical conflict; faith, on the contrary, in its deepest reaches is not linked to any particular time or culture, even if it has to be incarnated in them. Strictly speaking, an ideology does not attain to the truth of a situation; faith does.

Ideology, giving the term its precise meaning, is an expression of one social group in their concrete circumstances. It appeals to their solidarity and their agressiveness. It elaborates collective symbols and representations in view of realizing a project that presupposes defined ends and means; and justifies itself by reference to a system of values. Without strategy it is powerless.

Because of the values to which it appeals, ideology has a relationship with faith. By taking them seriously, it questions the believer who has a tendency to overlook them by escaping into an atemporal, nonspatial world. The great revolutionary ideologies of the modern era have all raised people's consciousness as to the values of liberty which faith cannot reject since they find in it their true solidity and full meaning. In promoting the values of liberty, ideologies have usually done so in an aggressive, and what might be called a "heretical," manner, partly because "the children of the new spirit" have run into opposition from "the children of tradition,"[4] who are often believers. This has happened partly because those pushing ideologies have thought that they could further what they affirm by the shock value of what they deny. Their enduring criticism of the Christian community is that it is a place for laggards and throwbacks.

On its part, the faith recognizes the necessity for ideologies but is against their innate tendency to make themselves absolute and sacred, to become transformed into a secular religion, as Paul Ricoeur has expressed it,[5] to take a part for the whole, to make some one value the only value. Faith holds out to them "a global vision of man and of the human race which the Church possesses as her characteristic attribute;"[6] and, by rectifying them, restores their true liberating function.

*The Church and power.* Every political ideology and strategy, if they are not to rest content with vain pronouncements and demonstrations, have a relationship to power in society as a whole. They are intended to win it, to exercise it, to control it, or to subvert it.[7]

Theology, basing itself on Paul's well-known directives to the first Christian communities, insists on respect for established power (Rom. 13:17). In reality, what it implicitly supports is something broader, the legitimate autonomy of the political enterprise, whether it has in view maintaining or rejecting the established regime. Perhaps those who take issue with the traditional doctrine would find it easier to accept if they grasped its import.

Just as faith has been given to the disciples as light, so the Spirit has been communicated to them as energy. Both must "renew the face of the earth" and change "the shape of the world." They are a liberating light and energy, since the powers of this world tremble and fall before them.

Yet this energy is not power, if the term is used in its precise meaning. The Church has no civil jurisdiction. It does not see itself as having the right to legislate, to govern, to administer, to judge, to restrain in society as a whole. It admits that it does not have the competence to substitute for an unjust law one that is just; it claims only the right to alert consciences. In this regard, Christ's words are definitive. The Church, like its Master, leads in a war but bears no arms, uses no means of constraint. Those who come to it do so because they respond to the sound of its voice. All the situations when it has been, or still is, otherwise are in direct contradiction to Jesus' most evident will.

Jesus simply reminds those who possess and those who seek power that whether it be the power to repress or to contest, it can only "lay down the law" because it is dependent upon and answerable to higher law that judges it, because "it has been given you from above" (John 19:11). Neither against one nor the other, however unjust they may be, does the Christian community claim to use either ideological or strategical weapons: all it can do is to make the voice of conscience heard and to take action that does not aim at the exercise, the control, or the conquest of power. It is not a party, not even a pressure group. If it sometimes confronts established power just as tellingly as the forces fighting against it, it uses, not political means, but the strength of the Spirit so that it can give testimony to the truth.

*Conflicts of conscience.* We can measure the extent to which the Church recognizes the autonomy that its members rightfully exercise in civil society by pointing out another principle: even to Christians as political beings the Church does not dictate what options they are to choose. The ultimate decision rests with each one alone. This becomes particularly evident when, in a political matter, a person's conscience sees a conflict between two ethical norms. Whether in the case of people in power or people in revolt, cases of this kind often occur. What happens most frequently is that an ethical norm of undeniable value is accepted, taught, and defended in the Christian community but cannot be converted into a civil law because it lacks sufficient acceptance in society as a whole. It is, in fact, a recognized moral principle but it is impossible to press for its adoption as civil law, even on the basis that it belongs to natural law, if a broad spectrum of the human community fails to acknowledge it. [8]

Here is where "the autonomy of the temporal" enters in, in one of its most important aspects; the Christian community does not claim to resolve the ultimate conflict. It leaves the final solution to the consciences of the faithful engaged in the exercise of power or in the organization of the opposition. The role it must play is to remind them of the values involved in their decisions and, in this way, to help them reach the discernment incumbent upon them.

Ordinarily, when a problem of this kind arises, we think of matters like divorce, the use of contraceptives, homosexuality, pornography, prostitution, abortion. They certainly come up and sometimes in a dramatic way. To estimate in each case whether or not an unquestionable ethical norm is sufficiently recognized by the whole body of citizens is most often very difficult. People will certainly agree that certain purely private actions like the use of contraceptives or homosexuality ought not to be punished under penal law. Difficulties begin when it is a question of personal conduct that has wide and deep repercussions on the mores of civil society and the lot of other human beings. To enunciate general rules for discernment is impossible. For one thing, societies differ from one another. An ethical norm which could find sufficient recognition among the body of citizens in one nation will not win the same acceptance in another, due to differences is the evolution of beliefs and customs. For another thing, ethical norms themselves can be more or less serious. For example, in some conditions questions of divorce and abortion cannot be settled according to the same criteria. The breaking of the conjugal bond established between husband and wife who clearly intended to bind themselves for life has many negative consequences but it cannot be compared to the voluntary and direct taking of the life of a innocent human being.

These questions are certainly extremely serious. The struggles for liberation also bring up conflicts of conscience just as important and just as difficult to solve. It is not merely a matter of the means to be used, whether for suppression or for revolution. Essentially, it has more to do with the very nature of the regime that people want to preserve or to establish. Politics admits of options between ethical values which are not necessarily completely reconcilable.

It would be impossible to go into each one of these discussions; but it is possible at least to indicate the criteria for discernment, which allow people to get their bearings in this field.

On one hand, the Christian community makes no claim to take the place of political people, whether they be in power or with the opposition, in order to make in their stead the choices that rest with them: the ultimate decision belongs to the people engaged in politics. It solves their cases of conscience only in extremely grave matters, such as, for example, torture and unjust imprisonment. It almost always leaves it up to citizens themselves to settle conflicts between obligations, for it lacks adequate information and is not close enough to the situation to offer a solution.

On the other hand, the Christian community requires believers, even if they would not be apt to do so spontaneously, to give their full attention to considering what the values involved in these options are worth. Its mission also includes emphatically reminding people of the gravity of what is at stake when unquestionably ethical norms are made the subject of dispute, not to intrude into temporal affairs but simply to fulfill its role as witness without claiming authority to exercise power of any kind. [9]

Vatican Council II certainly synthesized the twofold doctrine of the legitimate autonomy of the temporal, on one hand, and the necessary involvement of the Christian community, on the other, in a famous statement: "Christ, to be sure, gave His Church no proper mission in the political, economic, or social order. The purpose which He set before her is a religious one. But out of this religious mission itself come a function, a light, and an energy which can serve to structure and consolidate the human community according to the divine law." [10] If the mission of the Church belongs not to the political or economic or even the social order but to the religious, it should not then trespass on terrain that does not belong to it under pain of sacralizing the profane. However, if from its mission a function proper to the service of the human community is derived, that is because the faith has "political" import; had it not, the Church would be unable to deliver the world from its idols.

The Council contented itself with bringing together the two terms of this antinomy and did not undertake to show their coherence.

## False Alternatives

Dissociations and confusions so encumber the terrain that headway is made only with difficulty. At the outset, before placing ourselves at the point where all perspectives converge and apparent contradictions vanish, we ought first to clear the air.

*To change people themselves or to change society.* Sometimes it is said that Christ changes a person's heart, a person's mind or spirit, that his mission is not to transform society. What comes out of the heart is, in fact, what defiles a person, and therefore it is the inner being that must be converted in order that from a ferment of iniquity, the person may become a fount of justice. Christ's thought is clear: it is not eating this or that which condemns or saves a person, but the thoughts of justice or injustice which arise within one and issue in words and actions. There is no conversion of the heart without a conversion of behavior. But this "within" from which comes defilement is not just the individual heart, it is also the hidden source that inspires societies to commit their collective crimes and to construct their inhuman institutions. It too must be converted.

*Values or structures.* It will be objected that the gospel has to do with values and not with social structures. But that means forgetting that a structure like slavery or social discrimination implies a countervalue that must be transformed if the affirmation of conscience is not to be worthless. Conversion of judgment must go hand in hand with the transformation of structures; they mutually condition one another. Many blighted hopes of "the revolution" come from the fact that people's "education" is forgotten. There is also education that fails for want of a modified structure. Any given structure is an idea incarnated in an institution. If the idea is destructive for people, the structure conditions the interpersonal relationships that are established and, even if it does not absolutely determine them, it does tend to pervert them. An authentic relationship can be established between a master and a slave; but the relationship cannot remain authentic if it does not include an effort to abolish the structure of slavery.

*Individual sin and collective sin.* Currently, people speak of a society, even of a church, as in the state of sin. Properly speaking, sin is a uniquely personal action. Salvation and condemnation are alike personal. But each person in his or her own way can participate, actively or passively, in the injustice of a situation. This is so because we are conditioned by a collective ideology that weighs on our actions and provokes both our responses and our silences. The fact that these attitudes may be unconscious is generally not an excuse, for the unconscious can conceal a bogus sincerity. It happens, as John says(3:20) that sin consists precisely in turning away from the light because the light would condemn it. We do see the light, since we turn away from it, but, by turning away from it, we do not receive it. This situation often ensues when our judgments in a given milieu bow to the weight of accepted ideas, customs, and institutions. Then we can talk of collective sin provided that we do not lose sight of the fact that, strictly speaking, sin belongs to the person to the extent that that individual is responsible for the genesis and continuance of an unjust structure. Christians are constantly challenged to be converted in their own conscience and conduct but through that conversion to change the collective conscience and to transform structures.

*Temporal or eternal.* A more radical view is that the work of salvation, which concerns eternity, has nothing to do with earthly and temporal affairs that aim at constructing the city of man and making it habitable. Or again, that the Christian message addressed to the poor promises them happiness not here but hereafter. To make such a dissociation is absolutely contrary to faith. Through revelation we know that after death we will not perform free acts capable of affecting our destiny. The free actions that we are performing here and now—with all their implications—we will live by then; this is the tremendous stake which gives so much value in the Christian view to earthly affairs, not by turning them from their proper end but, rather, by bringing them to it. The stake includes not just one but every aspect of existence. All that many Christians relate to their salvation is their inner and family life and some attitudes about giving individual help to others. As elements within the compass of salvation, only love, sin, and prayer count with them. They therefore exclude, if not their professional life, at least anything that has to do with politics. When we are aware of the importance of "the political" in the creation of any new human relation, we recognize that such a view is an aberration. In the political area, perhaps more than in any other, a person's eternal destiny is decided. We have to conclude that the work of salvation, because it does concern eternity, has much to do with temporal affairs, which are oriented to building up an earthly city. The Christian message, because it holds out an eternal hope to the poor, gives them a human hope right now: it invites people to establish a relationship and build a city where the poor will not be exploited and will feel at home.

*Natural or supernatural.* The same response will serve to answer those who hold that the supernatural work of salvation has nothing to do with the temporal building of the human city. So tenacious is this misunderstanding that any treatment of it needs to be enlarged upon somewhat. We know that Vatican Council II at least in the constitution *Gaudium et spes,* carefully avoided the natural-supernatural vocabulary precisely because of the false dualism that it introduces into the whole notion of existence.

Since a famous lecture by Karl Rahner,[11] a good deal of light has been thrown on this exasperating theme. We do indeed need to maintain that grace is in no way a constituent of human nature; to deny that would be to revert to adulterating the divine with the human and the human with the divine, to return to the ancient mythologies which faith in the one true God completely rejects. Yet if the same truth is expressed in terms of existence, then each includes the other and both are included in their totality. Herein lies the reality of the Incarnation: the divine alliance is so sincere that human beings cannot be dissociated from God, nor can God be dissociated from them. The mystery of human existence—and of divine existence as well—is that God is necessary for human-kind and yet wholly beyond their reach. We know no other word within God than the one spoken to us, Jesus Christ. In that Word the divinity is absolutely distinct from the humanity. But the freedom of the divine offer and of the human response brings divinity and humanity together in a single existence, in a recip-rocality as true of God as of humanity. At this point, human beings have need of God and God has need of them.

At the human level, there is no purely instinctive existence, although there is a reality called instinct, which is radically dis-tinct from reason; or, to put it in psychological idiom, a reality of need radically distinct from a reality of desire.[12] There is no common measure that can be applied to these two realities: between them a threshold has been crossed. Yet there is a recip-rocal and total inclusion of both in a human being. An animal can safely be directed according to its instinct alone, but human beings cannot because in them instinct is partly substituted for, and wholly assumed by, human intelligence.

In a comparative way, at the human level there is no purely natural existence. To use traditional terms, human existence is at once natural and "supernatural," although no proportion exists between nature and grace, the human and the divine. And that is why humankind cannot be safely directed by any wisdom not open to higher light, the light of the Spirit.

These few elementary truths, without which the primitive faith in a divine alliance collapses, makes it possible to get a clearer insight into the question of the natural law, which relates to so many debates in the Church. The very expression itself has involved theological thought in an impasse because it poses a false problem of a "natural law" completely distinct from the law of the gospel, whereas both are rooted in the one great commandment of love.

Vatican Council II does not reject the reality of a law which humankind does not impose upon itself but detects in the depths of its conscience. [13] In this idea of the Greeks, which Paul received from the biblical tradition (Rom. 2:14–15), the Church has recognized three fundamental traditions needed to give coherence to its thought.

1. The law immanent in conscience is, first, all the unwritten laws, *agraptoi nomoi*, which Sophocles' Antigone invoked against the tyrant Creon when he forbade her to bury her brother's body. Every human law depends for its authority upon a higher law not made by human beings. Jesus testified to that truth before Pilate: "You would have no power over me if it had not been given you from above" (John 19:11).

2. This immanent law is a common fundamental *given;* without it dialogue between cultures would be altogether impossible. It manifests an apprehension of existence experienced differently in different cultures. Of course, general norms cannot serve to define the heterogeneous content of diverse cultures, but if no homogeneity existed between them they would be entirely sealed off from one another and that would amount to having no common language and, as a result, no common family in the human race.

3. Finally, this law keeps the Christian community from being a sect that would impose a separate and distinct ethic on its faithful. Christian ethics proposes no other norm than humankind itself.

These are indeed fundamental intuitions. But everything becomes confused when a particular vocabulary leads people to ask themselves if the "natural" law can be understood by reason alone and obeyed by natural powers alone. Reason and faith, humanity, and divinity, however radically distinct they may be in the sphere of essences, cannot be dissociated in the sphere of existence. A firm answer must be given that "reason alone" and "natural powers alone" do not, strictly speaking, exist.

To try to make distinctions between the natural law and the law of the gospel is not a useful pursuit. The gospel requires nothing else of humans than that they be human; its originality consists in proposing that they be fully human. Human existence reaches fullness only in a divine form: therein lies the whole mystery of humanity and God.

In no way does this thought lead to the idea of an implicit Christianity that could somehow be discovered in some form in every culture and religion, as if the gospel had no purpose. It is true that everybody has a presentiment of the law of love. Otherwise, how could we be saved, since, according to faith, we can be saved only by Jesus Christ? And it is a dogma that everybody can be saved. Faith gives human beings an incomparable revelation of themselves and so realizes their humanity as to make them participants in the divine nature. For the one faith, the one law, the one sacrament is the human being entering into the very life of God by being liberated from all credulities, all prohibitions, all superstitions. And that in itself is unique among religions.

## Resurrection and Revolution

Having arrived at this point, we can no longer escape the question posed by two paradoxical affirmations constantly present in very recent Christian thought; involvement in "the political"—and the autonomy of politics; unity of human and divine existence and therefore involvement—and the secular character of civil society and therefore its autonomy.

Not only Christian thought oscillates between these two truths, Christian action does so even more: some jealously maintain their dissociation; others plunge headlong into compromises.

Any progress is blocked by making fine distinctions between these affirmations, as, for example, that divine light and strength are useful in human undertakings and the latter are not without effect in the coming of the Kingdom. Affirmations must be radical: God is necessary for people, and people are not God.

Some seem to close themselves up in either of two alternatives: existential monism or dualism. All the confusion in present-day discussions stems from that fact. Both conservative and progressive positions alike are alternately polarized by these two extremes, both reaching the dead end of making everything of one undifferentiated kind of reality or of so dissociating politics and faith that the unity of experience is destroyed.

In this impasse there is only one way out: an interpretation of the Bible and particularly of the words of Jesus as an invitation to commitment; to adopt neither monism nor dualism but to perceive the sacramental and paschal unity of existence.

The world has been created as a paschal *figure,* the image of a reality not external to it but, rather, immanent within it as its definitive reality. Nothing will be which will not have been already. This world does not, strictly speaking, lead to "another"; this life is not the sign of "another." The fullness of life beyond death is this life fulfilled; *that* world is *this* world in its complete significance. The Kingdom to come is all that will have been lived as communion here and now, to the extent to which it is already among us as sign. Nothing is more essential to the faith than this. It is *our* flesh that will rise, as Christ arose in flesh marked by the thrust of nails and lance. It is not a matter of physical, chemical, or biological continuity; death is not an appearance, a seeming. It is a matter of an enduring sign of a definitive reality, of meaning for the spirit.

The whole Christian community is a sacrament of communion from which all conflict will be excluded—the Kingdom. The whole of history is paschal history; in spite of its deficiencies and contradictions it keeps moving in the direction of resurrection, for resurrection is its end.

The whole of human existence is paschal in its three fundamental societies— the family, the working community, and the body politic—all originally embodied in one and the same community; and in its three relations—domestic, economic, and political.

The paschal event that makes the world pass from its sacramental form to its final eschatological reality we call salvation, that is, liberation in the fullest sense. That Easter, that Pasch, the expectation of the universe, is, first of all, the elimination of the distance between sign and reality; it is not the destruction of flesh and sense but their complete transparency in the Spirit. The limitations of time and space will be obliterated; the here and now will attain their fullness in the everywhere and always. In very deed, the Pasch is deliverance from the servitude in which the "mystery of iniquity" enchains humankind. Iniquity consists in making passing figures and signs the ultimate reality, doing away with the paschal reality of history, eliminating society as communion. Person exploited by person, the weak dominated by the strong, the rule of jungle law, the "barrier" (Eph. 2:14) between races, peoples, cultures, sexes—all are to be overthrown.

In that sense, resurrection is "revolution," an event in which fetishes are overcome, and exploitation, domination, and separation ended. It calls for the birth of a new society; invites every Christian, every human being, to become engaged in actions continually needed for this advent; calls upon the whole Church for participation

But the resurrection is not to be confused with any revolution, for no revolution can definitively liberate human beings from their inner servitudes and every revolution is threatened by idols that are constantly being reborn, especially when revolutionists refuse the revelation of the one true God and are then all the more tempted to bow before false gods.

Revolutions need to do nothing else so much as to raise their eyes to the paschal horizon. Faith in the resurrection saves them from the temptation to take themselves to be definitive liberations. It constantly rectifies them and protects them against new enslavements, which they are apt to engender, not restraining their élan but, on the contrary, helping them to accomplish what is most essential in their promises and projects.

If existence is symbolic and if history is paschal, not because of something that the faith brings to them from without but by the very fact of the twofold touch of the creation and the Incarnation, then we can understand both why the Church is engaged in the political and why it respects the autonomy of politics, doing so not as a strategy or tactic but in virtue of what the Church itself is.

The Church's mission is nothing less than to give meaning to existence, all existence; it is only that and all that. All existence belongs to the Church, for there are no sections of life not included in the paschal mystery; but existence belongs to it only insofar as existence has ultimate signification. The definitive schema is not always in question when timebound choices are made. All existence must be transformed, finding its meaning only through a transformation that rights and completes it. Yet cultural choices issue from Christ and the community of his disciples only insofar as they have to do with paschal meaning.

Then let us recognize a consecration of the world, if you will,[14] but a consecration that is desacralization, radical secularization, simply because it eliminates all confusion of the divine with the human; a true consecration, however, because it directs the whole of existence toward the divine term desired by every human heart.

On the basis of these fundamentals and on it alone a solution is found to the problem of the Church's political role. Like Christ, the faithful are to be present in the political area to give it meaning; they are to be present as individuals by their personal choices and activities, which do not belong to the whole group, and as the whole body every time that the universal significance of existence is concerned.

The Church does, then, have a political mission and those who have given themselves to its service, pastors and ministers, are collectively involved in it. No action in the world has had such an effect on political history as Christ's, as the martyrs', in standing up against power in its insane attempt to be deified and absolutized. In order to fulfill a mission that it has no right to avoid, the Church has a duty to keep itself independent of "politics," refusing to be identified with any form thereof. For the Church nothing in the world is more necessary and nothing more liberating, than its independence, which leaves it free to testify against injustice, from whatever source that arises. We are unable to offer opposition to injustice if we do not denounce it wherever we find it, whether on the right, on the left, or at the center.[15]

To apply these norms is certainly not a simple task. It must be left to the discernment of spirits, which can only be done within the Church. Now the Church is a community of disciples together with their pastors. If, like Jesus, it remains faithful to its mission, people will often reproach it with not being involved or with being too involved. To put it more exactly, each critic will reproach it with not being committed in line with the critic's own partial and perhaps biased options and of being too involved in actions that tend to set these right. The reproaches made against the Church, like those that bore down upon Jesus, will come from every political direction. But, no more that Jesus, can the Church allow itself to be turned from its mission by criticism made on that basis. It can and must listen only to the voices that speak in defense of what is essential: the Spirit is at work throughout the whole of human history.

Sometimes unbelievers will be more sensitive than the faithful to certain manifestations of the Spirit. The Church must give them a hearing. Often the truth of their statements has to be disengaged from the context of their negations, which are apt to hide and alter it. In this sense, dialoguing with all men conditions the accomplishment of the Church's mission.

That does not mean allying itself with or becoming identified with a particular political entity; still less does it mean becoming an accessory to party bias. It simply means "to bear witness to the truth" (John 18:37). Independence of such a kind, at once sovereign and humble, implies no false neutrality, no antipathy, no evasion. It is simply the Church's radical involvement in the whole paschal dimension of history.

## NOTES

1. These pages were written before the French Episcopate's document, *Pour une pratique chrétienne de la politique.* Since it is impossible to quote it in its entirely, I will simply refer to it here. See *Cahiers de l'actualité religieuse et sociale,* no. 46 (November 15, 1972), which gives the complete text and a reader's guide by Heckel. Studies on the subject are multiply-

ing nowadays. La Semaine sociale de Lyon, 1973, chose as the theme of its reflections "Chrétiens et Eglises dans la vie politique." Many documents, particularly in Latin America, continue to take up the subject.

2. *Gaudium et spes,* no. 36.

3. The word "ideology" is being used here in a positive sense as being legitimate and necessary in political action. It becomes totalitarian to the exact extent to which it puts itself forward as a faith.

4. These expressions are Paul Bureau's, one of the very few Christian sociologists who belong to a new sociology still in process of formation.

5. Paul Ricoeur, "De la nation à l'humanité: tâche des chrétiens," *Christianisme social* (September-December 1966), p. 506.

6. Pope Paul VI, *Populorum progressio,* no. 13 (Boston: Daughters of St. Paul, 1967), p. 10

7. This is precisely the risk run by "clerics" who engage in politics—to turn it away from its object and convert it into a field for disputations simply because they can make no claim to power.

8. See, for example, Eichmann-Morsdorf, *Lehrbuch des Kirchenrechts,* 10th ed., Vol. I, p. 97.

9. The European theologian who has been most commented upon—one would be tempted to say "made use of"—in "political theologies" is Johannes B. Metz. Marcel Xhaufflaire has made his writings the object of a study, *La "théologie politique"* (Paris: Cerf, 1972). The German theologian stresses the "critical" aspects of the gospel: "All eschatological theology has to be political theology inasmuch as it is critical theology" (Xhaufflaire, p. 39). Such statements have often led, although the author has explicitly denied it (pp. 111–12), to theologies of revolution—which suddenly become theologies of identification when the prevailing ideology has been overthrown. By virtue of denying any content to political theology ("its only allies are impotent ideas," p. 43), does it not run the risk of ending in an "anything goes" position, with everybody making their own interpretation in accordance with their own ideology and in the most uncritical way possible? It hardly need be said that an informed theologian does not fall into this contradiction, but it can be asked whether, by saying that the gospel is, above all, negation, one does not create a terrain favorable to the very compromises one is trying to avoid. Is the revelation of the one true God only, or even principally, negation? Metz himself has realized the danger and makes some much more positive expressions, such as: "It is not a matter of developing conceptions properly socio-political but of bringing out the value of the social and political elements contained in the eschatological message" (p. 56).

10. *Gaudium et spes,* no. 42. It is interesting to note that the second part of the statement was included at the request of some Latin American bishops, including Bishop Manuel Larrain, then president of C.E.L.A.M. (Latin American Episcopal Conference at Medellín, 1968), who died shortly afterward.

11. Given at Paderborn March 14, 1959 and published in French in the collection *Mission et grâce* (Tours: Mame, 1962), chap. 2 See too his *Nature and Grace: Dilemmas in the Modern Church,* (New York: Sheed and Ward, 1964), pp. 114–43.

12. See Denis Vasse, *Le temps du désir* (Paris: Seuil, 1969).

13. *Gaudium et Spes,* no. 16.

14. The term has been used just once, by Pope Pius XII, on October 5, 1957 at the Second Congress of the Lay Apostolate, revealing a reserve that is probably due to the ambiguity of the term. See A.F. Utz and J.F. Groner, *Relations humaines et société contemporaine* (Fribourg: St. Paul, 1963), Vol. III, p. 3405.

15. If a strictly one-dimensional political geometry is adhered to, it hardly does honor to the French intelligence, which has disseminated it throughout the world.

# PART THREE

# A READING FROM MARX

## The Timeliness of an Explication

If the faith destroys fetishes and reveals the meaning of existence in the adoration of the one adorable God, we can see immediately where Marxism joins Christianity—it makes a more radical critique of the fetishism of goods than any other system of thought; and where it is at variance with Christianity—it is equally radical in its rejection of authentic adoration and therefore contains within itself the seeds of new fetishisms.

All Marxist ambivalence is encompassed in this contradiction: it has believed itself capable of reaching the very foundation of false adorations without going to their source. Being unaware of the radical presence of the absolute in people, it has judged itself capable of liberating humanity by depriving human beings of situating the absolute where it is to be found. In so doing, it has certainly done its part in disclosing the fetishism of money and the exploitation of people by people—this is its great truth; but it has also exposed humanity to all the risks of spurious absolutes and new slaveries—that is its great error. Here we have the source of all the difficulties experienced by Christians and Marxists when they attempt to dialogue with one another.

### The Identity of Marxism

Marxism is taken up again here[1] because it is argued about everywhere, particularly in the third world and among Christians. Besides, the oversimplifications of anticommunism and procommunism have made the whole question uncommonly confused. It is difficult to keep in view at the same time Marxist truth and Marxist error, along with all their consequences. Some seem to forget that Marxism, by denouncing the idolatry of wealth, has opened up a road that Christian faith cannot refuse to take. Others treat atheism as if it were just something incidental that will pass away. Both do violence to Marxism as it presents itself to the consciences of a large part of humankind and as it is imposed on the history of a whole segment of the globe.

The first task to be done is to rediscover and restore the identity of Marxism. That is difficult to accomplish at the present time because the way to its restoration is encumbered with many divergent interpretations, all claiming to remain substantially faithful to original Marxism. Some, the most negligible, content themselves with sorting out the elements into what attracts them and what repels them, holding onto the one and discarding the other, a possibility in the sphere of discourse but not in the sphere of reality. Others, of some importance, try to find in early Marxist thought, beyond Marx himself, fundamental intuitions on which to reconstruct a *real* Marxism. With this in mind, they appeal from the Marx of history to a Marx of faith. Their approach has some merit because through it they make a contribution to a process of discernment, provided that they keep in mind that it is no more possible to alter the course of historical Marxism than it is to send a torrent back to its source so that it will take a different direction. Other readings, on the contrary, repudiate these primitive intuitions, believing that they see traces of Hegelian idealism in them. They have no hesitation in tearing out whole pages of the *Capital* masterpiece itself, retaining what they regard as definitive Marxism. Without doubt they come closer to reality but turn aside from all that could help them arrive at discernment. All these interpretations have one thing in common: they spring up with no relationship to praxis, and without any party affiliation, which in itself puts them in flagrant contradiction with the principles of Marx and Lenin.

If the Marxist movement as it has actually taken place, rather than Marxist theoreticians,[2] is considered, it erupts into many forms, often in opposition to one another,[3] a fact that proves of no help in defining the identity of Marxism. That being so, those interested in the subject are inclined to concentrate on those countries where Marxism has really succeeded in transforming the economic and political structure in line with its own criteria. Even there differences,[4] indeed contradictions, come to light; the most striking is the head-on clash between Russia and China. Yugoslavia is an original experiment but is condemned by the two giants of communism. However, convergences continue to be more numerous than divergences. For that reason, a study of Communist countries seems to be based on more solid ground than concentrating on Communist movements or, even more so, on isolated thinkers, to discover the nature of Marxism. Experience has imposed upon Marxism certain changes in course, which were not observable at the start, and has modified some of its basic principles. Reality, rather than theory, seems a better critique of ideology.

The best method both for defining Marxism and for attempting to predict its future is to adhere as closely as possible to the thought of Marx as he himself expressed it in the works of his mature years, (outstanding Marxists, such as Lenin, Stalin, Mao, even in the ideological developments which they have introduced, have remained surprisingly faithful to his thought), and then to confront it with the reality of the socialist countries as they continue to evolve. Marxism refused to dissociate theory and praxis. To confront the one with the other is not to make any change in Marxism but, on the contrary, to acknowledge its fundamental intuition. Marxism is at once a way of apprehending existence and an economic and political analysis. We need to study it from both of these aspects if we want to appreciate its relation to our times, that is, its capacity to explain and transform society today.

## NOTES

1. Already raised in my *Marxisme et humanisme,* 3rd ed. (Paris: P.U.F., 1961) and much discussed today. I would point out two recent non-

Marxist works: Paul-Dominique Dognin, *Initiation à Karl Marx* (Paris: Cerf, 1970); Alfonso López Trujillo, *La Concepción del hombre en Marx* (Bogotá: Edición Revista colombiana, 1972).

2. A good list of Marxists who do adhere to Marx is given in Jean Guichard, *Le Marxisme*, 2nd ed. (Lyon: Chronique sociale de France, 1970), p. 298 ff.

3. To point out just one example, in Latin America movements claiming to be Marxist-Leninist are divided at present into a number of different groups, one following the Soviet line, another the Chinese, a third Castro's, a fourth Trotsky's, etc.

4. Gilles Martinet brings them out clearly in his *Les cinq communismes, russe, yougoslave, chinois, tchèque, cubain* (Paris: Seuil, 1971).

# IX

# MARXISM AS AN
# OVERALL VIEW OF EXISTENCE

Today many people, Christians among them, say that they find
that Marxism offers the only intellectual approach that makes it
possible for them to make sense out of contemporary reality. For
them, dialectical materialism not only presents no difficulty but is
the very science of existence.

Everybody is in accord in recognizing a definition of the Marxist method in the famous text found in the preface to *A Contribution to the Critique of Political Economy.* Nowhere either in this
passage or in *Capital* does Marx use the words "dialectical" or
"materialism." Yet no one is left in doubt that, at this point, Marx
is defining what is essential in the treatment of his subject.

In 1859 Marx was forty years old, a man of mature years with
his youth behind him, a man in full and conscious possession of
his thought.

> I was led by my studies to the conclusion that legal relations as well
> as forms of state could neither be understood by themselves, nor
> explained by the so-called general progress of the human mind, but
> that they are rooted in the material conditions of life, which are
> summed up by Hegel after the fashion of the English and French of
> the eighteenth century under the name "civic society"; the anatomy
> of that civic society is to be sought in political economy. . . . In the
> social production which men carry on they enter into definite rela-
> tions that are indispensable and independent of their will; these
> relations of production correspond to a definite stage of develop-
> ment of their material powers of production. The sum total of these
> relations of production constitutes the economic structure of
> society—the real foundation, on which rise legal and political super-
> structures and to which correspond definite forms of social con-
> sciousness. The mode of production in material life determines the
> general character of the social, political and spiritual processes of

life. It is not the consciousness of men that determines their existence, but, on the contrary, their social existence that determines their consciousness. At a certain stage of their development, the material forces of production in society come in conflict with the existing relations of production, or—what is but a legal expression for the same thing—with the property relations within which they have been at work before. From forms of development of the forces of production these relations turn into their fetters. Then comes the period of social revolution. With the change of the economic foundation the entire immense superstructure is more or less rapidly transformed. In considering such transformations the distinction should always be made between the material transformation of the economic conditions of production which can be determined with the precision of natural science, and the legal, political, religious, aesthetic or philosophic—in short, ideological forms in which men become conscious of this conflict and fight it out. Just as our opinion of an individual is not based on what he thinks of himself, so can we not judge of such a period of transformation by its own consciousness; on the contrary, this consciousness must rather be explained from the contradictions of material life, from the existing conflict between the social forces of production and the relations of production. No social order ever disappears before all the productive forces, for which there is room in it, have been developed: and new higher relations of production never appear before the material conditions of their existence have matured in the womb of the old society. Therefore, mankind always takes up only such problems as it can solve; since, looking at the matter more closely, we will always find that the problem itself arises only when the material conditions necessary for its solution already exist or are at least in the process of formation. In broad outlines we can designate the Asiatic, the ancient, the feudal, and the modern bourgeois methods of production as so many epochs in the progress of the economic formation of society. The bourgeois relations of production are the last antagonistic form of the social process of production—antagonistic not in the sense of individual antagonism, but of one arising from conditions surrounding the life of individuals in society; at the same time the productive forces developing in the womb of bourgeois society create the material conditions for the solution of that antagonism. This social formation constitutues, therefore, the closing chapter of the prehistoric stage of human society.[1]

Everything in this fundamental text is important:

1. Primacy is given to relations of production, that is, the relations that link man with nature and with his fellowmen in the social production of existence—work. At one stroke, a whole traditional outlook has changed. Interest transfers from what up until that time had occupied the center of the stage—political and military events—to the working person. The worker is what counts. That change is history-making.[2]

2. Specific relations within production correspond to some degree with the development of the forces of production. In agrarian society, everything takes place among a small number of people in a tight working and living community, within which each person has a sharply defined function. In an industrial type of economy, what is produced is the fruit of the work of millions; if we take into account the work of those who produce and transport the materials and merchandise and the machines necessary for production and transportation, a whole human ant-hill has played some part in creating it. The "social division" of work engenders a whole new world.

3. When new relations of production come about as a result of the forces of production, they come in conflict with the system of relations inherited from the past, that is, with the system of property ownership. Production has become collective; possession remains individual. Marx's later work has as its object the analysis of the conflict between the market and capital. Private property becomes an obstacle to development and revolution follows in an attempt to break out of this bind.[3]

4. The resultant change in the economic structure (Marx does not say "infrastructure") results in a change in the whole superstructure (the expression is Marx's own):[4] in law, politics, art, religion. But there is an essential difference between the two. The first can be foreseen, is as predictable as "the natural sciences." In other words, the development of the forces of production and the conflict that it generates are strictly determined. According to Marx, the second change, on the contrary, does not follow the same laws because it brings consciousness into play.

5. The role of consciousness in the process of transformation has to be analyzed according to the following principles. People's consciousness does not determine their lives; quite the contrary,

their social existence determines their consciousness. Among capitalist leaders consciousness constructs a legal, ethical, and religious justification for the system of private property. Among the proletariat it exercises a revolutionary role. It is worth noting that, in the text cited, ideology linked with consciousness has a negative or positive function according to whether it is elaborated by owners or wage earners. Ideology, like consciousness, is to some extent an independent variable. In any case, how it acts cannot be predicted with the precision of the exact sciences.

These are the statements contained in the key text. They suggest a comparison with Freud. Marx, too, is proposing an explanation by way of the unconscious. Collective humanity has no more perception of the phenomena that determine its history than has the individual human being. Marx explicitly put the two together in the quotation given.

The fundamental thesis to be evaluated is this: to what extent is it true to say that people's consciousness is determined by "their social existence" so that those with property inescapably draw from it the thought of what they want to preserve, and those without property are impelled in the direction needed for social change? As we have just seen, it is not a question of considering consciousness as a simple "reflection," a thesis not of Marx but of Engels[5] that became a part of the Marxist catechism. Consciousness has its own proper function. But there is no other consciousness than class consciousness, consciousness that is either reactionary or revolutionary. No element foreign to a perspective on class enters into consciousness. Consciousness is defined strictly in terms of the economic structure and, therefore, ultimately in political terms. Dialectical materialism consists in exactly that.

When we study this point of Marxist theory, we are apt to see it under one of its aspects, which is neither exclusive nor primary. We ask ourselves whether each person's consciousness is in fact *conditioned* by the social class to which that person belongs. A fundamental question, yet it leaves aside one still more basic: to what extent is consciousness *determined* simply by men's situation in production relations?

## Is Consciousness Conditioned by Social Class?

Marx has sifted out a truth: social class conditions judgment. All people find themselves implicated in the conflict between classes. Nobody escapes the burden that it places on one's consciousness: it is not a matter of will.

Social class is a universal reality, dividing people and setting them apart in groups where frontiers are neither geographical nor sociological. It is difficult to escape from the network of forces that it sets in motion. All are caught up in the conflict.

The privileged classes are always astonished at such statements. They do not feel themselves to be at all aggressive. Being in a dominant situation, they are not sensible of oppression. Class struggle is, on the other hand, an evident fact to those who find themselves crushed in a system of institutions that systematically organize private privilege and power.

So every one of us ought to question ourselves. Some of those who exercise the function of judges in society are led to believe that they are outside the conflict. In reality, it is so impossible to find impartial judges in this matter that in labor conflicts it has become necessary to institute shared and coequal jurisdiction between the parties involved, an exception to all norms of law and an admission of impotence.

Social class spares no one, in particular it does not spare those who, not because of their profession but because of their religious function, believe that they are above social conflict. Pastors and prophets in the Church, bishops, priests, and laity are in the same situation as everybody else and sometimes are all the more affected because they do belong to a social class that exercises an influence over them of which they are unaware. People in power are more in danger than others of getting distorted views by introducing into their judgments factors that have nothing to do with reason and justice.

Yet it is surely possible to tear ourselves loose from the conditioning of our social class. Marx himself witnesses to that possibility. By family, he belonged to the bourgeois class, as did Engels, a big industrialist. They had to escape from their past. Yet nobody can believe that such transplanting is easily done. To break away from the whole sum of affective and aggressive reactions generated by social class presupposes a freedom that is, in the end, rare. It must surely be the same with those who opt to share the common lot of classes and peoples without privileges. Those who change mental structures have a chance of keeping them stable if they commit themselves to some action to modify the social structures involved. In this sense, it is true to say that "social existence determines consciousness."

The social conditioning that we experience as one of a social class is, in the eyes of faith, one form of spiritual enslavement. We are marvelously apt at fabricating theories to justify our actions. When we cannot renounce the privileges and powers that constitute our social class, we justify them to our conscience. This is one aspect of the human condition, not the only one but perhaps the one of most interest to today's world.

The gospel, far from favoring this complicity, as Marx thought it did, denounces it in incisive terms. In Jesus' doctrine, this sophistication is called the sin against the Spirit. Every sin can be pardoned save it. I act against my conscience, I have been weak, and I acknowledge it: God will not condemn me. But if I compound a theory to justify my sin, how can God pardon my sin, since I have done away with it by covering it over and hiding it away?

When people or classes are unjust, they construct laws and institutions to cover up their iniquity. For them to break free of their lie, their consciousness of injustice would have to be reawakened; and that is possible only by participating, in one way or another, in the collective struggle against injustice. This fundamental liberation must not serve the inverse aggressiveness of oppressed peoples and classes when they themselves are unjust, but must cleave to justice, no matter how threatened it may be, and join in the combat that justice demands.

Marxism itself explicity admits that determinism does not operate with the same rigor in this field as it does in the exact sciences; so it allows to some extent for freedom of conscience. Therefore it ought not to deny the proper function of a capacity acting at that level; rather, it ought logically to appeal to it. It does not exclude such a function but entrusts it to the party.

Can the party fill the role of a church? Can purely political criteria take the place of ethical norms? Here we touch upon a much more important problem than the conditioning of consciousness—that is, its determination. In a dialogue with Marxism, this is the crucial point.

## Is Consciousness Determined by Social Class?

In this matter, Marx is radical: class consciousness is simply coextensive with consciousness, completely absorbing it. Lenin is faithful to Marx's thought when he writes, "We say that our morality is entirely subordinated to the interests of the proletariat. Our morality is deduced from the class struggle of the proletariat."[6] When Mao invokes it in regard to people and their education, a new accent can certainly be heard, but we are not left in any doubt as to the bedrock of his thought: the human being in question is a political person, a revolutionary person. Like all leading Marxists, Lenin and Mao are consistent: social existence determines consciousness. There is no other human being than the political human being.

Every human being who believes that a person has some dimension, intuitively perceives that persons cannot be equated with this fundamental thesis of dialectical materialism. The mystery of existence cannot be encompassed in a definition limited to terms of class struggle and revolutionary praxis. The liberation of humankind demands far more than the subversion of economic and political structures; it demands an inversion, a *metanoia*, of the human being in all components of existence.

Before this basic difference is taken up, certain questions should be asked. Are not the effective announcement of a new society and the contest with the one still in existence necessarily matters of conscience? Have not particular rebellions, particular political plans something to do with conscience?

*Has ethics a political dimension?* The answer leaves no room for doubt: ethics assumes polity, "a global vision of man and of the human race"[7] and a global renewal of both. Anyone who fails to see the injustice of certain institutions and makes no attempt to build new structures remains at the threshold of conscience. Anyone who does not denounce social inequities, systematized privilege, private power, who does not raise a voice for a society in which there will really be "no acceptation of persons," falls short of being fully human.

Property is necessary; it is a condition for freedom and responsibility. It provides room for the autonomy of persons and groups, but it should not become a source of privilege and power. A society must be built up in which privilege and power resulting from property are abolished. Action must be set in motion by wage earners and by those who have neither job nor salary, those excluded from all privileges and living on the margin of society. Inevitably, their action will arouse the resistance of those with wealth, culture, and power. It will take on, therefore, by the very nature of things, the form of a struggle,[8] the legitimate defense of the oppressed against the privileges and powers that oppress them; a conscientization and organization of people is therefore necessary.[9] Only at this price will class structure and the will to power reach their breaking point.

Today a person attains an ethical level only through action that consists in both a breaking down and a building up.

Structure, conscience: Marxism forged the link between them and so presented us with a great truth. Does its position depend upon a positive, an "exact" science, to use the terminology of *A Contribution to the Critique of Political Economy*? Marx explicitly excludes that thesis. To reduce Marxism to the dimensions of empiricism means destroying it. Its dialectic is humankind's own. Not only what Marx wrote in his youth but his most definitive works lose all their significance and import if they are relegated to the rank of an empirical analysis. From beginning to end, his whole approach is through humankind itself.[10]

But it is also his great inconsistency and the principle from which his errors emanate. For Marx has closed off any course that would allow him to define this mutual link between structure and conscience. His questioning of law, philosophy, morality, and faith are not just a critique of their adulterations but a denial of all spiritual values. From whence will come a function proper to conscience if not from the spirit? A function proper to conscience: not only the possibility for an individual to escape from being determined by social existence but, more radically than that, the freedom of conscience to define itself in terms that transcend any given structure.

Marx has absolute need of this authority for the consistency of his thought. If contradiction between the forces of production and the relations of production based on property set free revolutionary energy, it occurs not as if it were a response to an exact scientific analysis of a mechanism but as an outpouring that has its wellspring in conscience or, as Marx would grant, in consciousness. Consciousness is not, therefore, a mere "reflection," as some of those who relay Marx's thought have said. But then, whence comes its sovereign freedom?

By divine decree—the expression is Lenin's—or from the lucubrations of metaphysics? Neither surely, if we define them as Marxism does. But from some human authenticity, from a certain way of being human that does not belong simply to the order of events but to the order of existence and meaning; from a certain openness that defines human existence. Lacking that, there is no dialectic.

*Is the ethical reducible to the political? The political dimension is essential for conscience but does not determine it.* This is the most serious point of opposition between the Marxist analysis and Christian faith.

As we have just seen, Marx does not rule out a reciprocal action between "social existence" and "consciousness." In the latter he therefore recognizes some sort of autonomy, some sort of capacity to mold reality in conformity with its own criteria; but, to his mind, nothing apprehended that is unrelated to class struggle determines consciousness. Anyone who departs from this strict definition is no longer a Marxist. All leading Marxists adhere to it faithfully.

This doctrine is latent in the thought of a great number of today's militants, Christians included. They are inclined to identify a person's complete and definitive liberation with revolution. They conceive of class struggle not only as the most urgent task in the fight for freedom but as the only task necessary. They think that the dependence of oppressed classes and nations is not only the gravest form of alienation but alienation itself. In essentials they completely agree with dialectical materialism.

At this point an evaluation of this fundamental Marxist doctrine is in order, as it involves a number of consequences.

1. It entails the politicization of consciousness and social existence, that is, it requires that both be defined solely by their "political" aspects.

Ideology and strategy are certainly both needed to build a new society; but they cannot pretend to take in the whole field of consciousness and existence. They lack that penetration into the mystery of man which emanates from knowledge and action of a higher and more intimate kind.

In the Marxist view, revolutionary praxis determines the truth of information: any data that fail to serve the revolution must be eliminated. Revolutionary praxis defines culture: every artistic creation that does not comply with the ends of the revolution has no reason to exist. It defines the identity of persons: every effort at converting human existence through other than revolutionary means is condemned in advance.

This displacement of the criteria of truth, justice, humanity (Lenin would say morality) changes the very foundations of conscience.

Clearly, many people who call themselves Marxist do not go so far as to adopt these extreme consequences. But, by never explicitly submitting them to criticism, do they not come to accept them implicitly? Whatever ethics they claim as their own are insensibly modified according to purely political categories.

In their personal lives, many Marxists keep their distance from this position. But doctrinally, the principles remain intact, a permanent threat to the sovereign liberty of conscience.

2. Defining consciousness by its political dimension brings about deep discrimination between people solely by the criterion of social class.

Certainly conscience cannot put oppressors and oppressed on the same level, but condemns one and defends the other. It sees no need, however, when insisting upon one fundamental right to deny other rights, no less fundamental. It gives no acceptance to the idea that governments, assemblies, courts, mass media, educational systems are to govern, legislate, judge, inform, and teach with no other criteria in mind than those of the class struggle. "The people," as a social class, are neither infallible nor exempt from injustice in their judgments and reactions. No doubt they have some sort of intuition about what is needed to establish a society in which all share and share alike, yet that intuition is subject to passion and aggressiveness. It can happen that "the people," too, can be unjust.

Why have a revolution if it simply means denying to some what has been for all too long kept from others: the right to be judged according to a norm of justice not defined simply on the basis of class interests?

Every human being, every group attains equity only through a hard struggle against all that masks and alters justice in the human heart. That struggle is not purely and simply identical with revolutionary struggle. It implies a conversion that goes to the roots of iniquity and calls upon the most basic energies.

3. Dialectical materialism leads to a kind of violence that is exactly what conscience condemns: force that is a law unto itself. Of course, force is sometimes necessary in the service of justice; and in class conflict it cannot always be ruled out a priori. But violence in the precise sense in which Marxism defines it, that is, the use of all effective means in revolution according to no criteria save those indicated by a scientific study[11] of the situation and its revolutionary possibilities, destroys the very ground of conscience. Marxists show themselves capable of obeying other principles,[12] but if they do, it is for reasons foreign to the logic of dialectical materialism and a time can always come when that logic takes precedence over every other consideration.

Violence fashions a violent world, a consequence which Marx in his later writings showed that he fully understood. He saw clearly that class struggle, as he conceived it, would relentlessly pursue the path to "the revolutionary dictatorship of the proletariat."

The Marxist schema implies that societies erected on its principles will have a monolithic character. Nothing gives evidence that a system which makes revolution the ultimate criterion for conscience will offer protection of any kind to human liberties.

And if official protest does sometimes occur, for example, against Stalin's cruelties, it is done in the name of principles that have no place in the system.

Against the manifold consequences of Marxist logic—the complete submission of life to ideology, the acceptance of persons according to the criterion of class, violence exercised and liberties stamped out—people must give witness just as they do in the face of the exploitation of people by dominant classes. They have to cross the barriers of the same fear, lifting bare hands to oppose every form of power that has become oppression. Beyond the reach of any power stand truth and justice that no power can define or determine.

In them we find principles that lead Christians to join Marxists when they project a society in which all will really have equal rights and that make Christians oppose them when they attempt to reduce the whole matter of humankind and human freedom to revolutionary praxis.[13]

## NOTES

1. Marx, *A Contribution to the Critique of Political Economy* (Chicago: Chas. Kerr & Co., 1904), pp. 11–13.

2. We need to remember that Hegel first introduced us to this perspective.

3. In Marx's view, contrary to what is often stated, the modification of the relations of production (the abolition of private property) is secondary; the development of the forces of production is primary. Structural change is only a means. In the terms used in Latin America, we have to say that Marx is *funcionalista, desarrollista* before being *estructuralista, liberacionista*. He does not lose sight of the end in view—development. Marx's position stems from his fundamental idea that people's relation to nature is anterior to their relation to their fellow human beings and is the determining factor. Many interpreters of Marxism express themselves as if liberation were the end; basically, they are anarchists. True Marxists are realists; they do not forget the end of revolution—a rational economy. Because of that, Marxism remains open to what modification experience may suggest in its conception of social structure—if it were

proved that the functioning of the economy required some revision in its original analysis, even on substantial points.

4. On this point see M. Eubel, *Karl Marx, Oeuvres* (Paris: Gallimard, 1965), Vol. I, p. 1601, and note 1 on p. 273.

5. Mao explains, "While we recognize that in the general development of history the material determines the mental and social being determines social consciousness, we also—and indeed must—recognize the reaction of mental on material things, of social consciousness on social being and of the superstructure on the economic base. This does not go against materialism; on the contrary, it avoids mechanical materialism and firmly upholds dialectical materialism." *Quotations from Chairman Mao Tse-tung* (New York: Bantam Books, 1967), p. 125.

6. This passage is quoted in full in my *La doctrine sociale de l'Eglise,* 2nd ed. (Paris: P.U.F., 1966), p. 485. See V. I. Lenin, "The Tasks of the Youth Leagues," a speech delivered at the Third All-Russian Congress of the Russian Young Communist League, *Selected Works,* Vol. I, (New York: International Publishers, 1937), p. 475.

7. Pope Paul VI, *Populorum progressio,* no. 13 (Boston: Daughters of St. Paul, 1968), p. 10.

8. Pope Pius XI, *Quadragesimo anno,* no. 114 (1931), recognizes a legitimate acceptation of the expression "class conflict": "Class war, provided it abstains from enmities and mutual hatred, is changing gradually to an honest discussion of differences, based upon the desire for social justice. If this is by no means the blessed social peace we all long for, it can be and must be an approach towards mutual cooperation of vocational groups." *Five Great Encyclicals* (New York: Paulist Press, 1939), p. 156.

9. These thoughts are expressed in the conclusions of the Second Latin American Episcopal Conference at Medellín. See *The Church in the Present Day Transformation of Latin America in the Light of the Council,* ed. Louis Colonnese, 2 vols. (Washington, D.C.: Latin American Bureau, United States Catholic Conference, 1970), Vol. 2, pp. 80–81.

10. This point has been, I believe, established in my work *Marxisme et humanisme,* 3rd ed. (Paris: P.U.F., 1961), Part 1: "Lecture de Marx." In the works of his mature years, and particularly in *Capital,* Marx does not always seem aware of the direction his thought is taking. He meant to found an economic science and thought he had, a misapprehension which seems to explain why he never finished revising *Capital* to the extent to which he claimed to have verified his theses by empirical analysis.

11. Nothing is more contrary to Marxism than anarchical violence,

than "the revolutionary gesture," a useless provocation because it is not based on any "scientific" analysis.

12. In this way a Communist ethic is built up in which traditional principles of human morality are to be found. Since 1961, in the Third Program of the Russian Communist Party (the second was drawn up in 1919), the moral code of the builder of communism, is defined as follows: "The simple rules of morality and of justice . . . are, under communism, inviolable rules. . . Communist morality encompasses the fundamental rules of human morality . . . conscientious work for the good of society . . . honesty and sincerity, moral purity, simplicity and modesty in social and private life; mutual respect in the family, care for the education of the children . . . " Quoted in Michel Mouskhely, *L'U.R.S.S. au seuil du communisme?* (Paris: Dalloz, 1962), pp. 178,179.

13. Roger Garaudy, in *The Alternative Future,* trans. Leonard Mayhew (New York: Simon and Schuster, 1970), p. 74, sees a new opportunity for Christianity and Marxism. "Only through these parallel crises in Marxism and Christianity, only through their mutual recognition of the contradictions and confrontations of their past histories, can a new relationship develop along with an awareness that their futures are necessarily complementary." His manifestly sincere book puts the question to Christians whether or not they are capable of being open to all the truth to be found in Marxism, an interrogation that Christians, on their part, can address to Marxism in somewhat the same terms as just expressed here.

# X

# MARXISM AS AN ECONOMIC AND POLITICAL ANALYSIS

Marxism is put forward not simply as a science of existence but also as an economic and political analysis, literally as "a political economy." On this plane in particular those who sometimes begin with quite contrary presuppositions see it as a method of knowledge and action which, in their eyes, is the only one capable of making sense of the present and of offering discernment for the future.

At the level of such an explication, what value has the Marxist analysis today? What practical values does it have? And, first of all, in what does it consist?

To deal with these questions, we have to return again to Marx himself. Leading Marxists—Lenin, Stalin, and Mao—have been creators; yet they have been strictly faithful to him.

## The Economic Structure

In the view of dialectical materialism, the economic structure is primary and determining. Contradiction exists in social division, the fruit of the development of the forces of production and the structure of private property inherited from a former protective system based on the autonomy of the producer. In his master work *Capital*, written in 1869, Marx analyzes this contradiction at length and in two stages: by an analysis of commodities, that is, of the exchange market, and an analysis of capital, that is, of surplus value, two distinct and inseparable aspects of the same contradiction.

### A CRITIQUE OF THE MARKET

In order to make a study of commodities and their fetishism, Marx borrows from the founders of political economy, especially from Adam Smith, but he modifies them substantially in regard to the categories of use value and exchange value. In his eyes, use value is a mode of existence, a certain way in which people situate themselves in relation to nature and to others. Insofar as commodity is a use value it is an aggregate of physical qualities and is wholly due to human work. Insofar as it is an exchange value, a commodity obeys the market's blind forces of supply and demand and does not act in response to human needs.

This metamorphosis is a passage from the qualitative to the quantitive, from the physical to the metaphysical, from a "simple and transparent" relation to a "mysterious" relation, and, to sum it all up, from the human to the nonhuman. In regard to use value, Marx says, "The form of wood, for instance, is altered by making a table out of it. Yet, for all that, the table continues to be that common, everyday thing, wood. But, so soon as it steps forth as a commodity, it is changed into something transcendent. It not only stands with its feet on the ground, but, in relation to all other commodities, it stands on its head, and evolves out of its wooden brain grotesque ideas, far more wonderful than 'table-turning' ever was."[1]

In other words, the marketing universe of commodities evolves according to its own laws, without taking into account the world of human beings. Among primitive people this did not happen, since what an individual made was made entirely by and for that person.

In Marx's eyes, the origin of this phenomenon, a characteristic of "capitalism," is clear: it consists in the autonomy of enterprise in the exchange of commodities. Autonomy had a rational basis as long as a product resulted from the work of a few people. In a market where each product is the fruit of the collaboration of millions of workers, it makes no sense and leads to anarchy in production and distribution. People no longer control the mechanisms that at one time go full speed ahead and at another grind to a halt without any regard for human needs. An incoherent system of things sets the pace for a society of human beings.

Having determined the cause of contradiction, Marx then indicates a radical solution. In the future only the abolition of all autonomy in production will make it possible for collective humankind to regulate a system of collective production for their own proper ends. The passage is famous, one of the rare statements in which Marx describes the regime that will come after capitalism: "Let us now picture to ourselves, by way of change, a community of free individuals, carrying on their work with the means of production in common, in which the labour-power of all the different individuals is consciously applied as the combined labour-power of the community. . . The social relations of the individual producers, with regard both to their labour and its products, are in this case perfectly simple and intelligible, and that with regard not only to production but also to distribution."[2]

Thus millions of producers constitute one and the same social labor force: it is impossible to state more emphatically that the new system will leave no power of decision to the innumerable units of production. The Plan will be concerted; there will be consultation but no autonomy, even of a relative kind, in decision-making.

Here we have the Marxist schema. Of course, it has been modified during the course of a century. Nevertheless, socialist economies remain substantially true to it. Without doubt, the Yugoslav system has completely freed itself from the Marxist thesis by reestablishing a competitive economy but it is severely condemned by Soviet theory and even more harshly by Maoist principles. We can quite rightly consider it as non-Marxist in its conception of the market.

Since the Marxist analysis is presented as alone capable of interpreting reality and providing orientation for action, it must be submitted to scrutiny. To what extent must some relative autonomy in decision-making be left to the units of production? At this moment of examination, of analysis, the structure of these units of production, in other terms the relationship between capital and labor, is not being called into question but only the play of relations between the Plan and both of them.

Marx's critique is radical and opens itself up to some radical questions. To just what extent can an individual permit absorption into a collective system so that, together with millions of workers engaged in production, that person constitutes one and the same work force, "the combined labour-power of the community"? Marx's response is categorical and implied in his philosophical presuppositions that the individual has social and only social dimension. "But the essence of man is no abstraction inherent in each separate individual. In its reality it is the ensemble [aggregate] of social relations."[3]

To a great extent, the Marxist analysis of the commodity market is verified. Everything that has evolved confirms it. The recessions in capitalist economies, abandoned to the free play of supply and demand, give superabundant proof of it. A "concerted plan" is necessary. It is indispensable that the units of production conform to collective disciplines, that individual human beings therefore assume, in large measure, collective motivations. The whole transformation of thinking in economics, following Keynes, moves in this direction.

However, they do not go so far as to abolish the market, that is, competition between enterprises. Western economies seem to come up against a stone wall at this point, a limit that they are not ready to cross. What of the socialist economies?

They remain substantially faithful to the Marxist schema. The search for decentralization comes up against a sort of internal logic, just as the search for planning does in the market economies. Endlessly repeated difficulties occur, especially in agriculture and crafts, in manufacturing and merchandising ventures that do not lend themselves to integration. This has given rise to debates among Marxist economists that demonstrate the complexity of the question that Marx settled out of hand.

Liberman inaugurated the debate and his name has become associated with it.[4] Reduced to its essential, his thesis, the famous "bombshell," can be summarized as follows: the system that is actually functioning in the U.S.S.R. brings about a good deal of dissonance between the units of production and the interests of the collectivity. The latter impose on the former norms and controls for production and price. But the enterprises have engendered, in practice, a whole system of self-defense which allow them to escape norms and controls. In the consultations carried on according to the Plan, enterprises tend to propose very low norms of production and no one knows whether or not the decisions finally reached represent an economic optimum; enterprises do not utilize their productive capacity to the maximum and are always avid for new investments (since they benefit from them gratuitously without having to disburse any interest); they are inclined not to give a full account of their production in order to lower the number of products that will be required of them the following year, and so stocks accumulate; norms imposed are modified only with difficulty and delay, and this puts a brake on technical progress and keeps productivity at a low level, etc.

This situation is common to all socialist economies; Western technicians who have been called upon to work within them are unanimous in remarking it and the Soviet press cites abundant instances of the most glaring anomalies that result from it. As a remedy for the situation, Liberman suggests a substantial modification of the structures of production. Instead of being based upon the realization of imposed norms, the Soviet economy from now on should be centered around the income from the enterprise. A bonus for making a profit, a fraction of the income, would be left to the enterprise as a collective stimulant. The necessity to maintain a cost level below sales proceeds would inspire decisions in conformity with the interest of the collectivity. Direct relations could be established between suppliers and purchasers, the latter being left free to make contracts with suppliers who offer them raw materials of better quality at a cheaper price. A certain competitiveness would in this way reappear; a market would reopen, buying and selling would take place once more. The Plan would content itself with setting quantity indices and delivery targets. Each enterprise would establish its own production plan: indices for work productivity, level of wages, production costs, stocks, investments, and technical updating.[5]

To realize such an audacious reform, Liberman very logically introduces the payment of interest by enterprises on the social capital invested in them. This is the key to the system that he suggests. Without it, enterprises with large investments would enjoy a privileged situation in the market in comparison to those with little. The advantage of having capital to dispose of would not be gratuitous. Liberman estimates that the coefficient of capital efficiency is actually 20 percent for the whole of the Soviet economy and that it would be necessary to require enterprises, in addition to amortizing their debts, to pay interest on the proceeds and include that amount in the cost of production before calculating their income.

Actual practice in the U.S.S.R., at first opposed to these suggestions, whether because of the internal logic of a centralized system or because of the inertia of doctrinal orthodoxy, has finally adopted it in substance. Debate about it still goes on and socialist economies continue to have real difficulties. Marx's argument in *Capital* leaves no room for autonomy in enterprises, even to the limited extent suggested by Liberman, and no place for the payment of interest on invested capital.

It seems legitimate to ask: what then is the value of the Marxist analysis of the market? Is it certain that, as Marx thought, individuals can be identified with their generic being? Are we sure that producers can be actuated by collective motivations for the interest of the nation and even of the whole human race?—for, in the Marxist view, we must logically arrive at that point. Without such inspiration, individuals behave in an anarchical manner. Can they lift themselves immediately to the high consideration of the general good without approaching it by intermediate steps? Here we are up against the huge problem of a structured society, and both Marx and the liberal economists whom he criticizes ignore it.

The "fetishism of commodities"[6] results from the total absence of control over a market abandoned to its objective law of supply and demand: this is the truth of the Marxist analysis. But the abolition of relative autonomies and reliefs leads to another sort of absolutism in the centralized and omnipresent Plan. Economic reasons like Liberman's and political considerations as well make us question the theses of Marx on this point. Is such a total planning conceivable without an equally total dictatorship? This was the question asked by the Czechoslovakian defenders of liberty. It could not be allowed to go unanswered lest it undermine the very foundations of Marxism.

Today every economy is, in fact, familiar with a certain amount of planning, of falling in line with the conclusions of the Marxist analysis but also of having a certain amount of commodity marketing too—which goes contrary to Marxist conclusions. Just one area remains where the "fetishism of commodities" continues to reign supreme—in international trade as practiced by socialist and capitalist nations alike.

It is astonishing that, in these circumstances, a method that was elaborated a century ago and offers such an incomplete explanation even of socialist countries, continues to have such great prestige. Even in its contemporary and most thoroughly renovated forms, it reveals itself as surprisingly incapable of interpreting what has taken place. It is thinkable that Marx himself, as alert as he was to realities, would have modified a collectivist structure that would have had value for him only to the extent that it would assure greater economic development.

## A CRITIQUE OF CAPITAL

The analysis of capital follows from the preceding. Capital is the form that ownership assumes when in the market it encounters a unique kind of commodity—labor power.

For Marx, capital, like commodities, is a world, a mode of existence, a certain way in which people situate themselves in relation to nature and to their fellow beings; in brief, it is a relationship. But while commodities submit to the law of equality, capital is the locus for inequality.

Just as commodities are the result of a phenomenon of quantification, labor undergoes an analogous metamorphosis. Count just its quantity, that is, its duration: that duration is the "substance" of its value. A commodity has no other value than labor, for a commodity is purely and simply a relation and the human ingredient alone can enter into its composition. It is a quantified relation and the relation is just what is repudiated in such a way that the greatness of the work is at the same time its downfall. The value of a commodity is a person's working time reduced to the state of something dead.

In the process of production, labor power is calculated like any other commodity. It is bought at the same price, that is, at its value for production. In capitalist accounting, the cost of labor power is added, without any differentiation, to the cost of raw materials: together they constitute, according to classical categories, "circulating capital" and are added to the amortization of fixed or constant capital. And so, in the eyes of the capitalist, surplus value seems the natural fruit of the total capital invested.

But if we reestablish the reality of the "relation" behind the mask of things, what becomes evident is something quite different. At the level of "relation" only living work creates value,[7] because value is pure relation and that alone can enter into the composition of what people are doing, their work. At the level of things, work loses its character; as the dead work contained in raw materials or in machines it is no longer creative. A turnover has taken place and work is regularly found dispossessed of surplus value, which then appears to originate in capital, therefore in property, and not from labor.

The Marxist analysis strips off the surface of things and penetrates into the intimate reality of the relation, making the assertion that in production labor is the only material that reproduces more than its value, precisely because it is the very substance of value.

As he does in regard to the commodity market, Marx inquires into the origin and end of the exploitation of person by person, which constitutes capitalism. Its origin is clear—capital is identified with enterprise and everything proceeds as if it were the only source of all that is produced and overproduced. Its end can be looked for only with the complete eradication of the system of private property.

Many consider that this analysis of capital offers the only interpretation that gives an account of reality. What is the value of the Marxist explication today? What value has its radical condemnation of every form of interest paid to capital and every form of ownership within enterprise?

Without any doubt, Marx's thesis is in line with an immediate datum of contemporary consciousness, an image of a society in which work has primacy over property as a source of revenue and of decision. Since Marx, the phenomena of the self-generating accumulation of capital are no longer accepted as a matter of course—profits for no reason, undefined and automatic income from invested capital involving no real risks. No longer taken for granted is the identification of enterprise with capital alone, as if the worker were something outside of it, a supplier of some sort of raw material.

However, the socialist reality itself hesitates to follow Marx to the very root of his thesis, and that gives people pause.

In the first place, Marx himself accepts the creativity of capital in at least one instance. His thesis on qualified work, a multiple of simple work, is well known. But what is "qualification" if not the incorporation of social capital into the worker? And if qualified work has a right to a higher revenue; is it not as one sort of capital? Marx himself was conscious that he had in this way introduced inconsistency into his own theory. In his *Critique of the Gotha Program*[8] he considers this distinction as a remaining trace of capitalism in socialism and explicitly excludes it from the final Communist regime when prophesying its future coming.

Besides, there are in the U.S.S.R. as well as in China state loans that are paid back. Individuals can commit their savings to the state and receive from it the same kind of interest that capitalist countries pay: an admission of a certain productivity in capital, even at the level of a relation.

Furthermore, in Yugoslav socialism and in the reform suggested by Liberman, which is partly accepted in the U.S.S.R. today, enterprises must pay interest on the capital allowed them by state organizations. Since a certain amount of competition is being reestablished in the market, it would be inconsistent to allow enterprises with small public investments to compete with those with large public investments, and, for the same reason, to allow agricultural enterprises with only limited or poor land at their disposition to compete with those which have either a great deal of land or rich land for their use. And so, interest on capital and income from the land once more have meaning.[9]

All these "exceptions" to Marxist theory in socialist countries do, however, leave intact a fundamental principle, the abolition of the private ownership of the means of production. Yet we see that the principle itself is weakened when a private sector of the economy exists, which is the case in varying degrees in some peoples' democracies. When it is a matter of small or average

enterprises—in farming, crafts, merchandising, and manufacturing—socialist practice itself hesitates to make a radical application of socialist theory, as if the lack of accountability characteristic of socialist economies has in such instances negative
effects.

In reality, here as in the case of commodity marketing, what is
in question is the possibility for individuals to be at one with,
immediately identified with, their generic being. Beginning at the
moment when, for reasons of economic effectiveness and political liberty, people come to anticipate something that is completely foreign to Marx's thought—room for individual and
group initiative and responsibility in certain sectors of the
economy—it becomes necessary to reestablish remuneration for
the effort to save and to invest. Furthermore, it is no longer so
evident that the attribution of a part of surplus value to capital,
when it is engaged in production that involves real risks, should
be completely eliminated.[10] It would seem worthwhile for society
to give this some consideration in order to avoid structuring an
economy in which irresponsibility rules and freedom is excluded.

The Marxist principle that makes work the substance of value
and the only value capable of creating value is a principle of
radical equality. For all human beings are limited as to the duration of their own work, whereas they can make capital "work" for
them in many places at the same time. Yet, absolute equality is
unproductive. The modifications made in socialist regimes all
move in the direction of compensating effort and are, therefore,
ways of appropriating surplus value.

Not only is this evident in capitalist regimes but in socialist
countries, too, as they come to doubt some of the conclusions of
the Marxist analysis.[11] Even after having fully restored to value
and to capital their character as relations and to work its creative
primacy, the socialist reality is showing an inclination to recognize a certain creativity in the human initiative to save and to
invest.

*The critique of profit.* The Marxist critique of profit can be
evaluated within the perspective of the realities just touched
upon. We all realize that this critique holds a basic place in
Marxist theory and is accepted by all who claim Marxism as their

authority. It asserts that the units of production make their decisions in function of profit, the economy becomes a storm center of crises and conflicts, which prevent its development and threaten its survival.

The evolution occurring in socialist countries makes it necessary for us to go back over this ambivalent critique.

In any economic system whatever, those who produce must create more than they destroy. In this sense, the idea of profit, the positive difference between the values consumed and the values produced, is not a capitalist notion; it is an economic concept and socialism cannot fail to take it into account. It follows that the apparatus of production has to create more social values than it consumes: a law from which no system can escape.

When the profit of one specific enterprise and not of the whole of production is under consideration, socialism has gradually come to learn that it can no longer fail to recognize that law. As a result, it is reorganizing individual enterprises as centers of relatively autonomous decisions and, consequently, as units for profit. So profit tends to become the law of enterprise, even in socialist regimes. However, it cannot constitute an absolute law, for it is only at the level of the whole economy that the creative effectiveness of any single enterprise can be definitively evaluated. For this reason, the decisions of any enterprise must be subordinate to a plan. And, according to recent doctrinal statements, profit is partly accepted as a stimulant and as a norm for decision-making in the Soviet economy.

The appropriation of profit at least continues to be the object of radical criticism. On this point, Marxism evidently remains true to itself: the individual who allots surplus value to himself under any other title than work confiscates the fruits of others' labor. In reality, the disparities that exist between the salaries of intellectual workers and the wages of manual laborers are already an appropriation of profit under the title of capital, as Marx himself recognized. More than that, the interest assigned by the state to those who lend it money constitutes an appropriation of a like kind. A fortiori, the same is true of the profit gained by small and average entrepreneurs in the private sector of some peoples' democracies.

All this leads to a query: perhaps criticism ought to be aimed at some other point? It does not seem to be profit or even the appropriation of profit that creates a problem. Economic reasons—(maintaining the initiative of individuals and groups within the framework of the general plan) and political reasons (liberty is no longer possible when the collectivity is the sole entrepreneur) suggest that the significance of profit be acknowledged when it recompenses services rendered to society that are so regulated that they pose no danger to it. What must be denounced is profit to the extent that it allows an accumulation of resources without any proportionate reason and with the consequent and comparable power derived from wealth.

In the presence of the increasing demand for freedom within socialist countries, must not Marxist theory some day come face to face with a lacerating revision?

Is it not a mistake to construct an economic society in which all workers constitute a single category as wage earners of the state? And a more fundamental question: *is* work the only substance of value, the only source of surplus value?

The Marxist position is categorical: work is the only constituent of value; labor power is the only source of surplus value. Intellectual effort, saving, investment, management, the taking of risks—which often comprise the creation of an instrument of work—have no social import. The class of independent workers, that world of craftsmen, traders, farmers, small and average entrepreneurs, who fill in the spaces left open by the great companies in nonsocialist countries, must disappear from the face of the earth. All these producers, whose income is not a wage but the difference between cost price and selling price, have no reason for existing because they draw their resources both from work and from capital.

Reflection on the conditions indispensable for freedom and observation of the evolution taking place in socialist countries necessitate a reconsideration of this thesis. In reality, the experience of socialism has not proved that the dynamism of independent workers can find an equivalent, at least in the sectors unsuitable for concentration. In addition, it can be asked if peoples' liberties can be preserved when the state is charged with such far-reaching roles. Marxist doctrine, as well as the reality in socialist countries, gives a negative answer.

Marxism has underscored the conflict that sets two categories of workers against one another. Between workers who have no disposition of capital and workers who utilize the capital acquired by their own efforts stand opposing interests. To put it briefly, the wages of the one hold down the profit margin of the other. However, in the long run, their interests coincide: the salary of the one is also the purchasing power that supports prices and therefore the income of the others.

What about the homologizing idea of a classless society with everybody a wage earner of the collectivity? Does not history tell us that this is a mistake? Economically, in many sectors the dynamism of a people striving to better their own lot and that of their families through the creative instrumentality of work cannot be replaced. Politically, peoples' liberties are abolished in a society where every worker is directly dependent upon the public powers.

Marx's conception of class struggle as driving a wedge between two categories of workers so that they are irreconcilable enemies is a misapprehension. There are two classes of workers in society and they cannot get along without each other. For a government seeking to achieve a revolution for liberty, one of its most necessary and difficult tasks is maintaining their coexistence.

The abuses to which independent work can lead are all too evident. It is difficult to distinguish between creative work that merits a recompense and automatic accumulation of wealth that has no social significance. Everything must be done, therefore, to see that merited recompense is given and that unmerited gains are eliminated. But are there means to achieve the discrimination needed to do that? The experience of socialization in some nonsocialist countries has brought to the fore a series of effective measures, and social contrasts in them are perhaps less accentuated than in some socialist countries.

Chile's experience after 1970, under the presidency of Salvador Allende and his final defeat, confirms these views. The expropriation of big capital did not inflame public opinion. The nationalization of Chilean or foreign companies, the abolition of the *latifundios*, provoked no unfavorable reaction. Problems began when a whole class of workers—farmers, tradesmen, craftsmen, small entrepreneurs—felt that the structure on which they depended for a livelihood was being threatened. Better-paid wage earners with technical preparation have attitudes comparable to "independent" workers. These were the immediate causes of the failure of a freely conducted experiment which allowed the social body to voice its reactions to a Marxist model that some wanted to impose upon it.

It is easy to say that these reactions were *petites-bourgeoises*. On the contrary, they quite possibly represented a resistance to an economic and political system which more than half of Chile did not want, which certain categories of the working world saw as an impending menace, and which the majority of Chileans would have disapproved of if it had finally triumphed—and, by that time, been irreversible. [12]

Observation moves us to put the problem of social coexistence and economic dynamism in terms other than those of Marxism: democratic pluralism is conditioned by economic plurality.

## The Political Structure

Several times in the analysis of the economic structure it has been pointed out that ultimately what is concerned is the political structure of society.

*The dictatorship of the proletariat.* The Marxist positions that have become so well known Marx arrived at by degrees. That the economic structure determines the political structure is essential in his system. From his later works it is evident that Marx understood perfectly that the class struggle, with the radical and violent character that he never ceased attributing to it, would lead to "the dictatorship of the proletariat."

This holds at least during its initial stage, for Marx gives us his famous distinction between the two stages in the establishment of communism, which he stated in marginal glosses criticizing the German workers' party program, called the Gotha Program.

"Between capitalist and communist society lies a period of revolutionary transformation from one to the other. There corresponds also to this a political transition period during which the state can be nothing else than the revolutionary dictatorship of the proletariat."[13] The idea is clear—a violent process of transition must be followed for a time by violence in the new institutions. Lenin's contribution will be to define precisely the conditions for violence, particularly in his famous thesis on the supremacy of the party over the government. It is still very much with us, since it was challenged in 1968 by the Prague leaders and responded to by the intervention of Soviet armies in Czechoslovakia.

Marx is so conscious of the rigid discipline of this political system that, as a sort of compensation, he announces a second definitive stage in which the dictatorship will disappear. The passage is as famous as the one just cited and is one of those that leads people to speak of "Marxist messianism."

In the first phase we are surprised to learn, for reading *Capital* has not prepared us for such a revelation, that some traces of capitalism will continue and workers will receive wages proportionate to their work performance. Marx says that equality will consist in income being measured by the same yardstick—work; no one will have a right to revenue from capital; basically such a right, like every other, is a right to inequality, like the inequality between manual and "intellectual" workers.

> In a higher phase of communist society, after the tyrannical subordination of individuals according to the distribution of labour and thereby also the distinction between manual and intellectual work, have disappeared, after labour has become not merely a means to live but is in itself the first necessity of living, after the powers of production have also increased and all the springs of cooperative wealth are gushing more freely, together with the all-round development of the individual, then and then only can the narrow bourgeois horizon of rights be left far behind and society will inscribe on its banner: "From each according to his capacity, to each according to his need."[14]

So we see that Marx remains faithful to his system: the economic determines the political.

Plainly, not just the political necessity for the proletariat to defend the conquest of the revolution against internal and external enemies leads to the "dictatorship of the proletariat"; what does so is chiefly the economic necessity to organize a division of work on the basis of a centralized plan. It is only when abundance reigns that the whole apparatus, which must be maintained during the first stage of communism, will finally disappear and take the dictatorship with it.

The line of argument allows for no ambiguity. The coming of communism and the elimination of dictatorship are in no way attendant on a transformation of the economic and political structures of collectivism, on a sort of progressive liberalization and decentralization (an idea completely missing in Marxist thought). What it awaits is a reign of abundance. Each one will then produce as "a first necessity of living" and will freely take from what is produced. Then there will no longer be any need for repression.

Until that happens, collectivism and dictatorship cannot be dissociated. A monolithic economic system engenders a political monolith.

*Violent revolution.* In regard to the revolutionary process that will destroy capitalism and lead to socialism, Marx becomes more and more explicit in his later writings. In 1879, for example, when he and Engels responded to the three leaders of the German Social Democratic Party then exiled in Zurich, he violently criticizes *petites-bourgeoises* reforms, because they will be utilized by the *Ancien Régime* as a means of keeping itself in power. He rejects the idea that in this spirit the final catastrophe can come to be transformed into a slow process of decomposition that will take place in bits and pieces and, to the extent that it is possible, peacefully. In opposition to this *petite-bourgeoise* strategy, he states, "As for us, taking into account our past, only one way lies open to us. For almost forty years we have continued to insist upon the class struggle as a direct motive force in history, and, in particular, on the class struggle between the bourgeoisie and the proletariat as the great lever for modern social revolution."[15]

Nevertheless, in the same open letter Marx makes a point that shows an evolution in his thought. "The Party," he says, is not to "hit its head against a stone wall" or "throw itself into a bloody revolution against great odds" but rather to "utilize any big event in international politics and the furtherance of the revolution resulting from it, and even the victory won by the people in the conflict which can erupt from this base."

This doctrine is new with Marx. Very probably it resulted from his reflection on the 1871 Commune, in which the people of Paris, having revolted, set about organizing themselves in an experience which Marx, after some hesitation, ended by recognizing as a dress rehearsal for revolution. Up to that time, Marx had thought that revolution sprang spontaneously from the contrast between the growing mass of the proletariat and the ever restricted group of capitalist owners. In any case, the new vision is prophetic. In Russia, in eastern Europe, and in China the revolution was brought about under the favorable circumstances of an international conflict. In Cuba communism is a war communism; it can be explained only by the conflict between the American and Soviet blocs. In the passages just cited, Marx laid the foundations for the famous Leninist theory of the transformation of international war into a war of revolution. [16]

Such is the Marxist analysis of the political structure. Leading Marxists, Lenin in particular, made substantial contributions to the theory. None of them made any fundamental changes in the concepts of violent class struggle and the dictatorship of the proletariat.

To what extent is this schema necessary to explain history today? And can it serve as a model for every revolution? Because of the great number of people who say that they find the Marxist analysis the only adequate instrument for understanding and interpretation as well as for action, the question cannot be evaded.

Without a doubt, the requirements of a concerted plan demand the modification of democratic structures that have grown up out of a liberal revolution. All nations are looking for new forms of power capable of meeting the new functions of the state. A linkage exists, therefore, between the economic and political structures in industrial society.

But, for all that, do we have to accept a strict interpretation of the Marxist schema and conclusions? Is dictatorship inseparable from revolution? Is violent class struggle a condition for revolution?

As we know, some believe that they can adhere to the Marxist analysis without following it to its ultimate consequences. Some believe that they can build a Marxist socialism and preserve freedom at the same time. Can such an idea be insinuated into Marxist-Leninist thought in spite of the strong and explicit statements of the masters themselves?[17]

Of all the questions put to the Marxist conscience, this is probably the most serious. Up to the present, no socialist regime satisfying the Marxist definition has been able to set up a working democracy, that is, a democracy of the majority. Examples to the contrary that are sometimes adduced have not been cogent. In Prague of 1948, was Czechoslovakia a free country?[18] Was communism implanted there by a democratic process? Do not the ups and downs of the country twenty years later demonstrate that communism was imposed and maintained, there as elsewhere, by an active minority, in conformity with the Leninist thesis of the class struggle and the supremacy of the party over the government. As to Chile, the failure of its experimentation in a freely made transition into Marxism confirms the classic theory: a Marxist revolution never receives the backing of the majority.

Furthermore, the very people who dreamed of a revolution freely achieved and, therefore, of a revolution without violence, knew full well that they could only do it by the action of a minority skillfully using a framework of legality to impose it upon an opposing majority by surprise. Perhaps they were already conscious that such a revolution, supposing that it did accede to power, could never succeed in holding onto it while respecting the normal working of a democracy.

The rigor of Marxist reasoning is, in any case, unquestionable. A rigidly planned socialist economy can be organized and developed only under a dictatorship. Every true Marxist is realistic in thinking so. Beginning with the moment when the state crosses the threshold of the nationalization and planning of enterprises, it finds itself holding such heavy responsibilities that it cannot submit to the rules of a democracy: every manifestation of autonomy and freedom, the smallest strike, casts doubt upon the whole system and is therefore actually seditious. This became quite evident in Hungary in 1956 and in Czechoslovakia in 1968.

The armed intervention of the U.S.S.R. was logical: the cohesion of the system was at stake. Socialism is not freely established. It has to be done under anesthesia, that is, by preventing the expression of opinion and the organization of opposition. Marx laid down that law. Logic and events confirm it.

In the end, it is hard to decide what causes more wonderment about the Marxist analysis—the vigor of its intuition and the rigor of its reasoning or its capacity to explain the movements shaking up the socialist world itself. The revelation of Stalinist tyranny, the revolt of the Budapest workers, the Russo-Chinese conflict, the Prague springtime, the revolt of the Polish workers, the cultural revolution in China are not negligible happenings. The Marxist analysis, even in its most modern forms as offered by the most recent and original Marxist theoreticians, does not make a start at explaining them. No response has yet been given to the outstanding Italian communist leader Togliatti at the time of Khruschchev's 1956 report. Who, he asked, is going to explain to us how the Stalinist tyranny could be engendered in the heart of a system that claims to solve the human problem[19] and to mark the end of the prehistory of humanity?[20] Since then, how many questions, equally urgent, have been left unanswered! In China at least, and in the third world, will there not be a new Marxism?

## NOTES

1. Karl Marx, *Capital, a Criticism of Political Economy* (New York: Modern Library, 1936), pp. 81–82. It is impossible to repeat the analysis I made which led me to adopt this reading of *Capital*. See *Marxisme et humanisme*, 3rd ed. (Paris: P.U.F., 1961), pp. 44 ff.

2. Ibid., pp. 90–91.

3. Marx and Engels, "Sixth Thesis on Feuerbach," Part 1 and selections from Parts 2 and 3, in *German Ideology*, ed. C. J. Arthur, (New York: International Publishers, 1970), p. 188. See my *La doctrine sociale de l'Eglise*, 2nd ed. (Paris: P.U.F., 1966), p. 173.

4. An exposition of Liberman's theses and of their application in the U.S.S.R. and the reason why, in spite of some positive results, the

proposed reform reached an impasse can be found in Marie Lavigne, *The Socialist Economies of the Soviet Union and Europe,* trans. T. G. Waywell (White Plains, N.Y.: International Arts & Sciences Press, 1974).

5. Ota Sik went much further in the same direction than Liberman, proposing the establishment of workers' councils with power to choose their own directors. At the time of Dubcek's attempt at democratization in 1968 in Czechoslovakia, he was trying to get efficient management by big leaders formed along the lines of their counterparts in large capitalistic enterprises "who would feel the effects of their decisions in their skins and in their pockets." Quoted by Roger Garaudy, *La liberté en sursis, Prague 1968* (Paris: Fayard, 1968), p. 72.

6. *Capital,* p. 83.

7. This is why Marx rejects the classic category of "circulating" capital, in which work and raw materials are added together, and replaces it by the category of "variable" capital (work alone, the unique creator of surplus value) as opposed to "constant" or fixed capital (all the other components that go into cost price), which is incapable of reproducing more than its value in the process of production.

8. Karl Marx, *Critique of the Gotha Program,* Vol. I (New York: International Publishers, 1933), p. 3.

9. René Dumont makes this point clear in his *Soukhoz, holkhoz, ou le problématique communisme* (Paris: Seuil, 1964), pp. 235 ff.

10. In *Capital* Marx shrugs off, with easy irony, the objections to his thesis. Are these pages really definitive? See *Capital,* pt. 3, chap. 7, sec. 2, pp. 213–21.

11. Studying the economic growth of the U.S.S.R. and some of the peoples' democracies, Jean Marczewski comes to the conclusion that they are relatively ineffective and analyzes the causes for this. He also hypothesizes a probable evolution in socialist planning that would involve a revision of some of the fundamental principles of Marxist political economy.

12. The analyses given here took into account the Chilean experiment, which I knew at first hand and wrote up before the fall of Allende, September 11, 1973. In Alain Touraine's *Vie et mort du Chili populaire* (Paris: Seuil, 1973) are some reflections that appeared among Communist ranks. Perhaps in the European Communist milieu can be found the most apposite critique of this experiment and an explanation of the drama that brought it to an end. Marxist thought, however, does not go so far as to include a factor that seems to me most decisive in this crisis—the year-long division of a country because of the conflict between the two categories of workers who comprise its citizenry.

13. *Critique of the Gotha Program,* Vol. IV, pp. 44–45.

14. Ibid., Vol. I, p. 31.

15. Marx and Engels, *Selected Correspondence 1846–1895,* trans. Dona Torr, Letter No. 170 (New York: International Publishers, 1942), pp. 376, 371–72.

16. Here we have the reason why, from the Marxist point of view, the establishment of communism in Chile was an impossibility—the military machine remained intact and constituted the only obstacle that stood in the way of a Marxist dictatorship.

17. Nevertheless, new doctrines about the possibility of a peaceful revolution are appearing among Marxist writers. On this point see the Third Program of the Russian Communist Party. "Communists have never thought and are not now thinking that revolution must inevitably come about by war between nations. Revolution is not necessarily linked to war. Taking its stand with the majority of the people . . . the worker class can defeat reactionary forces and win a solid majority in parliament." Quoted by Michel Mouskhely, *L'U.R.S.S. au seuil du communisme?* (Paris: Dalloz, 1962), p. 217.

18. See François Fejtö, *Histoire des démocraties populaires,* Vol. I: *L'ère de Staline, 1945–1952,* 3rd ed. (Paris: Seuil, 1971), ch. 6, "Le coup de Prague." Nothing is more dramatic than the story of the alliance and finally the struggle to the death between the National Socialists headed by Fierlinger and the Communist Party with Gottwald as its secretary general under the presidency of Bénès, laid low by a stroke—all carried out within an international context that seemed to be foretelling a new German threat and gave Stalin the prestige of being Poland's only ally. Fejtö concludes: "A worker class that can count on the more or less active cooperation of the police and the army is an irresistible force. If such a worker class is led by men who believe in the necessity for and the opportunity of establishing a dictatorship, then a dictatorship becomes inevitable" (p. 216). The election of May 30, 1948, which gave the voters a choice between opting for the National Front candidates or not voting at all, gave 90 percent of the votes to the new power. The destiny of the nation was decided in the preceding months during which the Communist Party succeeded in paralyzing all opposition.

19. "Communism clears up the mystery of history and is fully aware that it does." Marx and Engels, *Gesamtausgabe,* Ite Abteilung, Vol. III, p. 114.

20. Karl Marx, *A Contribution to the Critique of Political Economy* (Chicago: Chas. Kerr & Co., 1904), p. 13.

# XI

# A NEW MARXISM?

*"The Great Proletarian Cultural Revolution" in China*

Insofar as we can begin to understand it, through official documents, travelers' accounts, and the analyses of experts, is the cultural revolution a new version of Marxism? Is it the one and only representative of Marxist-Leninist orthodoxy, as it claims, in opposition to the revisionism of Khrushchev and Liu Shao-ch'i? Or is it simply removing any marks identifying it with them by making the kind of protests typical of a new revolution?

Certainly Marxism-Leninism is its evident and enduring resource. In the famous *Little Red Book* as well as in the *Report of the Ninth Congress* of the Chinese Communist Party,[1] it is astonishing not to find even the slightest reference to the prestigious cultures of old China. The new world is fashioned according to an ideology that is, in every respect, a complete import. In this very orthodox context Stalin himself remains untouchable, although certain errors are attributed to him. According to the official interpretation, the letdown and falling off in the U.S.S.R. resulted from Khrushchev's abominable denunciation. Without a doubt no stricter Marxist-Leninist vocabulary is to be found than in the Chinese documents distributed in over a hundred million copies throughout China and the rest of the world.

It is all there. "To strengthen the dictatorship of the proletariat, to prevent the restoration of capitalism, and to build up socialism"[2] are the main objectives of the new revolution. There is no question of allowing the dictatorship of the proletariat to relax. "The class struggle necessarily leads to it."[3] A person who simply recognizes class struggle is not thereby a Marxist, but only those who extend their recognition of class stuggle to accepting the dictatorship of the proletariat.[4] Liu Shao-ch'i and his clique are reproached with being capitalists, bourgeoisie, "great lords," and imperialism continues to be the principal enemy. Class struggle cannot be peaceful but must be done with arms. "Political power grows out of the barrel of a gun."[5] The primacy of the working class remains intact in that immense rural country. "Our state is a people's democratic dictatorship led by the working class and based on the worker-peasant alliance."[6] The relationship between social existence and consciousness is exactly the same as Marxism defined it once for all. "It is man's social being that determines his thinking. Once that correct ideas characteristic of the advanced class are grasped by the masses, these ideas turn into a material force which changes society and changes the world."[7] There is no point in adding quotation upon quotation. Mao's whole work could be reprinted here. Actually, there is no more classic Marxism than the Chinese.

Nevertheless, we are conscious of new ideas emerging in this context. "*It is the first time* [Bigo's italics] in the theory and practice of the international communist movement that the idea has been put forward in an explicit way that classes and the class struggle will still continue to exist even after the socialist transformation has been achieved"[8] through the abolition of private ownership of the means of production. This is no empty statement. It is a constantly repeated requisite for the coherence of Mao's thought. The great leader never wearies of saying over and over again that "a distinction must be made between conflict among the people and conflict between the enemy and us."[9] Was the former foreseen by Marx? In the *Critique of the Gotha Program,* he admitted that antagonism existed between intellectual and manual workers, a consequence of capitalism to be found in socialism. But would he have stated that class struggle was to remain the dynamism of the new society? Mao declares that "the principal contradiction within a country is between the laboring class and the bourgeoisie." What bourgeoisie—after the private ownership of the means of production has been abolished? Nonetheless, the Red Guard are constantly raising the question of the famous "problem of power,"[10] which means maintaining the power of the working class and dislodging the bourgeoisie in communist China. Mao logically concludes from that to the necessity for permanent revolution based on the existence of armed force.

Marx certainly well knew that communism would be fully realized only in the distant future with the advent of abundance, as he admits in the *Critique of the Gotha Program.* But did he imagine that, within a socialist country, there would be a merciless combat such as China has experienced since the coming of the cultural revolution?

To move on to something more serious. "Often, correct knowledge can be arrived at only after many repetitions of the process leading from matter to consciousness and then back to matter"; then he immediately adds, "that is, leading from practice to knowledge and then back to practice.[11] Mind then does exist. But words are words and Marx never designated consciousness by the word "mind," a non-Marxist term.[12]

Reading our way through Maoist statements we come to ask ourselves whether the recurring reference to Marx is not partly a way of legitimizing new assertions which Marx never expressed and for which he would doubtless never take responsibility.[13]

In a very orthodox Marxist-Leninist context, certain contestations typical of a postsocialist revolution can be observed. Party bureaucracy within established socialism is challenged—a person has to be more "Red" than expert. A summons is issued to humankind and its consciousness—to remake people is just as important as to remake nature. People are educable and perfectible. There is no need to liquidate an adversary; instead, the adversary is to be made over—the new mission of the techniques and prisons for reeducation. Everybody must exercise vigilance through self-criticism, a process of continual reform that cannot be other than painful. Mind and matter have a reciprocal relationship, the mind being formed by contact with the material world and the form which the world imprints upon it. In myself I have only a small compass of existence; in the world I have a great sphere in which to be.

Here we have not just new accents but new ways of thinking that modify the traditional Marxist conception of dialectical materialism. The education of human beings, their inner conversion, the grounds justifying it, the means chosen to accomplish it, all this is a new contribution. Not only is personal ownership of political power abolished, as in the democratic revolution, and not just the private ownership of the means of production—but every form of proprietorship, even of learning, of technical skill, of bureaucracy. Perhaps it will be said that the socialist abrogation of ownership is pushed to its utmost consequences. But is not socialism itself logical democracy? In any case, education through manual work, the inversion of roles (a hotel manager becoming a bellhop),[14] the absolute equality between officers and workers on revolutionary committees in factories, are completely innovative practices. There is no question of suppressing learning or technical skill or office holding but only of eliminating the privileges which people have arrogated to themselves through these things. What is hoped for from this revolution is not change of structure, for dictatorship stays on, but a new spirit, inculcated by new methods of education. The official abrogation of material incentives in production (bonuses for high individual and collective production) and their replacement by heroic models of sacrifice and devotion demonstrate that an ideal is being appealed to.

The fact that the cultural revolution began with a revolution in opera, ballet, and symphonic music is symptomatic. Art must no longer be dominated by personages of bygone days. It must serve as dynamism for the people.[15]

In all these characteristics, the cultural revolution in China is consonant with the contestation in the West. It has elaborated and offers to the world a new basis for society, the commune. Spontaneously, the young in France and elsewhere actualize it in their own way by getting back to manual work and forming communities without any hierarchies whatever.

However, the Chinese cultural revolution is a far cry from the images that the West has formed of it, seeing it as a kind of refuge from lost illusions. Doubtless it is as different from what they conceive it to be as Stalinism was from the way it was represented in French "progressive" circles in 1950.[16] It is true that the Chinese cultural revolution is part of a spontaneous rebellion of the young and their boundless enthusiasm on finding Mao making common cause with them.[17] But it is being channeled into a monolithic system which may no longer be the party's but is no less strait and hard for having one man and one thought with absolute power over seven or eight hundred million people. Restrictions on information, speech, and association are stricter than ever. The education of the people and the reeducation of adversaries by manual work and by proven techniques of self-accusation and accusation by others can be a most subtle form of dictatorship, which touches the person in the most intimate recesses of his being.[18] The antireligious, and especially the anti-Christian, struggle is more relentless than ever. Even the autonomous nationalist church, at one time tolerated, has been, it seems, completely annihilated. If the cultural revolution in China seems to be a creative and lasting process, it is also a temporary process which Mao intended as a means of giving new life to the revolution and of gathering the reins of power completely in his own hands.

The question may well be raised whether this is a revolution within a revolution or the Marxist revolution pushed to its extreme consequences.

Will an evolution of Marxism in the third world make it possible for it to reach a clearer resolution?

## Marxism in the Third World

Marxism retains all of its prestige in the milieu of the universities and in intellectual circles, particularly in Latin America. As some see it, it is the only explanation that accounts for phenomena, the only revolutionary praxis that can free oppressed classes and peoples. Its eruption into a number of movements that follow the line of the Soviet or the Chinese or Castro or Trotsky, all engaged in ferocious attacks on one another, has in no way robbed it of a hearing.[19]

What is a marvel for anyone face to face with the misery of the people and the violence of social disparities is that Marxism has made so little progress with the masses. However, it plays a decisive part for them. Leaving aside a few particular cases,[20] its ideology has not caught on with the people. But has not that always been so? The Communist revolution follows a pattern. First strategy and tactic have the mission to detect, and do detect, the exceptional circumstances needed; then an active minority succeeds in stirring up the masses, making sure not to launch an abortive anarchical rebellion or a guerrilla movement committed to failure. When and only when the time is ripe, the revolution gets under way and triumphs.

Sometimes the governments of young nations are inspired by Marxist ideals and undertake some kind of new revolution. It would be impossible to list them all, much less to arrange them in a typology. From the socialism of Tanzania's Nyerere—which leans toward Christianity—or of Kaunda in Zambia to the aggressive socialism of Sekou Touré in Guinea, they have a wide range of variations. They are a new phenomenon, which Marxist theory has acknowledged and analyzed as a possible transitional stage.[21]

These "national regimes"[22] manifest common characteristics, which Soviet experts observe and isolate, all the while persisting in an attempt to determine the cadre with the best chance of realizing the desired transition to the only real socialism, proletarian dictatorship.

The experiment unfolds under the control of a single party[23] made up of a nationalist elite of intellectuals and bourgeoisie who have freed themselves from the yoke of colonialism. Agrarian reform with the distribution of land to poor peasants, nationalization of banks and the leading anonymous companies, economic planning, socialist education of the masses, and class struggle are the fundamental elements of this noncapitalist way of development.

Soviet experts carefully avoid mistaking such developments for socialist models. A wide gulf separates them from that. Communism is irreversible. Experience has shown, on the other hand, that these "national regimes" are unstable. Failures like those of Mobido Keita in Mali and Kwame Nkrumah in Ghana; about-faces such as Neméiry's in the Sudan; tragic events like what happened in Indonesia, where hundreds of thousands of Communists were massacred, have shown what direction the action is taking. China, as a rural country that can count only on the mobilization of a huge work force to build up its economy, has a greater attraction for the third world, a fact that suggests prudence to Russian observers.

It remains true that communism, whether Soviet or Chinese,

takes an interest in the third world and maintains a presence there though ambassadors, experts, and economic aid, rather as if it were taking soundings on its future there.[24]

Insofar as an impression can be gained by observation, it appears that even if the third world is prepared to accept many Marxist ideas, it is not disposed to slip into the rigid mold offered it by the U.S.S.R. or even by China. What is being elaborated there is not a new Marxism but an original model, or even a number of models, closer to cultural traditions, more in conformity with the general principles of people's consciences, as these are distinct from a revolutionary process in which socialism represents but one phase. The "choice of a society" by Latin Americans, Africans, Asians, and the Arab world, if it does include Marxist elements, does not seem to be leaning in the direction of a monolithic state.

No one can pretend to be sure of what the future holds but observation and reflection can at least lead us to some conclusions.

## NOTES

1. Since the disappearance of Lin Piao, *The Little Red Book* no longer appears in everybody's hands at demonstrations and official receptions. But nothing in it has been disavowed. As to Lin Piao's *Report to the Ninth Congress,* the official position is that, if it was read over by Lin Piao, it was not drafted by him and consequently retains its full value.

2. Lin Piao, *Report to the Ninth Congress of the Communist Party of China* (Peking: Foreign Languages Press, 1969), p. 4.

3. Ibid, p. 8.

4. Ibid., pp. 5–6.

5. *Quotations from Chairman Mao Tse-tung (The Little Red Book)* (New York: Bantam Books, 1967), p.33.

6. Ibid., p. 20.

7. Ibid., pp. 116–17.

8. Ibid., p. 10.

9. Ibid., p. 28.

10. See Maria-Antonietta Macciocchi, *Daily Life in Revolutionary China*, (New York: Monthly Review Press, 1972), p. 51.

11. *Quotations from Chairman Mao Tse-tung*, p. 118.

12. Almost as if he had forseen this objection, Mao writes: "While we recognize that in the general development of history the material determines the mental and social being determines social consciousness, we also—and indeed must— recognize the reaction of mental on material things, of social consciousness on social being and of the superstructure on the economic base. This does not go against materialism; on the contrary, it avoids mechanical materialism and firmly upholds dialectical materialism." *Quotations*, p. 125. It is doubtful that this language belongs to materialism. It can be found, too, in the Third Program of the Russian Communist Party of 1961. See Mouskhely, *L'U.R.S.S. au seuil du communisme?* (Paris: Dalloz, 1962).

13. Something of the same seems to apply to the situation with Mao. All the different factions claim him as their own (and this is officially recognized); as the *Report to the Ninth Congress* expresses it, they utter words that are apparently in line with the left but are actually rightist. But, after all, within the framework of a dictatorship, isn't this the only way left to express any new opinion?

14. Macciocchi, *Daily Life in Revolutionary China*, p. 29.

15. *Report to the Ninth Congress*, p. 29. Within Marxism this is certainly a novel conception of the superstructure and its role as a motive force. Liu Shao-ch'i was reproached just for being attached to an ideology and a superstructure by creating "departments of literature and the arts" appealing to "the dead"—the ideals and personages of old China. It is not the least paradox of the Chinese cultural revolution that, while it exercises such an attraction on countries that are jealous of their own cultures, it seems bent on repudiating the prestigious past of China.

16. Did not prominent thinkers in France exert themselves to justify, from a Marxist point of view, the famous Stalin purges? In articles in *Temps modernes*, "Le yogi et le prolétaire" (October and November 1946; January 1947), Merleau-Ponty came up with the hypothesis that the victims of the Stalin purges who were conscious Marxists, in agreement with the recognition that their actions, which were perfectly justifiable in their time, could in retrospect be considered criminal in consequence of the historical evolution that had taken place since then. The revelations of Khrushchev's 1956 report gave a much more realistic explanation of Stalin's purges.

17. The account given by Macciocchi makes this point clear. *Daily Life*, pp. 54-55. Written after a visit to China by a group of French Parliament

members, Alain Peyrefitte's *Quand la Chine s'éveillera* (Paris: Fayard, 1973) contains much valuable information.

18. These are the questions that can be felt surfacing in the *Memoires du garde rouge Dai Hsiao-ai* (Paris: Albin Michel, 1971), suspect as it is, like every account by a voluntary exile, and certainly utilized by propaganda, but a testament to truth nonetheless.

19. The review INDAL *(Información documental de América latina)*, 220 Waversban, Heverlee-leuven, Belgium, publishes (no. 1, November 1972) hitherto unpublished documents on the different Marxist currents running counter to one another in Latin America, for example, in Guatemala, Colombia, and Venezuela.

20. Not only Cuba, which is more radical than some peoples' democracies in its actualization of communism, but Chile too, where Marxism served as the inspiration of both the Communist Party (with its leaning toward the Soviet type) and the Socialist Party (with a leftist majority), which together collected a third of the votes when elections were still free.

21. On this point, see Robert Bosc, "Conceptions soviétiques du développement pour le tiers monde," *Projet*, July-August 1970. Experts have gone so far as to say that the study of this phenomenon is the most important contribution of recent Marxist theory.

22. The Third Program of the Soviet Communist Party (1961) explicitly recognizes their existence. *The New Soviet Society: Final Text of the Communist Party of the Soviet Union,* annotated and introd. Herbert Ritvo (New York: New Leader, 1962), p. 84.

23. This is the reason why it is questionable whether the Chilean experiment, in which the plurality of parties was respected, can be interpreted according to this model, although it came quite close to it in other features.

24. Philippe Richer, *La Chine et le tiers monde* (Paris: Payot, 1971), gives a comprehensive view of the effort Communist China has made to penetrate the third world. For the attitude of the U.S.S.R. in regard to the third world, see Henri Chambre, *Union soviétique et développement économique* (Paris: Aubier, 1967), pp. 372 ff.

# PART FOUR

# A READING IN THE FUTURE

## Choosing a Society

It is not the business of the Church to propose model societies. Its mission of liberation lies elsewhere—in exorcising the fetishes that introduce division and oppression among people and to communicate its faith in God, the source of every true relationship.

Yet its mission puts an obligation on Christians to look for models which, in a given situation, seem best suited to establish a new economic and political society in conformity with the meaning of existence.

The search must be carried on within the Church. Everything has been said and well said about the need for Christians to become engaged in undertakings for liberation. Yet most of the theologies urging them to do so leave the basic question open: what liberation? They come to a halt at this threshold and do not cross it. The Church does not limit itself to saying that we should engage in these undertakings; it gives us the elements for discernment so that we may make the necessary choices; it companions us Christians as we make our options and initiate our activities.[1] The silence of theologies on this point can encourage ambiguous positions, leave Christians without compass or direction, and even lead some to identify their faith with some particular theology.

However, the conclusions reached by this search will differ according to circumstances. Nobody can prescribe options that would fit every particular case. Yet it is possible, beginning with an analysis of revolutionary currents, especially those in the third world, and with the knowledge of existence emanating from the faith, to discern tendencies and open up perspectives. Analysis and reflection call for a definition of freedom, not in abstract but in historical terms. That kind of a definition could be of help in establishing the society toward which the whole human race, and the third world most of all, are feeling their way.

Starting with the liberation that took place during the last two centuries, we have, as we have already seen, not one definition of freedom but three: the democratic, the socialist, and the cultural. These three definitions have been worked out in confrontation and sometimes in bloodshed by three successive revolutions that are both related and opposed to one another.

All three definitions originated in a world marked by Christian preaching. Believers discover in the three revolutions, mixed with negations that contradict their faith and a selection of civilizations with sources elsewhere, options that form part of the gospel message.

While making no claim to delineate a model for a society, we may now have reached ground solid enough to allow us to determine the three fundamental elements in any liberation.

## NOTE

1. Alain Birou writes: "Perhaps it is even more urgent . . . to make faith in Christ live and grow in a completely political world and in our own very politicized selves than to push Christians who lack political maturity to become involved in politics. This is the reason why, after all those who have addressed themselves to the political in order to be Christian, I would like to address myself first to being Christian in order to keep the faith alive within the political." *Combat politique et foi en Jésus-Christ* (Paris: Cerf, 1973), p. 7.

# XII

# THE ALTERNATIVE

If we want to go ahead with a project for a society with greater justice, brotherhood, and freedom, we ought first to give consideration to the alternative now open to us, particularly those of us in the third world. In the third world the alternative is written in the clearest script. The question there is no fabricated dilemma, no abstract intellectual query. Reality itself, in its most concrete and, if one may venture to so express it, most real form, is causing a tragic schism.

Think of some country now in process of development. Within the country can be found everything needed for all the people there to live decently: the earth is productive enough, the work force is numerous, investment resources are not lacking (for foreign and private capital really exists), qualified workers, technicians, and officers can all be trained. Many developing countries are in this sort of a situation.

The material possibility exists of constructing decent housing for all, of giving everybody the necessities of life, of establishing enough schools, making primary education obligatory for all children and secondary and university education open to all on an equal footing, of creating dispensaries and hospitals where they are needed.

The question arises spontaneously in the mind: why would it not be possible to realize a program of equal distribution, of education and health, while preserving democratic structures and creating authentic basic communities? Everybody would profit by it, beginning with the most advantaged, for, in the face of so much misery, are not privileges a weight upon them, a lasting reproach? Why could not objectives in democracy and participation be reached?

A project of that nature is eminently humanitarian. In a sense, many goverments that are in no way socialist envision it at least partially in the reasonable, common-sense aspects of their programs.

Suppose a government wants to effect such a program in and through existing free political and economic structures, such as are to be had in many countries of the third world. What would happen? That government would immediately arouse the resistance of the assembled elect; it would provoke the opposition of the mass media, largely dependent upon the economically powerful. Why does this unjust and unintelligent opposition infallibly arise?

In order to establish schools, dispensaries, and hospitals, to construct decent housing, to create a system of family subsidies as protection against sickness and old age—everything, let it be said again, that would in no way exceed the material possibilities of the country—the government, having decided to act, will then have to procure the necessary investment funds to carry out the program planned. And where will the funds come from? In part, from freely invested national and international savings. But no sane government can expect to raise the whole sum by borrowing; it will also have to tax. And when it attempts to do so, it runs head-on into a double obstacle.

On one hand, private investment is needed to fertilize the economy and to do it freely. The government too must have the necessary financial means at its disposal. An indirect tax solves nothing—except when put on luxuries—for it augments in line with the expenditures that have to be made for a decent living and goes counter to the end in view, to raise the standard of living for the mass of the people. A directly and steeply progressive tax on income and capital, at least that portion not invested and not creating new employment, is the solution. A determined government should have recourse to it, in the interest of economic and political freedom, to exploit the existing resources of the country and put them at the disposition of the people as a whole.

And that is just what will not be allowed. The leisure class of the country are not disposed to lower their style of living in order to cede to the poor classes some portion of their income and assets. This is a fact. And, as they have at their disposal a whole

arsenal of means to bring weight to bear on governmental decisions, by a slanted communications system—press, radio,
television—and the bias of elected assemblies (through electoral
campaigns, pressure of every kind); and as they can use other
weapons at least as formidable—fiscal fraud, sending their capital abroad, and, in particular, withholding investments—the
government in question is going to encounter an unsuperable
barrier.

Such a program—equal distribution of goods and services
within democratic structures and basic communities—provided
that it is divested of its agressiveness towards the leisure class
and of every intention to do away with legitimate liberties and
autonomies, in no way contravenes the Christian ideal; more
than that, the Christian ideal absolutely demands it. No doctrine
regarding social matters has been invested with greater authority
than that concerning the designation of existing resources for the
general use of all. No other program can actualize at once the
triple liberation called for by the human conscience today.

Granted all this, the program is unrealizable economically and
politically because of the irrational but unfailing resistance of
those who hold onto incomes and fortunes above the average.
Psychological mechanisms are at work against which the government is defenseless, especially if its action has been accompanied by general measures of expropriation and provocative
steps against the social categories whose collaboration is necessary.

Experience demonstrates that, in these circumstances, the
government has to resort to one of the two following possibilities.

1. It abandons the idea of raising the standard of living of the
masses by putting the disposition of existing resources on a truly
equal footing. Instead, it puts its hopes in free enterprise, allowing people to accumulate income and assets in the expectation
that, after the privileged classes have been abundantly provided
for as individual consumers, they will save and invest, attracted
by the opportunity for new revenues and increased capital. A
government that follows this policy is assured of support from
the mass media. And, if public opinion is lacking and thus the
support of the elected assemblies, it has the resources to put

democracy to sleep and to perform an operation under anesthesia—the creation of a dictatorship. Yet the very logic of economic efficiency leads to a rise in the standard of living for the less advantaged (beginning with the best-off among them) and will create a market within the country and maintain the development of enterprises based on the expectation of increased profits and, therefore, of sufficient sales. What results is a type of development characterized by economic efficiency and the social contrasts that it engenders. Violence has apparently been vanquished; in point of fact it has been made an establishment.

2. Taking an opposite tack, the government renounces democracy and participation and puts its hopes in a people's dictatorship, that is, with one person or one party in absolute control of the situation, deciding, without any possible opposition, whether political or economic, on the allotment of resources to be made to meet the people's needs. Marxist socialism begins with this premise. Gone are public liberties and basic communities, but the standard of living among the most deprived classes does rise. In this situation, too, violence has not been overcome but has been institutionalized in a irreversible way.

## Two Worlds in Opposition

Today the third world is being urged to align itself with one or the other of these two models. Anybody seeking a way out of that alternative should first discern the values and defects of each.

### THE MARXIST MODEL

Those who come from the other, non-Marxist world to a country that embodies the Marxist model get a surprise and a shock. If they want to become acquainted with it other than as an official visitor or a tourist, they must manage to forget that they are soon leaving it and really to put themselves in the place of the people who must live there all their lives; then the shock becomes, for those capable of going behind and beyond it, a stimulus for reflection and an approach to discernment.[1]

*Values.* All socialist countries structured according to the Marxist plan exhibit the following traits.

1. They have only one social category. Setting aside the new class of directors, high functionaries, and party leaders, who enjoy a privileged but precarious position—for when they fall into disgrace they lose everything—the standard of living, without being exactly equal, is comparable for all. Fortunes, which establish the most glaring differences in capitalist countries, have vanished. Incomes, if not all exactly at the same level, are close enough. Salary coefficients may range from one to four in one country and as much as one to fifteen in another. The inequality that results does not lead to distinctively different lifestyles,[2] for even the best-off can purchase only the products offered on the market and what and how many these are does not depend on demand. To a large extent, money has lost its value. Rationing and the lines waiting at the shops—where these still exist—have tellingly limited its power. Then, too, individuals often have no other option than to lend the money that they have saved to the state, which, in this way, absorbs any excess buying power.

By way of illustration, the capitalist world could be compared to a building of many stories, including underground cellars. Socialism makes everybody either go down or come up to the ground floor—which explains both the satisfaction and the discontent that it evokes.

2. All children, in actual fact, attend primary school, as their parents are obliged to send them. Enormous effort has gone into creating a substantial system of schooling. In some countries, if it is necessary to take children from their parents in order to have them attend school, that is done. Not only is secondary and university education free but students even receive a salary. The selection of an intellectual elite is not made on the basis of social class.

3. Medical aid and care in dispensaries and hospitals are completely free. In this instance, too, an enormous effort has gone into providing indispensable and jointly held equipment. There being an insufficient number of buildings and doctors, all those who formerly could pay for medical care now present themselves like everybody else in the long lines that wait at hospital doors. This should be but a temporary situation.

4. The all too famous shantytowns, a sore in the side of all big

cities in the third world and even in some capitals of the industrial nations, have disappeared. Housing is often still deficient. Each family has the use of a tiny but relatively decent space.

5. Save for some exceptional cases, there is no prostitution. The incidence of delinquency is comparatively low. In general, corruption among officials has disappeared, although a black market has developed. Drugs are effectively prohibited and pornography is unknown.

6. Manual work is honored. Sometimes, as in China and Cuba, all—officials, employees, students—are obliged to do manual work for more or less extended periods of time. In the same countries, farming is held in equal esteem with factory work. Elsewhere the peasant or field worker is still looked upon as a poor relation. Idleness no longer exists. Everybody is obliged to work.

There are, of course, many shades of difference between the one socialist country and another, which could be brought out in an outline of this kind. In summary, it can be said that among them as a whole money has largely lost its power. It no longer serves as a means of speculation and accumulation, the real cause of social inequities. It is no longer the only power that decides what is to be placed at the disposition of consumers. It is no longer the creator of economic privilege. Finally, it is no longer the fetish denounced by Marx.

For many, these values are decisive. The matter is settled. They have made their choice.

*Defects and deficiencies.* It should be clear, however, at what price these values have been bought.

1. From a political point of view, the dictatorship of the proletariat has been established in the form forthrightly defined by Marx and organized by Lenin with the supremacy of the party over the government. Public liberties are abolished. Universal suffrage is maintained in a form that allows voters to have no choice as to their candidate or candidates. "The masses" are the final authority but can be interpreted only by and through the omnipresent and omnipotent party. Police action complements party action. Generally, revolutionary committees exist in each housing group, in each commune, in each factory; the network is

such that surveillance is perfect. No clandestine action is possible; no persons express themselves on political questions in public; the right of criticism belongs to a single person or a very restricted number of leaders. Insofar as consulting the masses is concerned, it is always done through organizations in which the party is present. Prisons, psychiatric clinics, and work camps are crammed with interned people incarcerated after trials in which the defense had a hard time getting presented, whether the trial was held in public or behind closed doors. Freedom of speech, of association, and of education are abolished. The option to move from one place to another, even within the country, is restricted.

2. From an economic point of view, the Marxist model functions with unquestionable effectiveness in heavy industry, in overall operations for development that necessitate the use of huge resources, in sectors where, for reasons of strategy or propaganda, the government has decided to put forth the necessary effort. The endlessly recurring troubles in agriculture, crafting, small and average industry, trade, and housing, the outdated techniques still used in nonprivileged sectors demonstrate that the dynamism of a responsible worker "on his own" has not been replaced by an enormous bureaucratic apparatus in which each one tries to shift responsibility onto somebody else. The creation of material incentives reveals the failed expectation of socialism to replace individual self-interest by motivation for the collective. Where material incentives have been discontinued, absenteeism and low production have become such that a real campaign against laziness has been found necessary,[3] unless, as in China, the masses are kept in a continual state of exaltation. If unemployment is nonexistent, it is because jobs are created with little use or effect. Growth, when taken over a long period of time, is comparable to the most advanced capitalist countries—which leaves socialist countries still behind. But, apart from the fact that in the two groups of countries the gross national product is calculated from two different bases, it seems that, if the products put at the disposition of consumers are considered (not including the equipment of the collective), the standard of living is still generally lower in socialist countries, although it is rising steadily.[4]

3. Finally, from a religious point of view, socialist countries forbid all proselytizing and maintain freedom of antireligious propaganda. There is no official persecution but a slow stifling of the faith, especially through discrimination in regard to top posts at the university and in the party. It even happens that a declaration of atheism, that is, an act of abjuration, may be required of someone about to enter the party or the Young Communist League. The state's agressiveness and the austerity that living in a Communist state demands of Christians leads some to bear themselves with heroism but, on the whole, the people are out of touch with the faith.

In regard to the revolutionary dictatorship of the proletariat, the complete collectivization of the economy, and antireligious propaganda, Marx's thought has been determinative.

Those who would like to see only the second part of this triptych have thereby made a clear judgment and a choice as well—not to embrace but to condemn a system in which all three parts are essential to the whole.

Nothing has been said about the great disadvantage of this system if comparable drawbacks in the system that is its opposite have not also been weighed. What then is the situation in the Western democracies?

### THE WESTERN MODEL

Discerning its value, its defects and deficiencies presents no great difficulty. They are just the opposite of the socialist world's.

*Defects and deficiencies: capitalism.* 1. Social inequities, automatic accumulation of money, and unjustified profits, keep right on in spite of a socializing process. Enormous distances are created between different people's incomes and fortunes. In the third world destitution exists, sometimes in horrible forms; malnutrition and often famine remain the lot of the great mass of the people.

2. Educational advantages are distributed unevenly. The children of workers and, most particularly, those who do farming, have slim chances of being admitted to secondary schools and universities. In the third world, illiteracy is an acute problem.

3. The system of health care maintains the privileges of the

most fortunate. In less developed countries, the great mass of the people are completely deprived of health services for lack of money.

4. Housing conditions in shantytowns, and even more so in rural areas, are deficient. In the third world they are absolutely inhuman.

5. Prostitution, corruption, pornography, delinquency, and drug abuse are showing an alarming increase.

6. Manual labor is looked down upon. The hardest and lowest-paid work is left to the marginated. Underemployment, open or concealed, is the rule.

In a word, wealth retains its power. Money is the source of more money and confers privilege and prepotency in every sphere of social existence.

The indictment is harsh. Is there a plea for the defense?

*Values: democracy.* 1. Countries inspired by the Western model that have managed to stay free of reactionary dictatorship keep the values of liberty alive. In proportion to their freedom from preoccupation with the necessities of life, people prize those values. The rights of the individual person do not always receive recognition, but they are defined and their violation arouses public censure and demonstrations. Freedom of the press, of speech, and of association is often restricted by the intervention of big-money interests and parties in power. Perhaps people have to be deprived of their liberties to appreciate their value and to recognize that their actuality is relative. Pluralism of groups and parties obtains.

2. On the economic plane, an incomparable dynamic creativity is at work, especially in sectors that do not lend themselves at all or hardly at all to centralization, since crises of overproduction and unemployment are limited for the time being. As long as this continues to be so, the outlook should remain the same. Even in the third world, the standard of living is slowly rising in absolute value. The example of Brazil and the less known example of the Ivory Coast demonstrate that there, too, material development is possible if a coherent economic plan is put into action.[5] Where the capitalist economy shows itself deficient is not in production but in distribution.

3. Although a diffuse materialism seeps through societies of abundance, religions enjoy complete freedom except when militant secularism or dictatorship imposes limitations upon them. Even so they in no way encounter the aggressive opposition that they come up against in the socialist world.

## Two Classes of Workers

If analysis were to stop at this point, it would not reach the root of the schism dividing humanity.

The opposition between the two worlds has its source in structure—a structure with two classes motivated by divergent interests. Each seeks to build the sort of society that conforms to its life pattern and so is unconsciously inclined to exclude the other.[6]

One group gets their income not from fixed hourly or monthly wages but from the difference between the cost of production or purchase price and the selling price of their products. These are the farmers, the artisans, the tradesmen, the small and average entrepreneurs.[7] In this category should be added workers who, because of their skills or their professions, are able to obtain higher salaries. If being either skilled or professionally trained constitutes social capital integral to the individual person, the characteristic of this group of independent workers is that they draw their revenues both from work and from the capital which they personally invest in work. The rest comprise the mass of simple wage earners.

Now the interest of these two groups do not coincide. Briefly, in the short run, their interests are at variance with one another. Every increase in the fixed wages of the mass of wage earners is experienced as a burden by workers whose income is realized from the difference between cost and selling price. Higher wages for the mass of workers means higher cost price, endangering the price margin that makes it possible for farmers, craftsmen, tradesmen, and people in small or average businesses to survive. Conversely, every rise in the profit margin on which these workers live, and every drop in the salary range of the mass of workers, is resented by the latter as a threat to their livelihood.

The category of independent workers constitutes half of the

population in third-world countries. In developed countries, if those who possess technical training and, therefore, capital are added to the independent workers, altogether they represent at least half of the population.

In these circumstances, the class struggle does not erupt principally as a conflict between capital and labor, as Marx thought it would. Its nature has changed; now it consists in the antagonism between two groups of workers and, if it is systematically fomented, it tends to bring about the disappearance of a class of people with more modest resources than wage earners. It creates an irreducible opposition between two halves of a country, causing a definitive cleavage between them and destroying the balance of their coexistence.

As the experience of all socialist countries shows, if the state is the only entrepreneur, or if the category of independent workers becomes quite reduced and tightly controlled, bureaucracy rears its head and freedom is finished. Marx leaves no room for ambiguity on this final point: socialism is established by violence and with dictatorship.

Two major conditions are needed to bring forth justice in liberty. One is negative; the other, positive. First, the negative. The psychological reactions of the middle class are by their nature already strong enough. Those committed to achieving a just and free society need to avoid stirring them up by useless initiatives and especially by aggressiveness on principle. The nationalization of great holdings or of huge capital is not what arouses resistance. What does spark it are actions that go beyond the end in view and threaten independent workers in the fruit of their work and savings and, above all, in the very structure of their profession. Then, as to the positive condition, it is just the reverse. It means not posing a threat but being conciliatory to this class of workers, allowing them to maintain the ownership of the capital they have invested and so stimulating their efforts.

That said, it is important not to lose sight of another part of the active population who also have a right to exist. It is a matter of primary concern to secure for them what they legitimately aspire to—a decent living, that is, conditions of life that put them on an equal footing with the rest of the nation. To keep up anachronistic and revolting social conditions simply drives them to despair. Effective steps must be taken to see that they have means comparable to those of other classes of workers.

The whole logic of liberalism tends to leave independent workers free and to allow them to realize a high income in order to stimulate investment and that implies keeping a strict control on salaries. And so it is that the social contract, the foundation of a free and just society, is destroyed.

To revise this trend necessitates a certain mobilization of the wage-earning masses. In the third world they are often passive, unaware of their stake in concerted action. First of all, then, there has to be a struggle to arouse them from their inertia, an undertaking of patient work in awakening them to consciousness of their rights and in organizing them: the lever for every transformation that aims at integrating the mass of wage earners into social life. This is the reason why syndicates or trade unions have such status and importance.

But if the mobilization of one group means an intent to do away with the work structure of another part of the people, then that goes beyond the objective sought and needlessly stirs up defense reactions.

So the battle has to be carried forward on two fronts. If we want to avoid violence on one side or the other, the mobilization of each group must not be done in such a way that it does away with every chance for their coexistence. The class struggle, as liberalism implicitly and Marxism explicitly conceive it, is as contra-indicated as it could possibly be if people really want to bring about justice and freedom. Liberalism knows that and sets itself against every stable organization of the mass of wage earners. Marxism is perfectly conscious of it; in its view, the class struggle takes away from independent workers every chance for survival. Both make the process of violence and dictatorship irreversible by setting in motion the massive opposition of one class against the other with a whole series of measures that go counter to the necessary objective—the coexistence of two social categories of workers.

The two violences, one on the part of the independent workers and the other on the part of the mass of wage earners, both caught up in a systematic struggle, are mutually engendered. The greater the number of those who become embroiled, the more insoluble the dilemma becomes. Nothing is harder for people to do than to keep their heads in this maelstrom. Everything must be done to give both groups the means to better their lot—a difficult accomplishment, for the two classes have different interests and are always ready to rise up against each other. It takes good seamanship to sail through a narrow channel. The first duty of a statesperson is to keep in sight both classes of workers, who make up a free nation, seeking to maintain impartiality towards both, for both are part of the people. Economic policy must be clearly oriented to a twofold end: to allow skilled and independent workers the margins necessary for them to make a decent living, stimulating their initiative and encouraging them to make investments; and to see to it that the mass of wage earners are paid a salary that makes them a real part of their country.

This policy is possible only under two conditions. Independent and skilled workers must become concious of the interests of wage earners making the lowest salaries and, when confronted with a policy to better their working and living conditions, must not block the economic machinery necessary to achieve that end (by withholding their investments) and, a fortiori, they must not close off the functioning of democracy by establishing a dictatorship to serve their own ends. For their part, the mass of wage earners must not achieve the same sorry result by making impossible demands that will also finish by submitting them to the regime of a dictatorship.

One one hand, independent workers must become convinced that the privileges and powers which have become attached like parasites to the structure that serves as the basis for their existence end by justifying and institutionalizing existing social inequities. Once so convinced, they should accept the suppression of unjustifiable privilege and power. Does it really take so much intelligence to come to that point? On the other hand, those who earn salaries can and must comprehend that absolute equality is impossible. For the economy to be effective, it must recompense good production, real qualifications, and saving. To eliminate independent work and individual initiative in an economy would throw the whole social and political equilibrium of a nation off balance.

If there is a real will to escape the undesirable alternative, both classes have to agree to coexist. Without either one of them, no just, free, and responsible society is possible.

## Two Philosophies

In addition to the existence of two categories of workers with different interests, there are two opposing yet complementary philosophies. Reaching them, we are touching the source of difficulties that are continually arising in Western democracies as well as in socialist countries—the ends or aims of economic society, the point at which misunderstandings and conflicts arise.

Economic society is composed of all the people who contribute to production, in the first place by work, and in the second by the investment of funds.

Contrary to what is asserted by liberalism as well as by Marxism, economic society is not indentified with society in general. An increasing number of "nonproductives"—children, old people, housewives—are not a part of economic society but are, nevertheless, full members of society as a whole. Economic society has its end not within but outside itself. Society in general, on the contrary has but one end and that lies within itself, the common good of all its members.

Because of the nonidentity of economic society with society in general, two disparate philosophies are at work in economic society; the result is a distortion of which both liberalism and Marxism remain unconscious. First, there is a philosphy of effectiveness and production. It is primary, for productive activity must provide consumers with goods and services that are both cheap and of good quality. No system can lose sight of that fundamental law. But then economic society also obeys another philosophy: it aims at the betterment of all those who participate in production. Workers have their rights; they must not be forced to perform work so long and so intense that their human existence is threatened by it. All must be done so that working and living conditions go beyond providing for a life that is no life at all.

In a subsistence economy, individuals themselves arbitrate the conflict between the needs of the work and the needs of the worker. It is peculiar to industrial society that it has, by introducing the division of work into separate tasks, entrusted work production and the advancement of the worker to two different authorities.

In the short run, the two philosophies do not meet and merge. The need for cheap products of good quality imposes work hours and output quotas that go counter to the spontaneous inclinations of the workers and diminish their potential for living. Looking at it from the other side, conditions that will promote the dignity and advancement of workers demand a reduction in work hours and rhythms. It is only in the long run that these two aims come together. Society as a whole is not benefited by the deterioration of the work force to which it looks for its subsistence.

Although neither liberalism nor Marxism has explicitly recognized this contradiction, systems inspired by each of them have had to face up to it. Where wage earners have been permitted to organize freely, the capitalist world has had to take into account their needs and demands; the strike has been their means of bringing themselves to the attention of those apt to consider economic society as an improved machine performing in a purely mechanical way. The strike was needed to introduce the elements of the human and social advancement of the workers into economic calculations.

On its part, the socialist world, although it did not in the beginning foresee the cross purposes of the general good of society and the individual good of the workers, has had to organize material incentives for workers, a proof that this contradiction exists. Where attempts have been made to do without motivation of this kind to further production, whether in the case of individuals or of communities, it has become necessary to maintain a high level of collective consciousness by means of psychological pressure that, it is doubtful, could keep on being effective or even possible. The masses cannot be sustained in a state of tension indefinitely. In any case, the very existence of that continuing and continual education shows that no system has succeeded in automatically bringing the two ends of economic society in alignment with one another. The ''disharmony'' between the interests of the worker and the purposes of work performed has a tendency to reappear.

Behind the opposition between the two classes and the two worlds, a contradiction between the two philosophies can be discovered. Straining for efficiency and productive output, the class of independent workers care little about inequality. They would rather have as their goals a reward for effort, work, and investment that assures better service for the whole society. Holding out for dignity and advancement in their work, the mass of wage earners, those for whom work is, in Marx's trenchant words, simple muscular, nervous, and mental expenditure, are little concerned with making blows for liberty; any thrust should be, to their minds, for equality, which is for them the primordial good.

In any case, it can be said that the first group, to the extent that they have equality at heart, expect it to come about through liberty; and the second group, insofar as they have liberty in mind, think that it will result from equality.[8]

Both philosophies are needed for the cohesion of society; the two classes must think through and organize their existence together in order to live in harmony, if they want both liberty and equality to prevail.

Failing that, there appears no other escape from the impasse facing humanity that is created by the confrontation of two worlds, each of which responds to only one philosophy and gives only one class a chance. The intent here is not to propose some third way but simply to indicate the possibility of a human solution to the problem created by industrial society.[9]

A self-directed, self-controlled society favors a reconciliation, since it commits the management of the economy to those actively engaged in it. However necessary such a society may be, it cannot assume every social function. Socialism is with us to serve as a reminder that the decisions of partial units of an economy do not automatically add up to a rational whole. As to the economy itself, it must remain subject to the higher exigencies of political reason according to the democratic concept. There are three immediate givens, three fundamental principles, that have taken possession of the modern conscience. Three revolutions will be required to put them into effect.

## NOTES

1. We are surprised that the masses seem to accept a Communist dictatorship so easily. Is it not just as astonishing that we keep on living surrounded by what we well know to be "the scandal of glaring inequalities," to quote *Populorum progressio,* no. 9.

2. Unless, as in Moscow, special shops, reserved to the new ruling class, offer articles that cannot be found elsewhere or products that are generally available but are on sale there at prices lower than elsewhere.

3. In Cuba an antilaziness law has had to be promulgated. It states that work constitutes a "social duty" and provides for punishment up to two years of forced labor for those who do not work or absent themselves regularly from work. During 1973 Fidel Castro announced that material incentives were to be reestablished, after being abolished too soon, as if Cuba were able to skip over the stage of socialism before advancing to communism.

4. The socialist René Dumont writes with his usual forthrightness: "Socialism must also find ways of becoming more efficient, since that is its weakest point." René Dumont and Marcel Mazoyer, *Socialisms and Development,* trans. Rupert Cunningham (New York: Praeger, 1973) p. 101.

5. Throughout Latin America, this is the model most often put into operation and the rate of growth is on the rise in a number of countries since 1970.

6. This problem has been raised in regard to Marxism. See pp. 178 ff.

7. This group still constitutes almost one-fourth of the active population in a country like France. In no place in the Western world has it disappeared completely. Industrial society even creates new kinds of crafts. The term "middle class" has purposely been avoided as a designation for this group, for its income and social advantages are often inferior to those of wage earners.

8. Is not this whole political problem most urgent at present? Those who could bring about social reform because they have the confidence of those who could back them with funds and so would be assured of financial success, do not do so. And the mass of wage earners are

unequal to bringing about social reforms because they have no capital at their disposition and cannot make a go of it financially.

9. In his apostolic letter to Cardinal Roy on the eightieth anniversary of the encyclical *Rerum novarum*, Pope Paul VI dealt with the political responsibility of Christians and defined the two "violences" in the following terms: "Now a Christian may choose to live out his faith by pursuing political action as a way of ministering to the needs of others. In doing this, however, he cannot without inner conflict adhere to doctrinal tenets which, at their roots or in their main points, are inconsistent with his faith and his notions about man. Thus he cannot support Marxist doctrines: their atheistic materialism, their dialectic propounding violence, and lastly their manner of absorbing personal liberty in the community while denying any transcendent excellence to man, his personal history, or the history of the world. Nor can he support so-called liberal doctrines which claim to exalt personal liberty by freeing it from any regulation, urging it to seek only power and advantage, and regarding social ties among men as the ready result of spontaneous initiatives, rather than as the aim and primary criterion of a well-ordered society." *The Pope Speaks* 16 (1971) 150. Reference here is indeed to the circle within which humanity finds itself enclosed and from which it is trying to escape.

# XIII

# THE CULTURAL CONTRIBUTION:
# THE COMMUNE

For about the last decade in every domain, in civil society as well as in the Church, ideas have been fermenting that gladden some and worry others. A current has been forming that is a mixture of the best and the worst, as happens in all major historical transformations that inspire people with an idea and spark an event in history. Under the name of the "third revolution," I have attempted to encompass some aspects of this "crisis." It has picked up some elements from previous "crises." Just as they were, it is critical of society, now of a society of consumerism, a technological society, standardized and centralized, in which people no longer live but have their living done for them in a system of decisions imposed from "above." The new revolution is also recovering structures of participation and community, in which people can express themselves and captain their own destiny. Neither democracy nor socialism has fathered this new idea. Their mechanisms are not equal to dealing with it.

What is being confronted is no longer the fetishism of power or of ownership but the fetishism of the system, the institution, the "technostructure."

Without disputing the accomplishments of the revolutions that preceded it, the new revolution distinguishes between itself and them and has no fear to oppose them in order to be able to state what new things it has to offer. Political and economic views are no longer the predominant interest but human beings themselves as they struggle for survival by freeing themselves from a form of oppression which neither liberalism nor socialism anticipated.

To the extent that the movement does not sink into pure anarchy, it seems to be organized around several key ideas

—participation, self-determination, and basic community. It is worth remarking that these new ideas have sprung up within both of the two opposite and equally reprobated "systems." They originate in the same critique of consumer society and the centrally planned and controlled society, both of which make human beings feel overcome.

## The Idea of Community

It would be foolish to try to discover within Christian tradition the model of the commune which is being sought in all recent contestations, but let us not forget that for more than a century Christian thought has defended a form of social relationship which both liberalism and socialism were in accord in rejecting.[1]

The doctrine of intermediary or subsidiary bodies has, it is true, ambiguous origins. It seems to have been inspired, first of all, by a certain nostalgia for a reconstruction of the medieval guilds destroyed by the French Revolution and the coming of the industrial era. In the first of the great social encyclicals, *Rerum novarum* (1891), the thinking oscillates between the memory of the old guilds and the new reality of the syndicates or unions. However, Leo XIII's contemporaries were not deceived—the Pope was indeed defending the right of workingpersons to form associations or unions—to the enormous scandal of liberal thought, still prevalent at that time among Christians. A distinction was not clearly drawn between the one-time guilds and the unions. Hesitation to do so was apparent in the very formula which proclaimed the new right as the right to form either common associations in which employers and workingpersons would meet together or separate associations for each group. Obviously, those who prepared the draft of the encyclical were still obsessed by a great memory; yet, at the same time, they were looking for something beyond it that would be adapted to the new society.

Forty years later the encyclical *Quadragesimo anno* (1931)[2] was still calling for "corporative organization" as a possible solution for putting an end to economic anarchy; however, it no longer identified these with the oldtime corporations or guilds but openly criticized the latter as no longer adapted to the times. For its part, it did not revive the idea of a common association or union for employers and employees. Without denying that associations for workingpersons and their employers ought to be established separately to defend the special interest of each group, it expressed the desire that they meet together in an economic organization in order to deal with their common interests and the branch of production that they were operating together to serve society as a whole.

Pius XII was not favorable to a partnership of management and workers and on this point tended to retreat to a position beyond his predecessor's. He gave great importance, on the other hand, to what he called "the public organization of the economy." He also resisted and constantly denounced government-controlled centralization. He proposed an organization, with no rigid hierarchy, that would be "organic," and presupposed responsibility on the part of those taking part in production.

In *Mater et Magistra,* John XXIII proposed, under the term of "socialization," a concept in which both the public powers and the associations have a big place. Furthermore, he pointed out the risks involved when socialization encroaches upon the legitimate initiatives of groups and individuals. For the first time in the doctrine of the *magisterium* the communal character of enterprise was forthrightly stated. The encyclical thus goes beyond the reticences of Pius XII to rejoin the still timid assertions of Pius XI in *Quadragesimo anno* and open the door to a much bolder development.

All this doctrinal work has been carried out on the margin of the dominant currents of thought, liberalism and Marxist socialism, and in opposition to them both. The recent cultural "explosion" everywhere exceeds the boundaries of those elements of it to be found in the Christian milieu. It retains the idea of some sort of basic organization as the best expression of its aspirations. The germ of this notion existed in all that was sought, especially in the third world, for ten years or so under the title of "community development."

THE RURAL COMMUNE

The first mission of an agrarian reform is not to initiate expropriations. That is only its negative aspect. Its chief function is to form basic communities. Without these, the rural world, broken up into far too small productive units or gathered up into gigantic farming projects, is not in a position to take charge of its own destiny in a responsible way.

We hear it said, and said again, that human beings must be the agents of their own destiny. To state the necessity is easy. To organize responsibility is difficult in a world dedicated to mass production and consumption, because to do it means warring against the innate tendencies of people to leave decisions that concern their very existence to those central powers, whether private or public, demanded by a tightly planned economy geared to high productivity.

Understanding this fact means recognizing that developing the fabric of a new society is a challenge. But it is an indispensable task if people wish to respond to the basic demand of the cultural revolution; and the task is going forward through the patient building of basic communities.

Wherever a real community exists, miracles are accomplished. Apparently passive and inert peasants quickly reveal a surprising dynamism when organized into communities. The sudden surge of new energies that they reveal have to be seen if one would form some idea of the potential there.

Formulas are many; they are not what matters most. The spirit that animates them is what really counts.

*The cooperative.* When cooperatives are not "administered" but are really taken charge of by their associated members, they have given and always give surprising results.

The credit union is the easiest to organize. It touches only one aspect of social existence but has the merit of giving birth to a mystique: leading persons, instead of accepting their lot, to rise up together to face their destiny. The considerable sums that have been lent and faithfully repaid with a relatively minimal return on capital are cause for astonishment. It is easy to smile at the effort of thousands of peasants to maintain organizations that depend solely on themselves, but if we think it over, we will see that only an effort of that kind could ever combat the inertia of a consumer society. Putting it into effect is worth more than many verbal protests; it is contestation in action.[3]

The possibilities for cooperatives do not end with the organization of credit unions. When growers group together to sell their produce, to buy seed and fertilizer, and to make common use of farm machinery, they are making even greater advances in cooperation. They also encounter greater difficulties, those that stem from and will always stem from individualistic tendencies. When they succeed, their achievements can only have that much more value.[4]

Cooperatives can also undertake the construction of decent homes in common, in rural areas as well as in the poorer sections of the cities.[5]

To move onward to production in common is to pass a threshold—the production cooperative or the community enterprise. In an agrarian economy there is no assurance that collective cultivation is always the best solution. For reasons related to the very nature of farm work, in which a few men may find themselves distributed over wide areas, control of yield is impossible. In collective farming, it is inevitable that the lazy profit from others' labor.[6] Then too, it is doubtless generally necessary to look for a formula for community farming by assigning individual plots, all services being done in common, at least when the work of heavy cultivation has to be done.[7] In many cases, a mixed system of land cultivated in common and of individual holdings can prove a reasonable arrangement.

What should be emphasized in organizing farm work is that unwarranted intervention from outside, when it reaches the point of taking over the responsibilities of the farmers themselves, is a menace. The encyclical *Rerum novarum* made the early and wise observation that "things move and live by the soul within them and they may be killed by the grasp of a hand from without." Intervention "from without" can come from bureaucracy when the cooperative reaches a certain size. The virtues of the cooperative come to an end when associated members no longer feel responsible for it and lose their faith in it. However, public powers and political parties are the chief meddlers.

The state certainly has a role to play in the organization of these groups, for it is impossible in every case to wait for the peasant masses to organize modern-day agriculture on their own.[8] But the mission of the state consists not in taking the lead or assuming the direction in these projects but in creating conditions that make it possible for those who work the land to organize themselves and in providing them with the technical assistance that is indispensable. Inopportune intervention can destroy at a single stroke long-standing endeavors to educate and organize.[9]

What is most needed in the domain of rural communities is faith in people and in their potential to establish for themselves their own place in the sun.[10]

*Agrarian reform.* The establishment of basic communities generally presupposes expropriations, which cannot be done without impetus from the public powers, as such a move inevitably encounters resistance, whether on the part of the established regime or on the part of revolutionary ideologies that do not favor it. In the Marxist view, community enterprise is "an anarchist fantasy."

Agrarian reform is the order of the day in the majority of third-world countries and is now written into all their legislation. It is far from being effectively carried out.

The motivations inspiring it need to be distinguished. Referring to Latin America alone, the agrarian reforms that have really transformed the rural world can be put into three different categories.

1. The agrarian reforms in Mexico in 1910 and in Bolivia in 1952 had no other purpose than to give the land to the peasants. They were done with violence and were connected with the first of the three revolutionary currents analyzed earlier. We cannot forget that in 1789 France also carried out agrarian reform by an extensive expropriation of the land held by aristocrats and clergy. Private property was the objective of that irresistible movement.

2. Cuba's agrarian reforms in 1959 and 1963 and Chile's beginning in 1970 were of a socialist kind. There was no question of giving the land to the peasants but of integrating them into a collective organization. Fidel Castro has taken good care not to dismantle the expropriated *latifundios*, the great estates; he has done just the opposite, preserving them in their original size under the form of *Granjas del Pueblo*. In Chile, the agrarian reform law voted on during the presidency of Eduardo Frei, a Christian

Democrat, and still in force, provided for the expropriation properties of more than eighty hectares and the regrouping of the peasant beneficiaries into cooperatives called *asentamientos;* according to the law, at the end of a three- to five-year period, peasants would be able to choose between an arrangement with individual plots of land integrated into a network of cooperative services or an arrangement of collective proprietorship. After the socialist Salvador Allende[11] came to power, expropriations took place in much greater numbers; all the *latifundios* disappeared but property titles to the land did not pass into peasant hands, as the law provided. Agrarian Reform Centers were even set up, consisting of many thousands of hectares. They were a sort of "commune" like those in China; they broke up the structure of the *asentamientos* and absorbed them, showing a clearly collectivist trend on the part of the government.

3. An agrarian reform that would be commensurate with what can be called the third revolution would try to form cooperatives managed by the peasants themselves in a system of individual or collective cultivation, not imposed a priori but determined by the kind of production and the will of the cooperative members themselves. That was the first idea of the Chilean law. The agrarian cooperative movement opened the way in that direction. But governments and parties, whether socialist or of some other kind, are not generally in favor of it, for they do not find it easy to accept people's organizations not under their control.

The foundation for real agrarian reform exists. And the cooperative movement has the advantage of addressing itself to a problem which other agrarian reforms have passed over completely—the *minifundios,* the small holdings, a matter just as urgent and difficult as the *latifundios.* In Colombia there are families who must draw all their resources from a lean one or two hectares; no other destitution, even that prevailing in the most infamous shantytowns, can compare to theirs. No government has succeeded in buckling down to the task of regrouping the cultivation of holdings of five hectares or less. The public powers do not wish to upset a numerous electoral following. Besides, in this case, initiative can only come from within with assistance from the government. Yet not a single successful experiment in this most important area can be cited. Perhaps that is due to the fact that neither capitalist nor Marxist ideology is capable of bringing to birth a real cooperative movement.[12]

### THE INDUSTRIAL COMMUNE

*The syndicate or union.* Although the cooperative is easily engrafted on the peasant world, it is the union or syndicate that stands out as the basic cell of the workers' world. Consumer cooperatives in urban areas have either achieved only modest dimensions or have become commercial enterprises. Cooperatives for production have not been developed on a large scale and are to be found only in the sector of small enterprises, an experiment not to be considered negligible, however, since it points a way to go, but with no adequate solution for the problem as a whole.

We must then look to the union or syndicate. In its structure it is quite different from the cooperative. By the very fact of its situation in private as well as in nationalized enterprises, in capitalist as well as in socialist countries, its object is to defend the interests of wage earners in their confrontation with both public and private owners of capital. In the existing structure, whether capitalist or socialist, its fight is a procedural method for advancing the worker in the world of work. Were it to give up, working people would no longer be masters of their fate but would again be exploited or crushed.

Where alive, the union has succeeded in organizing passive and subservient as well as aggressive and violent people. Full recognition should be given to the efforts of its leaders, often anonymous, who managed, during a century and a half, against every kind of opposition and the inertia of their fellow workers themselves, to unite wage earners in the defense of their rights and by so doing to contribute to the formulation of national and international legislation. They have often paid for their dedication to the workers' cause with their liberty and sometimes with their lives. During the heroic period when any coalition and association was regarded as subversive, pitiless repression was exercised against them. Now that the right to form unions and the right to strike are recognized, repression still takes the hidden form of reprisals against the most active union leaders. As a matter of fact, the organization of a union or a syndicate continues to exact of its leaders an abnegation and faith deserving the esteem and trust of the mass of workers, even when the latter hesitate to follow them into actions that invite their participation but are obviously onerous.

Just as in the case of the cooperative, the greatest threat to the union is outside intervention. Here, too, the public powers have a role to play and the manner in which the United States, for example, has eased the way for union organization through legislation cannot be made little of before becoming familiar with it. But if the state means to control the union and make it march to is tune, leaving it only subsidiary functions and reducing its role to acting as a transmission belt, then the worst has happened to the workers' organization, which, to be true to its title, must be the workers' own.

Political parties, too, of whatever persuasion, pose a threat to the union. It is impossible to deal in a short and simplistic manner with the question of the link between them; yet their independence has to be maintained. Their ends being distinct, each organization ought to keep its own autonomy. The vast majority of workers think that political divisions and partisan interference are one of the principal causes of weakness in their movement, for these militate against its unifying vocation and devitalize it by placing it at the service of ends not directly in line with its own.

The existence of unions is fully justified but unions are not a complete solution to the problem of the working community, for they are grounded in the dissociation of ownership and work within enterprises. This is as true in capitalist as in socialist countries and in private as in nationalized enterprises. And so it is that the question of self-management arises.

*Self-management.* Neither the cooperative, except when it takes the form of a production cooperative, which is rare, nor the union fully represents a real workers' community. Perhaps what is needed for enterprises and workers is to go a step further and opt for autonomous control. Everywhere this indisputably important question is being asked. Some seem to see such a step as the solution to the alternative of choosing either capitalism or collectivism. [13]

In free market economies, some experiments point the way. They encounter almost insurmountable difficulties—so they are few. When they have succeeded they have all the more value for being few and hard pressed. Everyone who has had some contact with these enterprises, carried out as a community under the direction of a manager, usually a very stable person, [14] elected by fellow workers, has unfailingly observed the atmosphere of freedom prevailing in them in contrast to the climate in other enterprises.

In socialist countries there exists only one example of workers' self-management, the famous Yugoslav example. Worker self-management or autonomy must not be confused with the different forms of consultation at the grass-roots level. These exist everywhere, particularly in China, but that sort of consultation does not make the enterprise a center of autonomous decision-making. [15] The Yugoslav example is unique.

Much has been said and written about this experiment. Many put all their hopes in it. To make a closer study of the conditions that make it possible is not to diminish its importance. [16]

We know, in broad outline, how the Yugoslav concept of self-management is worked out. Today it is the usual arrangement in all the most import enterprises and farming projects: in each enterprise all the personnel constitute "a collective worker" and elect a workers' council, whose members in turn name a board of directors of from three to eleven members. The workers' council is actually fully autonomous in choosing a director. The communal council has a supervisory role, which tends to diminish. The functioning of the model is subject to two conditions, which have not perhaps been emphasized enough.

1. The enterprise does its own accounting and has its own accountability based on profit: it must, therefore, sell more than it buys or, in any case, balance sales and purchases. This is a very real control because an enterprise with a deficit is condemned to disappear: the state will furnish the credit needed for its survival for two years and no more. At the end of that time, if it has been unable to reestablish a budgetary balance, the enterprise is li-

quidated and its workers have to find work elsewhere. Unemployment exists in Yugoslavia, so there is an enduring interest in the working community to be sure of good management, to show prudence in determining salaries, in increasing work productivity, etc. Of course, an enterprise must pay interest on the social capital put at its disposal.

2. A free market has been completely reestablished in Yugoslavia under the guidance rather than the direction and control of the central planning bodies. Business ventures are, therefore, in competition with one another. Retail business can purchase materials from among suppliers who offer products of good quality at a fair price and the same freedom is exercised at all levels of production, providing, in this way, a stimulant that a system of autonomous enterprises cannot do without.

In Yugoslavia, because of the continual pressure to balance the budget and to meet competition, the community itself is able to arbitrate between the interests of society as a whole and its own special interests, between economic and social needs. The capacity to do this is absolutely essential for an autonomous management. The very nature of an enterprise demands that it reconcile both of its ends—the advancement of the common good of its members and the service of society as a whole. The realization of the general good of society must be effected through controlling mechanisms instituted by those in charge of directing the enterprise.

That said, it must be added that in Yugoslavia the political context plays a role in the functioning of self-management that is difficult to evaluate. Although greater freedom exists there than in other socialist countries, thanks chiefly to communication with the outside world and to emigration, the Yugoslav regime remains a Marxist "dictatorship of the proletariat," attenuated, it is true, by an antiestablishment tendency that tends to show up at every level. The Communist League continues to be the only party and is deeply entrenched in every place of work.[17] As in all socialist countries, the police are everywhere.

As a result, the Yugoslav regime compensates in some measure for the anarchistic tendencies that are generated spontaneously in a system where autonomy is general and threatens to circumvent the public powers by initiatives and demands contrary to the public interest. In that country these tendencies do in fact come up against a central power capable of repressing them. The great unknown about the system can be put into the question: could it be transferred into a context other than a dictatorship?[18]

In any case, it throws light on the structure of enterprises, whether in one regime or another. The end of an enterprise is not simply the good of those who form its membership. It is first and foremost the service of society by supplying it with good products at fair prices. A democratic structure is fully committed to society as a whole and the end of society is the general good. That being so, a democratic enterprise is conditioned by its service to the general interest, to the commonweal, and has no final end in itself. Even before learning whether an enterprise of this kind is more effective than any other in enabling workers to discharge their responsibilities, it must first be asked whether it ensures as well as any other the service of the whole social body. It can aspire to do that only if it accepts the obligation, inherent in any enterprise in any kind of regime, to create a greater social product than it consumes. This is an obligation of the working community, who will feel it as a constraint, but it is a necessary constraint.

To explain the difficulties of a community enterprise, people often allude to it in the context of a "capitalist" regime in which the competition of huge company and corporate enterprises prevent it from functioning. There is some truth in that. As long as the economy remains a jungle, the strong do prevail and the weak are eliminated. And a community enterprise, even when aided by the public powers, has not the strength to equal the giants of enterprise and remains their inferior.

If anybody thinks that an enterprise can avoid the properly economic constraint of productivity (which, in the case of an autonomous enterprise, must be imposed by the workers' councils) through some useful mechanism in planning or marketing or whatever, what he could have in mind would be the construction of a nonviable system.

The community enterprise offers a solution; it opens up to workers the prospect of making something of themselves through exercising responsibility. The difficulties that it encounters are not due to a particular context, whether capitalist or Marxist, but are part of every business venture, whatever its structure. To point these out so that they may be faced and overcome is to give the community enterprise its best chance to succeed.

*Joint management.* These difficulties, observed by all who have long experience with self-management, open up the question: should it not be adopted freely and productively?

The most difficult problem of a self-managed enterprise has to do with capital investment. Since workers cannot save, at least in sufficient amounts, investment must come from one of two sources, public funds or the private funds of people outside the enterprise. In either case, investors are unlikely to place blind trust in an enterprise for which they furnish funds. They intend to participate in its management and in its profits. In reality, except in the case of a rather exceptional communal type of enterprise in which the workers themselves invest their own savings and so offer a guarantee of good management, which allows them to borrow with less difficulty, self-management becomes in reality joint management. Even in Yugoslavia, central planning bodies maintain control and the Communist League supervises the carrying out of the objectives of the Plan. In the strict sense the words "self-management" or "autonomy" cannot be used. Since participation is entirely hypothetical, it can be questioned if the private investment of capital and the participation of the investors can be envisaged in this case as well as in the other.

What we have here is a political problem. If autonomy in a socialist regime is really joint management, and if joint management is viable only in a one-party system of dictatorship, there can be political reasons for preferring another type of joint management, which would not involve the same servitudes.

However, we need to recognize the enormous difficulty that would confront such a project. Private capital, sensing how much its assistance is needed, shows itself authoritarian and peremptory; it will have full charge or none. What is left of joint management for the workers? A few concessions to "participation," to "involvement," which are most often ways of depriving the workers of any decision-making power, and of completely "un-involving" them.

We are brought then to a structure of conflict, of powerful directors and management and, eventually, of powerful worker organizations capable of confronting each other on equal terms. This could be called a form of joint management, but is it the only one possible?

To count only on the initiative of enlightened heads of industry to create a community in which capital and labor each have defined responsibilities is to cherish illusions, although some initiatives of this kind, necessarily limited in number, do open up a difficult course to follow. What is needed is the combined action of people who represent the workers and people who contribute capital and are both convinced that a solution does exist. Requisite too is the imposition by law of an institutional framework in which joint management can function, for example, by using successful experiments in a specific sector to form a model suitable for general use.

The principle obstacle arises from the fact that the two parties, workers and investors, take exclusive positions. Those who represent capital want to have direction in their hands alone and find it unacceptable that "humanitarian" considerations should be appealed to when the fiscal balance and the survival of an enterprise are under discussion. Wage earners find it unacceptable that financial calculations should stand in the way of their working and living conditions being improved. Both sides in this dialogue of the deaf have solid grounds for their positions. The survival of an enterprise, by balancing sales and costs, is a necessity in any system. The betterment of working and living conditions for working people is also an urgent necessity. Any business venture must undertake to do both.

Experience proves that those in charge of the workers' interests, that is, the union leaders, are capable of rising to an economic frame of mind when they are responsible for the running of a business and that the latter itself is faced with external pressures, which force it to be highly productive. Experience also proves that those in charge of the interests of capital are capable of becoming attuned to a social way of thinking when they find themselves subject to the pressure of union power.

The question then is whether the two together can really arbitrate and reconcile their antagonistic points of view, the unions taking co-responsibility for the economic aspects of the enterprise and the capitalist bosses responding in kind in regard to its social aspects.

If this is not done, joint management would simply mean carrying the conflict into the very heart of the decision-making body, the workers' representatives unloading the full onus of the enterprise's economic function on the representatives of capital, and the latter reciprocating by leaving everything that has to do with its social aspect to the workers' representatives. That would no longer be joint management but its antithesis.

Joint management presupposes a radical change in mentalities both in those who act for capital interests and those who provide leadership for the workers. Both must, in large measure, abandon their exclusive points of view in order to settle a debate in which each position has a right to be heard. A modification in attitudes is blocked for the time being by defense mechanisms that act as protective shields for each group and by ideologies that tend to justify their intransigence. Liberalism demands that capital have the whole say. It can have none, declares Marxism. In every direction the principle of class struggle seems to be at work. Under such conditions progress is impossible.

If directors of capital would become aware that the interest of working men and women cannot be left out when business decisions are made and that unions have to defend their interests either by conflict, as the case is at present, or through collaboration, the hypothesis of joint management, and if union leaders, on their side, would become cognizant that in any regime there has to be some outside constraint to make sure that capital is well managed and properly remunerated—then a way would open out for them both.

Since divergent interests must be arbitrated in some way, does it not seem preferable to replace an establishment of conflict by a structure of collaboration?

Marxism entertains the hope of eliminating capital from business. In reality, it does not exclude it but makes it all-powerful by putting it into the hands of a dictatorial state and by reducing the unions to the role of "transmission belts." And the structure continues to be one of conflict. Is collectivism anything else but capitalism turned upside down?

In these circumstances, it is not clear that excluding private capital from any role in business would serve as a solution. For, if the communal enterprise cannot become a general thing immediately, that kind of exclusion would leave open only one possibility, collectivism, that is, the control of enterprise by state capital alone. It is not obvious that this solution would be more favorable to an evolution in the direction of self-management or autonomy.

*Industrial reform.* Agrarian reform is an accepted part of the contemporary scene. That there is so little question of industrial reform is astonishing. If a *latifundio,* a large estate of a hundred hectares cultivated by some twenty or so workers, seems an anomaly, it is hardly larger than a small fellowship of craftsmen when compared to industries that engage hundreds and even thousands of employees.

The reason for the delay in industrial, in comparison to agrarian, reform lies right there. The expropriation of great rural estates leads to the distribution of the land to farm workers or to the establishment of small cooperatives. The expropriation of sizable industries makes their nationalization a necessity, at least to begin with. Taking them out of private hands poses an immediate political problem, the need for a state organization of unquestionable power to undertake the direction of all the industries in the country.

Under these circumstances, governments that want to effect progress in industrial enterprises without becoming entangled in the matter of civil liberties look in another direction. They do not renounce all nationalization. It becomes a necessary weapon when enterprises wield great power that lies outside the law and is dangerous for the nation or when the state, having had to take charge of the finances of an enterprise, must, by the same logic, administer it. Outside of these cases, governments are inclined to allow enterprises to retain their autonomy based on a structure of participation.

The new government of Peru, in promulgating its new industrial legislation,[19] has moved in this direction. In every enterprise an industrial community composed of all its wage earners is set up. Ten percent of the profits must be given to the wage earners, 15 percent must be reinvested in the enterprise and becomes the property of the industrial community. To begin with, the industrial community appoints a representative with deliverative voice on the council that manages the enterprise; in proportion to the increase in its capital through putting profits back into the enterprise, the industrial community designates new members on the council, prorated according to the amount of capital held. At the same time, it collects corresponding benefits. A worker no longer employed in a particular enterprise loses all rights to its profits (art. 27). When the industrial community acquires 50 percent of the capital, each wage earner receives stock in the enterprise.[20]

This reform has the advantage of being gradual, leaving to the representatives of the wage earners' community the timing for their takeover of the complex management of the enterprise. It is not, however, ineffectual, because it opens the way for the eventual joint worker-owner management on an equal footing. It has aroused some criticism. From a Marxist point of view it is unacceptable because it leaves the representative of capital the right to have a place in management and organizes the workers' participation entirely on the basis of their ownership of capital. If rigid ideas are put aside and the fact is faced that in big and average enterprises, capital, whether private or public, cannot, as a practical matter, be excluded from the running of any business, then worker participation on the basis of capital ownership proves itself to be a sensible formula. As to the fact that, in this case, workers may be sharing the management of an enterprise with representatives of private rather than public capital, this need not constitute a drawback for them and can even represent an advantage.

In the domain of industrial reform no ideal model exists. There is always the obligation of reconciling antagonistic needs, the one of managing well high-cost capital, the other of looking out for the living and working conditions of working people. It remains true that, when capital has been acquired by real effort on the part of the workers themselves, this twofold condition has the best chance to be realized. When that is impossible, then indeed some type of joint management has to be envisaged, at least for a transitional period.

## The Limitations of the Basic Community

Many seem to think that rural and industrial communities are the solution to all the problems of society; that they are, of themselves, liberation in act.[21] But to ascribe to basic communities roles that do not belong to them means endangering them. Certainly a "cultural" problem and a community problem exist but so do economic and political problems, each with its own specific character.

The basic community cannot reach up to the level of macroeconomic decisions, which have to be of a general nature. It must, therefore, be integrated into a public organization, in which the state has to have a role. This is a condition for high work productivity and the just distribution of commodities throughout society. Basic communities cannot, moreover, assume a strictly political function, consisting in taking over power and exercising it in society as a whole; that is a role for other structures. If they do not accept within themselves a pluralism of options, they are going to destroy themselves.

It must be said that the claim to solve everything by developing communities has done much harm to getting them established. It has given weapons to their opponents. On one hand, the basic community or commune is not everything, although it is a necessary organ in the whole structure. It is disquieting to see an all-encompassing role attributed to it, which it cannot claim. On the other hand, the commune is not a place for politics. Debates that concern society as a whole ought not to be taken up there and brought to nothing.

Strictly speaking, the commune has neither an economic nor a political vocation. The part it plays is something else and a prime necessity: to organize personal communication and individual responsibility within the great mass of society.

If it abandons this essential function in order to assume activities not its own, then it will give a handle to the objections made against it and will inevitably be absorbed by more powerful collectivities. Ideologies that conceive of education and basic organization as political action in no way conceal their intent: to their mind the commune is only an instrument. The day that the regime which used it to come to power is established, the basic community is to be made strictly subject to the central apparatus.

At the present time the education and organization of communities encounter the unanimous opposition of dictatorial governments, whether they draw their inspiration from liberalism or Marxism. Weapons must not be given to this opposition by politicizing communitites.

The pretension of the basic community to supplant all other organs in the social body leads to anarchy in the literal sense of the term. An *arche* is necessary on the economic as well as the political plane. Of itself, a self-directed autonomous society provides no surety that the ends of either socialism or democracy will be met.

Only after having defined its limits can the basic community lay claim to all its rights against the unjust opposition directed against it by both liberalism and Marxism.

## NOTES

1. Primitive socialism, as it existed before Marxism, gave a prominent place to this idea, especially in France, where it was at times inspired by Christians like Buchez. This socialist current has a whole history of its own and is still very much alive.

2. An article by one of the drafters of the encyclical in 1931, Father Oswald von Nell-Breuning, makes some revelations regarding his draft forty years later. "Octogesimo anno," *Stimmen der Zeit* (May 1971), pp.

289 ff. See also Georges Jarlot, *Pie XI* (Rome: Gregorian University, 1972), pp. 247 ff.

3. Anyone who has been present at the initiation of a credit union with some poverty-stricken and frequently completely illiterate people and has seen the extraordinary interest and earnestness that it evokes from those who, for the first time, realize that they can be persons, can never forget the experience.

4. In the region of Santa Fé, Panama, Father Gallego (whose abduction in June 1971 remains a mystery) organized the social advancement of peasant communities on the basis of consumer cooperatives, with astonishing results that have endured. A number of such achievements can be seen throughout Latin America.

5. In Santiago, Chile in 1969 I saw about fifty houses being built by their future owners outside of work hours on land made available to them by the government, with water, electricity, and sewerage already laid on. All these houses, still unfinished when I saw them, had reached exactly the same height, the outcome of a decision by the community—who were realists—that all the homes were to be finished on the same day so that there would be no early birds tempted, as they inevitably would be, to escape the collective work. This "autoconstruction" was organized in different sections of Santiago. Together with other systems of construction it had succeeded in changing the face of the city and in doing away with the principal centers of *callampas*, shantytowns equivalent to the Brazilian *favellas*.

6. On this point, see the pertinent reflections of the socialist René Dumont, *Sovkhoz, kolkhoz, ou le problématique communisme* (Paris: Seuil, 1964), pp. 233–34. In sub-Sahara Africa I have seen "communities" of young farmers working the same field together to the accompaniment of drums. Doubtless, outside an area where this is customary, it would be difficult to make it generally acceptable.

7. In the northern part of Colombia I have visited a peasant community that had been established on land drained for road construction and which was then cultivable. Each plot of land was well cultivated but the land had been prepared by the common work of all, and all services were in common. The peasants themselves conceived and carried out this organization.

8. In the Ivory Coast, state agencies, sparked by a spirit of decentralization, have achieved an organizational task which, without a doubt, would not have been possible without them.

9. In sub-Sahara Africa, I was on hand at the inception of a peasant community under the fine leadership of illiterate men. All the hopes of

this community were dashed when the country's single party intervened by imposing its own directions and directors.

10. In *Options méditerranéennes*, no. 5 (February 1971) Eduardo Bastos Norena presented one of the best studies on the rural commune in a comparative examination of the models to be found in five countries of the Mediterranean basin—Algeria, Spain, Israel, Italy, and Yugoslavia. Well documented, it shows both the possibilities and the limits of autonomous management in agriculture. For an exposition dealing chiefly with the blighted hopes of agricultural self-management in Algeria, see Gérard Viratelle, *L'Algérie algérienne* (Paris: Editions Ouvrières, 1970), pp. 129 ff.

11. See Jaime Ruiz-Tagle, "L'expérience chilienne face aux élections," *Études* (February 1973), pp. 225 ff.

12. Other kinds of basic communities should at least be mentioned for they have had remarkable success—neighborhood groups, communal action, buyers' cooperatives, etc. Under various names and composed according to a number of different formulas, these communities aim at the same end—to give people some opportunity to make decisions as against having them made for them by anonymous bureaucracies. This serves as a means of giving life to the social body. In Peru, as early as 1963 I saw the astonishing achievements of some Indian communities. While preserving the primitive structure of Inca society, they succeeded in pressing modern developments into service—electricity, roads, schools, means of transportation bought and held in common, all this almost without government help. Seeing things like this, one cannot help but think of all that would be possible if confidence were placed in basic groups and if even a little assistance were given them to organize themselves.

13. Yvon Bourdet considers that self-management throws the whole opposition of directors and executives open to question and reconciles Marxism with the freedom realizable beyond the stand taken by Lenin. The author is rather representative of those for whom self-management solves the whole social problem. *La délivrance de Prométhée, pour une théorie politique de l'autogestion* (Paris: Editions Anthropos, 1970) pp. xii–xiii.

14. What hopes can be placed in this kind of enterprise and the difficulties that it meets are well covered by Albert Meister, *La communauté au travail* (Editions Entente communautaire, 1959).

15. The Liberman reform in the U.S.S.R. (see pp. 170–72) does not constitute a form of self-management: the directors are not elected and decisions are not made in community.

16. An historical treatment of the experiment, not concealing its difficulties but affirming its universal significance, is Milojko Drulovic's *L'autogestion a l'épreuve* (Paris: Fayard, 1973).

17. According to an account in the press covering the ideological purge in Yugoslavia, the Sixth Conference of the Communist League particularly stigmatized the theory which held that a self-managing or cooperative society can originate in an organized work force, in substance, in the Communist League, on the pretext that the worker class would not be capable by itself of moving toward socialism and of protecting itself from the danger of going astray. *Le Monde*, February 7, 1973.

18. Albert Meister, in his recent book *Où va l'autogestion yougoslave?* (Paris: Editions Anthropos, 1970), gives a rather different picture of the Yugoslav experiment in self-management than the one that could be gathered from his earlier work *Socialisme et autogestion* (Paris: Seuil, 1964), in which he published the results of a sociological investigation. Yugoslav socialism has established the fact that incentives other than gain do not stimulate productivity, that equality is unrealizable, that socialist ideology must be replaced by notions about consumption (p. 10). The salary differential, which was 1 to 4 in 1960 rose to 1 to 7 (pp. 69–70). The same skilled worker can receive 30 to 400 dinars, depending upon what factory he works in (p. 72). The workers' council is less and less a representative organism and more and more an arm of management (p. 88). The author goes so far as to say that "We have to realize that the primary end of enterprises is to produce and only after that to form and integrate individuals. Perhaps self-management and participation have nothing to do with the sound management of enterprises" (p.94). Delegates must have qualities, both human and technical, which puts strict limitations on their choice to the extent that the democracy of self-management is a democracy reduced to a fraction of the worker class (p. 97). Besides, the Communist League continues to be "the nerve center from which all initiatives radiate" (pp. 87, 97 ff., 199). The author puts forward the view that a person feels much freer in Russia or in Poland (p. 150). He thinks that the reform of 1965 marked a turning toward liberalism (p.268), that it brought back profit and money as the standard of value, reestablished the autonomy of enterprises, replaced the Plan by more supple mechanisms of intervention, abolished the fixing of prices and subsidies by the administration, devalued the dinar, and integrated the country into all forms of international cooperation with foreign enterprises of a capitalist kind (ibid.). The mining of uranium deposits, for example, has been entrusted to the United States (p. 311). Under these circumstances "a good part of worker attachment to self-management is linked to the exceptional job security which it

guarantees" (286), except in the case of a deficit, since in that case the enterprise must close down (p. 376). In conclusion the author asks whether a changeover has not occurred from a self-directed enterprise to a cooperative in a liberal economy (p. 342). He perceives a contradiction between worker democracy and development (p. 366) and even asks whether self-management is not a strong shield set up by power against democratization (p. 370). It hardly needs to be said that an analysis of this kind provoked reactions from Yugoslav leaders. It would have been conclusive if the author had proposed an overall view of the structure of the enterprise and of the economy that would offer a possible reconciliation between a workers' democracy and development. Here we are met with an irreducible duality in the ends of an enterprise, which does not admit of any ideal solution.

19. Law no. 18350 (1970).

20. The Peruvian government also foresaw "a sector of social ownership." New enterprises, in which wage earners were to become the owners, would be established, with the financial and technical assistance of the state playing a preponderant role in the early phases of the enterprises but relinquishing its hold as the workers learned self-management. A part of the profits were to be distributed, not within the enterprise, but within the trade. "We want," said President Velasco, "solidarity among enterprises, so that the factory with a deficit would be salvaged by one in the same sector of production which is making a profit." *Le Monde,* February 3, 1973.

21. Michel Crozier aptly points out the limitation of self-management: "I do not know that self-management can be a solution. Talking about self-management seems to me to be a far too easy way of settling everything, of reconciling contraries, and laying all difficulties on the back of an unjust system. Our behavior as working people expresses values that are difficult to bring into accord: equality, initiative, liberty, authentic human relationships, material and psychological security, efficiency and the opportunity to learn through experience. We complain of the way the game is being played today but it is not easy to change over to new rules . . . It seems to me that it is too soon to say that the reason for such a change is that changes made within the framework of the capitalist system cannot succeed but that a more radical change would allow us to control all the elements in play. On one hand, important changes have been able to succeed within the framework, and on the other, all the radical changes have, in fact, failed, at least from this particular point of view." "Dialogue sur la société bloquée," *Projet* (February 1971), p. 221.

# XIV

# THE SOCIALIST CONTRIBUTION
# THE PUBLIC ORGANIZATION
# OF THE ECONOMY

Socialism has put in our minds the idea of a society in which work has primacy over capital, and people over money.

It has set in motion a central organization capable of actualizing both a higher standard of living thanks to greater work productivity (the development of the forces of production) and an egalitarian distribution of the social product (new relationships of production). As a whole, it has not been a mistake. All the great developed economies owe their continuing growth in part to the intervention of planning bodies. Without them, the national economy would founder in crises that would make the great depression of the nineteen thirties, the principal cause of World War II, seem like a minor crisis. As to progress in the equalization of incomes and wealth—and progress has been unquestionable in some of the most developed countries—they too are due to legislative and fiscal interventions emanating from the public powers. This is the reason why basic communities must accept some form of public organization of the economy, something which they can in no way pretend to supply.

Nothing demonstrates more clearly both the historical role and the threat of socialism: it transfers to central bodies all or part of the decisions hitherto left to peripheral bodies.[1] The evolution of industrial society makes it impossible for us to dream of being able to retreat from this point. Socialism is a phase in the complete organization of society as a whole. Like other systems, it becomes dangerous if it is exclusive. It then amounts to an economic apparatus of a consumer society or of a centrally controlled society, which, in either case, is opposed to basic autonomies and civic liberties, and consequently prevents the at-

tainment of the very ends of the "cultural" and democratic revolutions.

The kind and degree of centralization envisaged depends upon
the accepted notion of liberty in all its dimensions: at just this
point socialism is asked the big question.

## Community of Goods

Christian thought has never accepted the view of property as a
source of privilege and power. In the eyes of faith, ownership is
only a condition needed for responsibility and freedom. Tradition is unanimous on the point and continues to express the same
position. Under the pressure of the ideas of the first revolution,
which made owning property an absolute and "untouchable"
right, Christian doctrine became parenthesized —a proof of how
dangerous it is for the Church to give way to revolutions and to
forget its own message. Even then, however, some voices were
raised. And, beginning in 1891 with the encyclical *Rerum
novarum*, the great tradition reawakened.

A doctrine thousands of years old, with its source in the Old
Testament, is expressed by the doctors of the Church in an
absolutely incisive manner and is repeated in all the documents
emanating from Church authorities: economic goods cannot be
made the object of ownership in regard to their use, they must be
available to those who need them; those with possessions can
only use them to the extent that they have a real need for them.
Ownership is simply the power to administer and to dispense
things; it cannot turn them aside from their purpose to be at the
service of humankind. Repeated time and time again throughout
Christian thought is a radical condemnation of privileges and
powers that originate in the ownership of property.

*Economic privileges.* Of course, Christians are realistic enough
to recognize that absolute equality—"to each according to
need"—is a will-o'-the-wisp. They accept the fact that recompense for work, for effort, for service, creates disparities in society. This is not due to sordid individualism but is a consequence
of an internal structure: people can rise only by degrees to an
effective consideration of the good of society as a whole and to the

abnegation which that demands. Nature has, with reason, arranged for a "complicity" between the good of society and the good of the individual.[2]

Inequality that acts as a stimulant is a condition, not an end. If conscience accepts it, it intends to keep on contending against those powerful forces that have a propensity to systematize it and, consequently, to turn being-more-than-equal into a privilege through the complicity of institutions themselves. Privilege is inequality, when it no longer stems from any contribution by the person who enjoys it, when it is definitively established and, above all, when wealth becomes the source of wealth simply by being wealth. Inequality then gives place to a process of auto-accumulation, which is the cause of excessive social disparitites between members of the same society.

*Private powers.* These have their origin in privileges and contribute to making them irremovable. As a rule, the mass media are strictly dependent upon their financial sources. Big capitalists can bring pressure to bear on them so that opinion is slanted in their favor. Often they influence even more directly the source of public affairs by the prestige which they enjoy with those in power. The latter learn all too quickly the cost of dispensing with their support. In many cases, these abuses go so far as the direct or indirect corruption of people in power with remuneration for services rendered, financing of electoral campaigns, etc.

It is normal for leaders in business and industry to exercise authority in relation to their responsibilities but their power must be used only within their own sphere, the organization of production. It certainly happens that their responsibilities require the support of the public powers. Experience has taught us just how questionable this intervention is when private interests, in order to obtain favors from the government, for example, by protective tariffs, turn to good account the vital needs of their enterprise when it is a matter of making conditions more comfortable for business but not always more conducive to the general good. In any case, it is important that in such negotiations the government should have the final say.

Business leaders abandon their role completely when they put the economic power that they exercise at the service of their own favorite ideology and claim the right, with no foundation in reason, to direct the course of public affairs.

The Church opposes all that, not because it has come to terms with some prevailing ideology but in the name of what is essential to the faith. Unwarranted privileges and powers are nothing else but the fetishism of money within the context of industrial society. It is still impossible "to serve God and mammon." The ignoble idol of money is the chief obstacle to the birth of a society of brotherhood. Those who adore the living God cannot bow down before it.

## A New Society

Those who believe in the one true God want to build a new society in which all people are to enjoy the same possibilities in the face of life's difficulties and no power is conferred on anyone because of wealth.

Such a society, after a century of socialization, is not simply a projection; it has become an actuality, however far from it capitalist regimes remain and however deformed is the image of it presented by socialist regimes. In spite of delays and deformations the lineaments of the structure that the world longs for can be discerned. It will be a popular, some say a classless, society. Terms are not what matter. What we need to do is say what they mean.

First, it will be popular, a people's society in the sense that everybody in it will find themselves in the same situation when it comes to resolving the essential problems of life—food and housing, health and old age, education and leisure. What people are looking for, what appeals to the contemporary conscience is an interdependent society, in which no small group of well-heeled people have means not open to everybody else for meeting life's basic problems.

This is a principle of unity. A believer, above all others, cannot reject it. Christians are people who hold their goods in common, as the practice of the early communities show (Acts 4:32–35): those better provided for no longer want to receive special treatment.

This unifying principle will surely manifest itself and is already manifested in a number of spheres. In the area of health, for example, it will soon seem unbelievable that society would not treat all the sick under the same conditions, whatever their financial means may happen to be. For an example we do not need to go to socialist countries. Great Britain, with free medical and hospital service, is a pioneer in this development. A unitary health organization, however, can and must respect people's freedom in choosing a doctor. In such an intimate domain of life, liberty has to be safeguarded.

The educational system is also moving toward unity so that each person has the same possibility of access to positions of leadership and intellectual endeavors. It is much to be desired that society recruit its elite from the broadest base possible, in this way also helping to do away with privileges. Furthermore, a unitary organization is compatible with the freedom of individuals to choose an education in conformity with their own religious and ethical ideas.

In all areas, including leisure, the new society inclines toward a fundamental equality in circumstances. Leisure, particularly (the word comes from the Latin *licere,* to be allowed), presupposes freedom and can become an actuality only in a permissive society.

It is difficult to imagine the change that a revolution of this kind would bring about in the habits of today's privileged and, as a consequence, the resistance that they would put up against it. Experience teaches us that they will do everything to keep from falling into the commom condition of other people. The best of them, however, can understand that people do not lose anything good by sharing it, for, in sharing, they gain by no longer living apart from the human community.

In every way, economic privileges will one day be as inconceivable as the onetime privileges of the aristocracy and the clergy in the *Ancien Régime* and the change will take place contrary to all the expectations of the privileged themselves.

Second, the new society will be a society of the people, in the sense that in it the structures of capitalist countries will be broken down.

Some kind of inversion of the powers that the privileged classes enjoy today is necessary. The people, that is, all those least advantaged, must be in a position to make themselves heard on an equal footing with those who, having both culture and wealth, have the ear of the public powers.

There is no question of simply inverting power by passing it over to an opponent group. Dictatorship by a class, even if it be the proletariat, is a kindred kind of power. Public authority does not belong to one class but to the nation.[3] But to bring down both privileges and the powers derived from them, people normally use force against powerful private individuals and groups who intend to maintain the established disorder.

The destruction of the social prepotency generated by the ownership of property and the managment of capital is a difficult thing to do. It means the end of oligarchies and of the imperialism of industrial metropolises. It means anticipating that the world of unwarranted power will not give way without resisting with every last one of the many means at its disposal. However, it is plain that not to make a move against that world is impossible. Nothing can justify the existing state of affairs.

## Central Bodies

Taken as a whole, these objectives require a concentration of means in the hands of public power, a requirement that is both new and essential. All the difficulties of democracy today spring from the fact that the public powers find themselves having to deal with economic tasks which the liberal model not only did not anticipate but excluded on principle.

Everywhere, even in non-Communist countries, a plan is indispensable. It takes different forms, it is true, in order to come to terms with the prevailing concept of public liberties. The term "plan" itself is sometimes still rejected, for liberal orthodoxy is tenacious. But how can we avoid applying the word "planning" to the intervention of the President of the United States in tariff and fiscal matters? Does it not have to be admitted that these interventions follow a certain line, have a certain consistency?

Is it not preferable, since there is a plan, to call it a plan and to organize it within the framework of democratic institutions rather than to leave decisions to improvisation or to the arbitrary decisions of the government?

To the extent that a free market is necessary for an effective economy (and we have seen that socialist countries have reestablished certain elements of it for that very reason), the plan must not destroy free-market mechanisms. It should, on the contrary, often reestablish them by eliminating the complicated network of protective devices and private agreements that hamper its functioning.

Is this to say that a plan is to be simply advisory? The word neither represents the reality of existing modes of planning nor the needs of present-day economies. Planning bodies cannot be simple information bureaus, which place all their statistical data at the disposition of enterprises. They must also be in a position to set in motion the public interventions that they find necessary.

The name that should be given to this aggregation of global forecasts and partial interventions is of small importance. What does matter is that coordinating bodies of this type have a wide hearing among the general public and, even more important, among the great public administrative bodies that often question their authority, as well as among economic agencies, so that their forecasts do not remain a dead letter, as is unhappily the case in most developing countries.[4]

Only in this way will public decisions on economic matters have a chance to be articulated—and all governments, even in countries where the liberal doctrine is still dominant, have come to such decisions.

The principal task of the public powers has, in fact, two aspects. On one hand, they must maintain conditions of fair competition in a market where cartels and accords, when they are not those of the public powers themselves, accumulate protective measures that tend to distort the normal play of the market. On the other hand, they must be able to intervene effectively in order to have certain trends followed, which the blind working of supply and demand are incapable of prompting.[5]

Paradoxically, this double objective sometimes seems to be achieved more successfully at the level of supranational agreements because, at that level, governments can more easily free themselves from the pressures to which enterprises subject them in the inhibiting intimacy of national affairs.

## Peripheral Autonomies

In order to suppress the illegitimate privileges and powers that originate in enterprises having autonomy, must we go so far as to abolish autonomy itself? Marxism gives a decisive answer: it condemns every peripheral autonomy within the planned economy. The plan must be "concerted"; decisions on the general level must be based on consultation with producers, but planning bodies allow no place for autonomous decision-making centers anywhere in the whole economy.

The Soviet reality is making substantial correctives in Marxist doctrine in this area.[6] Beginning with the time when enterprises started to keep their own accounts and were charged with their own accountability for profit-making, when they themselves decide on the internal organization of production, freely sign contracts with suppliers and buyers, administer the capital they have realized through profits, plow profits back into the enterprise, they really are autonomous business, small groups using some power of decision within the collective whole. The same is true, a fortiori, in Yugoslavia.

Those who think that ownership consists essentially in the administration rather than the appropriation of goods have no hesitation in seeing this as a way of returning to the ownership of productive goods.[7] Certainly it is not a question of going back to the private ownership of capital; this belongs to the enterprises themselves as collectivities and to individuals only during the time when they are working in them. This arrangement is a particular kind of capital ownership, neither private nor collective. The categories of "public" and "private" do not apply in this instance.

This evolution of socialism, no matter how timid it still remains, except in the case of Yugoslavia, can be compared to a tendency observable in free economies. The juridical reality of actual enterprises is less and less amenable to interpretation in terms of private ownership. Legislation and jurisprudence are contributing to the creation of a new branch of law, sometimes called institutional; directors of private enterprises can no longer be considered as owners, even if they possess the capital.

These two evolutions, one occurring in planned economies, the other in free-market economies, although still far away from each other, are converging toward a point in common, an enterprise that belongs in neither the private nor the public domain[8] but is an institution. Its power of decision, that is, its ownership, is neither private nor collective. It is "social ownership," a term that can be used, provided that it be defined.

In any case, some autonomy for the enterprise is slowly coming about, both in the whole socialist collectivity as well as among private investors in the capitalist world.

## A Structured Economy

If an enterprise is an "institution" in the precise sense that has been envisaged here, if it belongs to neither the public nor the private economy, then its organic bonds with both need to be determined, for its autonomy cannot be absolute, whatever its internal structure may be, that is, the kind of relationship existing between capital and labor within it.

*The enterprise and the public economy.*    According to economic liberalism, there is no public organization of the economy and there should not be. An enterprise is a reality in itself. In its internal structure it is identified with private capital. As to its external structure, it is sovereign and is limited only by competition in a reputedly free market.

According to socialism, an enterprise is not a center for decision-making. It is a small particle of social capital without power.

These two extreme theses being rejected—and we have seen how greatly the socialist and capitalist realities differ from one another—we are led to discern links between an enterprise and the central bodies, to define their competencies, and to envisage a structure of mutual relationships.

To give an a priori definition of that structure presents some difficulty. That experience alone makes progress possible in this area is equally true in both planned and market economies.

Within the latter, in cases where a plan exists that is not merely advisory or unreservedly mandatory—since it allows for partial interventions—programs can be established only on the basis of preliminary consultations. Concerted action, in which both employers' associations and workers' unions act together, provides the embryo for such a structure. In such cases the settlements made are never entirely satisfactory to the different parties. The arbitration that must take place fails to satisfy all those involved. Nevertheless, here is an experiment with potential for progress.

It would be preferable for capital and labor to be united in doing the work that they carry out together. As long as enterprises do not develop a type of joint or self-management, dialogue with the public powers can be contemplated only in its present form, with the disadvantages that entails, especially for the workers' interests, since their representatives do not have access to the same sources of information as the representatives of the owners.

In no way are the owners' associations and the workers' unions, on one hand, and the public powers, on the other, on an equal footing when they dialogue. The periphery inevitably tends to be anarchical; the role of the central bodies is to impose needed coordination. This being so, it is all the more important that competencies be clearly defined to prevent centralizing trends from taking full possession of the field.

*The enterprise and the private economy.*  Every socializing process poses a threat to the sphere of private life; being inspired by economic ends (a high standard of living and equitable distribution) it can represent an intrusion of the economic into the most intimate domain of personal existence—whence the necessity to define carefully private liberties in the economic order, people's freedom as workers and consumers. Both socialism and liberalism find that difficult to do, for they lack the principles to form such a definition.

1. The pressures that threaten the freedom of the consumer do not exist in the same form in economies where the market dominates and in economies where decisions are centralized.

In market-dominated economies, the advertising of the big firms is intrusive and, to many people, characteristic of a consumer society. Some advertising in the trades has always been authorized; it used to be carefully limited by corporative regulations that forbade enticing customers "by word and gesture." It was not unpleasing; shop signs emulated one another in artistry. But in industrial society an obsessive and offensive advertising has taken the form of a hydra with a hundred heads. Through the mass media—the press, television, and radio—which are strictly dependent upon advertising for their survival, through public billboards in cities and along the roads, advertising invades and destroys the environment necessary for artistic enjoyment and close human relationships. It is amazing that at the very time when so much talk is going on about protecting ecological structures against physical destruction, so few questions are raised in international congresses and public opinion about the psychological deterioration of our life environment. The pressure of the mass media only partially explains the apparent resignation of the public to the aggressiveness of commercial firms.

The inaction is all the more surprising, since it would be relatively easy, in certain areas, to take adequate measures to contain the invasion. Just one law would suffice to rid the countryside and the cities of the billboards littering them. It is hard to see what society would lose by that. Action in the sector of the mass media would be more difficult. In brief, putting any strict limitation on them must wait upon the education of the public, must find all of us willing to buy newspapers at a higher price, to pay for radio and television programming. In any case, we are all being charged without our knowledge, for advertising is a tax on consumers. Educating the public will take a long time; while awaiting improvement, the law could at least intervene, for example, by limiting the time given to advertising on television and radio. What harm would be done if a commercial, instead of being repeated three times in an hour were run only once and charged the same price? Anyhow, is psychological bombardment effective? Would it be a drawback if advertising, as in the case of some national television stations, were allowed to be presented only in the form of artistic programs?

As long as the public remains passive and comes to no decision to pay freely for what it is now paying for by constraint and force, a ruthless suppression of advertising would in fact result in putting the means of communication into the hands of the public powers, leading to government financing and, consequently, control.

Advertising cannot be denied any economic function; it makes concentrated production possible and, in some cases, products of better quality at better prices. It should not be completely eliminated, but when it ends by giving a monopoly to the most powerful firms, it can have a negative effect, even from an economic point of view alone. Everything suggests that public opinion and governments should exercise strict control over it. To do that requires courage and initiative, for the ordinary means of influencing public opinion—the mass media—are diametrically opposed to any diminution in the advertising on which their lives depend.

Rather than continuing to carry on a discourse of denunciation about a phenomenon so humiliating for us human beings, would it not be preferable to undertake some remedial action? In some countries, consumer associations prove what individuals can do when they unite for common action and what they could do if the public powers would support their action.

Faced with these difficulties some seem to think that the advent of socialism is the only radical means open to us. It does, in point of fact, eliminate the phenomenon at a single stroke.

Planned economies too, in their own way, bring pressure to bear on consumers. Buyers can no longer choose commodities to suit their individual tastes. The plan set by authority without consulting them determines the kind and price of products to be put at their disposition. Probably the queues of customers in the shops inform planning authorities about consumers' wants; but this is very incomplete information and very costly for the public, and for women in particular. In reality, the economic burden on the individual is at least as heavy in socialist regimes as in consumer societies. This occurs not by the invasion of private life by hucksters, but by the arbitrary and more or less blind decisions of central planning bodies about what consumers want and what is advisable to make available to them. There is no certainty that it would be any easier for people to put up a fight against this other form of economic intrusion into their lives.

Among consumer liberties, one is particularly important to defend against the process of radical socialization—the freedom to take costly initiatives with no view to profit and no public interest at stake but with real justification for society.

Central bodies and institutions for social security cannot and ought not to take care of everything. They cannot, because a number of social cases always slip through the meshes of their net, no matter how fine these may be. Society cannot cover every need. Moreover, it ought not to, for needs exist which it cannot relieve. In the domain of leisure, of artistic creation, for example, and still more, of religion, there are people who undertake to cover the expenses of activities that they judge necessary. To do that, they must have some margin of income and reserves.

A process of socialization that claims to limit revenue and reserves strictly in accordance with what the central bodies recognize as necessities turns society into a mob satisfied with food and amusement, *panem et circenses,* that it clamors for and with which it comes to be content. This is no free society. Liberation consists in creating room for individual decisions, which the socializing process is ever inclined to dispute.

2. Pressures that threaten freedom to work are just as different in the two systems.

In consumer society, unemployment without a doubt puts the greatest limitations on freedom. As a matter of fact, when it reaches a certain percentage, unemployment means a take-it-or-leave-it choice for many workers. They are told, "Take that job or the door." And the door leads to long months without work. Unemployment is what most weakens labor organizations. When it is considerable, employers and not the wage earners do the choosing and apply pressure. That is why liberal doctrine is so indifferent to any theory of full employment and, particularly, to the actions that they imply. In all third-world countries, the creation of new employment is surely one of the essential objectives of planning. In this matter the intervention of central bodies serves as a source of freedom. Their impotence and passivity in this domain is deplorable.

In planned economies, unemployment no longer exists. Every individual has a job although not necessarily a productive one, for the number of jobs offered is determined by the working population and not by productivity, as it is in the case of market economies. In principle, people are free to choose their work, but, in a system of full employment, workers are very frequently obliged to accept the jobs and working conditions offered to them. The limitations put upon moving from one place to another and the prohibition to emigrate (save in the case of Yugoslavia) are a kind of bondage. So it is true to say that in a socialistic regime the employer, a single employer in this case, is also the one who chooses what pressure techniques to use. The trade union or syndicate is reduced to playing a secondary role and, in any case, deprived of the right to strike.

In either system, people in all professions strongly resent the intrusion of economics in their private lives. A regime in which absolute freedom to work here or there, in one branch or another is unimaginable, but if we want to get away from a concentration-camp kind of world, a world that is at present the special locus of the most deprived workers—immigrants from rural regions and from foreign countries—we must, while organizing to secure people's right to work, also preserve their freedom to work.

In all these matters, liberalism and socialism run headlong into fundamental human demands. The role of the cultural revolution is to bring to light, in opposition to the blind forces of the market and of bureaucracies rigidly committed to the Plan, the necessity to leave individuals and groups room for freedom. Without that, no society is worthy of the name.

## Anarchy in the International Economy

In the domain of international economy, socialism is experiencing its most flagrant failure and the third world has been its major victim. Not only have its objectives, the increase and equitable distribution of products, not been attained, but they seem to be moving further and further out of reach. If a rise in the standard of living throughout less developed countries is unquestionable, in most instances it is excessively slow and the contrast between these nations and the most highly developed countries continues to increase.

In a world now and hereafter interdependent, the differences between the misery and poverty of some peoples and the opulence of others are just as insupportable as those which set one class against another in the same country. In the long run, these disparities threaten international as well as social peace. They are a grave form of iniquity and are so apprehended today by the conscience of humanity.

Why has there been so little advancement in this area? Why have the means put into effect not been able to put an end to the disorder they were meant to remedy?

Up until now, efforts have been made to find a palliative in two different directions, aid from rich to poor countries and an amelioration in the exchange rates between the two types of countries.

International aid has not been negligible, yet it remains minimal in the face of increasing inequalities. And it stays at the level of assistance and does not reach to the roots of social contrasts. It inevitably engenders some form of dependence in the countries who receive on those which give, especially when the giving is of a kind not favorable for the autonomy of nations and of the third world.[9] It would be absurd to reduce this assistance; rather, everything ought to be done to increase it and to eliminate those conditions associated with it which promote dependence.[10] In this terrain, however, movement meets a roadblock either because of the egotistical reaction of public opinion in rich countries or because of the innate incapacity of assistance to resolve a permanent relationship problem which has its source neither in delinquency nor in disaster.

Reform in international trade between rich and poor countries has been on the agenda of four conferences of the United Nations Conference on Trade and Development: at Geneva in 1964, New Delhi in 1968, Santiago in 1972, and Nairobi in 1976. Reform in trade and development is the official purpose of the organization. Everybody knows that the results of these great gatherings have been, if not nil, at least insignificant in view of the enormous problems that have to be resolved.

In this area, however, we do stand on more solid ground, the matter of trade relations rather than of simple assistance. The ax is struck at the root of the tree: the very structure of decision-making must be changed if we wish to reach the source of disorder in international economy.

Of course, here we come up against a wall of defense that seems almost insurmountable. No country, capitalist or socialist, great or small, rich or poor is prepared to yield one iota of its national sovereignty.

The more we reflect on it, the more we see that this intransigence is the basic cause of powerlessness in this domain. A problem of justice between nations is not essentially different from a problem of justice between classes, the very question raised by socialism. The failure of efforts undertaken on the international plane is explained by the fact that, at this level, the means employed, generally those of socialization—to wit, the establishment of central bodies provided with adequate powers—have not been put into effect. Nations, whatever their size, their degree of development, and their political regime are not ready to scale down their concept of absolute sovereignty in order to actualize the coordinating and unifying processes without which socialization is a doctrine empty of any reality.

The cause of incapacity for any action lies in the structure of international relations or, rather, in the absence of any structure at this level. What characterizes economic rapport among nations is the isolated stand maintained by each of them. Every one, whether great or small, fears to part with its liberty. Consequently, everything is done on the basis of mutual concessions, on the simple promises of nations, without any obligation either to make them or to keep them. Here is the principal defect. Although in our day national economies are content to have some internal power exercise control over them in a more or less direct manner, the international economy remains a locus of anarchy. Just as in the jungle, the powerful dominate; the weak are subject to the law of the strong; and violence, not law, reigns.

The world's peoples could be freed from this disorder and the oppression resulting from it if nations would reach the point of establishing bodies in which the interests of all those in face-to-face conflict could have an equal hearing and decisions would be reached not simply as the result of economic and political pressures but by an interpretation of the general good made independently of pressures.

A first stage in that direction ought to be worked out on the regional or subcontinental level. The European Community has succeeded in according the same footing to big and little countries, as well as countries at very different stages of development, for example, West Germany and Italy. The less developed countries have probably benefited the most from the powers initiated within the Community.

A way to go has therefore been indicated. In Latin America, the Andean Pact brings together into one community Colombia, Ecuador, Peru, Bolivia, Chile and, a little later, Venezuela, and is attracting Argentina. It has moved from the talking to the acting phase. It represents at the same time hope and an uphill path provided that, like Europe, it is animated by a faith strong enough to surmount one by one the countless obstacles that it will certainly meet as it moves ahead.

Today the economy can be organized only by combined action on a broad scale. Leaving aside nations like the United States, Russia, China, India, and Brazil, all subcontinents, integration can only assure the development of the third world by establishing plurinational regions and markets, in this way putting an end to the economic nonsense of dividing peoples up piecemeal.

What puts a limit on efforts for subcontinental integration is the fact that they do not reach a level where determinative relations are established for less developed peoples. Rather, integration as it now exists unites people whose development is already advanced, as in the case of the European Community. In spite of real attempts at understanding, these nations are ignorant about people who, in comparison to them, live a marginal and dependent existence. In any case, they do not integrate them into their community on an equal footing. The relationship between Europe and Africa, which seems written into geography, remains marked by a lack of organization and the presence of dependence.

Regional grouping brings together countries that have not advanced very far in development, as in the case of the Andean Pact. A powerful economy, therefore, lies outside their orbit

—yet, by the way it functions, it has a far greater effect on them than their mutual dealings with one another.

The relationship of the United States and Latin America is also written into geography. It too continues to be marked by the inequality of those who share it.

We are face to face with a formidable and unavoidable problem. The unknown element in it is whether Europe in relation to Africa, and the United States in relation to Latin America, have decided to rise above their nationalism, which is really an unconscious imperialism, in order to enter into a system of decisions made on an equal basis. The problem is unavoidable because it is vain to think that the countries of the American continent can develop themselves without increasing and organizing their mutual relations—the example of Cuba would serve as proof of that, if proof were necessary. It is a formidable problem, for just the idea of establishing a real community modeled on the European Community between the United States and Canada on one side, and Latin America on the other, with all the members having equality in decision-making, provokes real panic in North American opinion.

Europeans need not find this amusing, for their own reaction would be exactly the same if it were a matter of establishing a real economic community based on equality with either the Arab world or black Africa. However, let us think about it. Justice and wisdom are pointing to a system of that kind and in no other direction. Endless talk goes on about the dependence of Latin American countries on the United States and of African countries on Europe. But talking is useless if we do not get to the root of the evil. Adopting socialism means nothing, for the dependence of the East European countries on the U.S.S.R. is just as great. The organization that presides over their relations, the Comecon, is just as open to question as the Organization of American States (OAS),[11] the object of so much criticism in Latin America. The only solution for countries forced by geography to live together is a community in which each plays an equal part in making decisions. Regional organizations put forward by the great powers, like the OAS or Comecon, do not eliminate dependence. They consecrate it.

Of course, we have to be realistic. Community in the full sense, like the European Community, is possible only if economic disparities are not too great. Developing nations must then utilize all the capital assets put at their disposal by highly industrialized countries and, at the same time, keep them under their own national control. They must also supply the internal effort of working and saving in order to accelerate their own development and follow a clearly articulated and intelligible economic policy. The example of Japan and soon, perhaps, of Brazil demonstrates what growth is possible. Although a country may be dependent to start with, growth gives it the necessary vigor to treat with more powerful nations as an equal. A case in point is the relationship existing between Japan and the United States today. If Latin American countries and, as time goes on, the countries of Africa were to follow the same route, it would be much easier to establish a continental community in the Americas and an intercontinental community of Europe and Africa. Only their formation can obliterate the dependence now existing, given the fact that isolation means the definitive establishment of underdevelopment and oppression for the third world.

Economic organization is also possible in the marketing of particular products. Some efforts have been made in this direction, not without success, for products like cacao, thanks to agreements between selling and purchasing countries. In the absence of any organization based upon agreements oil producers have achieved spectacular results by forming a syndicate in their sector. It is true that the resultant situation places an unjust burden on Europe, which is almost entirely without this natural resource, and puts the oil-producing countries in a dominant position. The completely unforeseen reduction in oil deliveries by a certain number of producing countries is creating a chain reaction that throws doubt upon a continuing growth rate in developed countries and seems to be introducing a new era.[12] At a time when some of the world's reserves of raw materials are becoming exhausted and some mineral and argricultural products are reaching very high prices, a combination of circumstances is resulting in a trend that favors some third-world countries. Suppliers could profit by these circumstances and agree among themselves how to regulate the market and obtain the best prices. The union or syndicate, demonstrably effective as it is in the hands of workers, can become equally so in relations between nations. Will the example of the oil syndicate become contagious?

In any case, the organization of a region or a market is not enough to establish an international community and, if we are to be realistic, we have to face the problem of organization at this stage. This became evident when the United States in recent years made a unilateral decision to devalue the dollar, with the result that the whole monetary system reverberated with uncertainty, as it was based on the worldwide acceptance of the dollar as a standard of value, a store of liquid wealth, and a medium of exchange. Minting money has always been the privilege of the prince. Issuing bank notes is a reserved right. It confers on those who enjoy it an inordinate advantage: that of creating for their own profit a purchasing power recognized everywhere. To leave the mechanisms of international money in the hands of a single power is a mistake.

Voices were raised against such hegemony, first of all on the European continent. A proposal was immediately made to replace the monetary system of one nation with a system organized by the ten most developed nations, but they could reach no agreement and their debates provoked laughter in dollar land. Replacing a one-power hegemony with a hegemony of ten major powers was absolutely no solution to the problem, which was a concern for the international community. The only adequate measure would be to cede to the prince the right to mint money. And "the prince" in this case could only be the United Nations itself.

Of course, people will say that it is utopian to think of such a solution and, consequently, vain to present the problem. If so, what is the good of continuing to carry on long discussions about dependence? Progress is not made by denouncing the injustice of a system but by putting into effect those actions that alone can replace it with a system marked by greater justice. We can turn the problem over and over and find no other defense against the imperialism prevailing today than true community.

Socialism in its Marxist form is no help. If the completely centralized model that it proposes has been found inapplicable for just one nation, as the evolution of socialist countries demonstrates, there is no possible chance of imposing it at the international level. Soviet doctrine, more than any other, insists upon national sovereignty.[13] A theory that leans toward completely suppressing any autonomy within the economy arouses unparalleled reactions from the world community, and above all, in any ambience where national sovereignty is conceived in the most absolute manner. If the national reality rebels against an over-centralized economic organization, the international reality absolutely rejects it.

It takes courage to state the kernel of the matter correctly. Nothing will be done if the world's peoples are not resolved to abandon their narrow idea of sovereignty in order to work together to reach a decision sufficiently free of special interests to rise to the level of the general good. Some kind of international authority is necessary. Until it is established, the world economy will stay as it is, a jungle where the great carnivores hold dominion.

Evidently there are ways that open up possible approaches to the ideal, still too far away to be attained immediately. So, while we await something better, we must enter upon the intermediate stages courageously; these consist in the organization of markets and regions. Without despairing of people and of humanity in general, we also have to look the global problem in the face and do battle against the centrifugal forces that prevent its solution. Socialist countries are no more disposed than any others to enter upon this path. The most powerful among them give an alibi by invoking the class struggle between imperialist and proletarian nations in order to justify their own imperialism. And in capitalist countries, their ideology is in full swing. We must hope for a new energy capable of lifting the enormous weight of national prejudices and passions and engendering a current strong enough to move on beyond them.

Failing that, it would be better not to keep people thinking that "dependence" can be brought to an end; for, as far as relations between nations are concerned, no other liberation is possible.

## Multinational Enterprises

The multinational trust or corporation is, like the national, a spontaneous creation of the free enterprise system. The technical need to master, through information and decision, the great economic aggregates in order to organize them explains their rise.[14] Questions arise when this great concentration creates, in the hands of industrial leaders, economic and political power which they then use to bring weight to bear on people's destinies through all the means within their control. The whole matter becomes even more crucial when the great powers place at the service of their own nationals means of pressuring small nations. In the anarchy of the international economy, it then happens that powerful private groups and persons exercise in public life the most excessive unofficial power, derived from owning property and managing capital. Here we have one of the most negative aspects of capitalism to which socialism, of itself, brings a solution. For the socialist countries substitute for multinational enterprises a system of direct intervention, unencumbered by any intermediary, by one nation in the life of another. In that way, the hold of one country on another, for reasons at once political and economic, is at least as strong. Here we again meet a characteristic of socialist organization: to cram into the same hands both economic and political power. The result is dictatorship, something equally dangerous for national and international relations.

Everything has already been written about the power of multinational firms.[15] The biggest of them produce more on a global scale than many small and medium-sized nations. If we consider the hundred largest economic entities (grouping under that term nations as well as enterprises), fifty-one are enterprises, and thirty-nine of these are North American; only forty-one are nations. General Motors is thirteenth on the list, between Mexico and Sweden.[16] Obviously, the conscience of humanity cannot remain indifferent to a phenomenon of that magnitude.

As in the case of national trusts, the development of multinational firms is in response to reasons of a technical order. Manufacturing a product today often requires making use of resources not usually found in just one country; and the social division of work brings people together across national borders: so the logic of industrial society leads those responsible for production to try to coordinate the general economic process by establishing a unity of power and profit at a plurinational level. From that point of view, multinational firms respond to a more urgent need than national firms, for, in the absence of any real international organization, it is impossible to see just who would be the conductor of so vast and varied an orchestra. The direct power of just one dominant nation could be even more dangerous than the present activities of multinational corporations. However, these pose huge-scale problems of both the economic and the political order.

Socialism has alerted us to the big economic problem of production becoming so completely solidified and autonomous that it comes to consider itself an absolute and thus introduces a troublesome factor in the whole manufacturing and distributing process. No matter how wide-reaching it may be, it represents only one part of a whole and cannot pretend to confuse its own well-being with the general good. Whatever the rationale of a firm's decisions about its own production, there is no certainty that these decisions will be best for the functioning of the general economy. Using aggressive publicity, a firm can launch into manufacturing new products that do not necessarily correspond to people's most urgent needs. It can go ahead so fast with technical modernization that it makes extremely expensive equipment out of date before it has been paid for. In the absence of any control over the economy at the international level, nothing gives us any assurance that the strategy of multinational firms might not some day provoke crises of overproduction. Problems concerning the environment and pollution and the use of the ocean beds, if not considered, make nonsense of technical progress and extend far beyond the vision of the whole of big management together, no matter how broad its horizon may be.

Even when multinational firms are strictly apolitical, as some of them are, they are the subject of serious concern. And if their directors abandon neutrality and intervene in the destiny of nations by means of the mass media, which they can easily control, or mobilize them to give direction to the dominating nation to which they belong, then multinational firms present an extremely grave political problem, especially for third-world countries.[17] There is no reason why the management of huge capital should earn those who exercise it influence in the political decisions of a nation and even of the world.

When a trust or corporation is developing in the framework of a national economy or a plurinational economic community, authority can impose strict controls on it, although to do so is never easy. The big firm has at its disposal many means of escaping such controls. But an authority does exist in that instance and can be envisaged as extending its power to make the great powers subject to a common law.[18]

The absence of any authority within the international economy, as the result of the jealous notion that each nation has of its nationhood, makes impossible any effective intervention to prevent multinational firms from assuming political competence, to which they have no right. In the economic sphere, which is theirs, no apparatus exists to make them subject to any other more general authority.

It is possible to envisage "rules of good conduct" that would comprise ethical norms. But what police would be on hand to enforce these traffic laws? The consciences of those in management and directorship should be appealed to; to have great expectations of them is to overestimate, if not their moral worth, at least the possibility that they will rise to the level of keeping in view the general ends pursued by humanity. The responsibility for society as a whole cannot be confided to one particular authority, no matter how wide the field in which it operates.

To do away with multinational firms offers no solution, for technological objectives exist which cannot be achieved without them. To replace them by the direct intervention of the public powers in some leading nation has a least as many disadvantages. So we come back to the same need. The anarchy reigning in the international economy is in no way lessened by the existence of huge production entities; order can only be imposed by the progressive establishment of an international authority in a position to control these power groups.[19]

That sums up what is truly one of the most difficult and most needed tasks of liberation: on its outcome the fate of the third world directly depends.

## NOTES

1. "We denote as socialist every doctrine which demands the connection of all economic functions, or of certain among them, which are at the present time diffuse, to the directing and conscious centers of society." Emile Durkheim, *Socialism and Saint-Simon*, ed. and intro. A.W. Gouldner, trans. C. Sattler (Yellow Springs, Ohio: Antioch Press, 1958), p. 19. This definition covers neither all the aspects of socialism nor all its historical forms. In France particularly, a libertarian socialist ideology has been developed. Proudhon, as well as a number of others, including in more recent times, Charles Péguy, have been its adherents and supporters. See Jean Bastaire, "Péguy, prophète de la liberté socialiste," *Etudes* (February 1973), pp. 245 ff. Anarcho-syndicalism represents a similar version held in France, beginning with the Charter of Amiens. In 1906 at the Congress of the Confédéracion générale du travail at Amiens, syndicalism separated itself from political socialism as to means—the general revolutionary strike instead of action through elections and parliament; and as to ends—the appropriation of the means of production by the workers rather than by the government. A resolution of the congress, which was baptized with the name of the Charter of Amiens, proclaimed that "Syndicalism is sufficient unto itself." But these tendencies have been largely supplanted by the collectivism of Marx and Lenin. However, do they not speak to the postsocialist contestation becoming more and more evident today? For syndicalism see E. Dolléans and G. Dehove, *Histoire du travail en France* (Paris: Domat-Montchrestien, 1953), Vol. I pp. 408–10.

2. Consider, for example, the propagation of the species. If a man and woman procreate, it is, above all, because they love one another. The collective end is present in their action but, as persons, they are scarcely conscious of it and seek it only through personal ends.

3. Gaston Fessard makes this point quite clear in his book, *De l'actualité historique* (Paris: Desclée de Brouwer, 1960), Vol. II, pp. 149 ff.

4. In my book *La doctrine sociale de l'Eglise*, 2nd ed. (Paris, P.U.F., 1966), *passim*, a number of sectors in which the government can act are pointed out: fiscal policy, policy regarding credit and money, public

investments, social security, family benefits, the salaries of public employees, etc. A lack of coordination rather than a lack of means is the reason for most failures in the third world and, even more than that, a lack of will to put means into effect. The greatest difficulty is in reconciling the interests of fixed revenue (an increase in salaries) with variable revenue (sufficient profits to stimulate private investment).

5. In a comprehensive study, Pierre Bauchet points up the principles that serve to inspire planning in a democratic structure. *La planification française* (Paris: Seuil, 1966).

6. See above pp. 169 ff.

7. "No one has yet been able," Sévérac says, "to draw a judicious line between decentralization of economic administration—so necessary for its efficiency—and certain forms of private ownership." Cited in Dumont and Mazoyer, *Socialisms and Development,* trans. Rupert Cunningham (New York: Praeger, 1973), p. 226.

8. This subject will be taken up again, pp. 277 ff.

9. See above pp. 32 ff.

10. See Henri Perroy, *L'Europe devant le tiers monde* (Paris: Aubier, 1971).

11. See Jean-Yves Calvez, *Politics and Society in the Third World,* trans. M. J. O'Connell (Maryknoll, N.Y.: Orbis Books, 1973) ch. 2. For the socialist countries, see Jean Caillot, *Le C.A.E.M: Aspects juridiques et formes de coopération économique entre les pays socialistes* (Paris: Librairie générale de Droit et de Jurisprudence, 1971).

12. Henri Madelin, *Pétrole et politique en Méditerranee occidentale* (Paris: Armand Colin, 1973), p. 317, brings out the uncertainties in the new situation.

13. See Jean-Yves Calvez, *Droit international et souveraineté en U.R.S.S.* (Paris: Armand Colin, 1953), ch. 2, "La souveraineté nationale."

14. It is estimated that multinational enterprises control 50 percent of world production in market economies.

15. The article by Philippe Laurent, "Un pouvoir envahissant, les firmes multinationales," in *Projet* (September-October 1971), gives an excellent idea of the present state of the matter. It is symptomatic that the International Labor Congress in Santiago, Chile, April 1973, took this subject as the theme of its discussions.

16. Ibid., p. 896.

17. There is widespread knowledge of the revelations of the U.S. Senate Committee investigating the interventions of the powerful I.T.T. (International Telegraph and Telephone) in favor of the American government when President Allende came to power in Chile in 1970.

18. Action taken within the E.C.S.C. (the European Coal and Steel

Community), which has supranational authority in economic matters, can be cited as an example. Although it has not always attained its objectives, it tries to discern what agreements are harmful (tending toward monopoly) and what agreements are helpful (tending to coordinate the manufacture of products).

19. It is in this sense that Raymond Vernon includes in his book *The Economic and Political Consequence of Multinational Enterprise: An Anthology* (Cambridge: Harvard Graduate School of Business Administration, 1972) a discussion of the idea of a world society with a definite organ, "more likely than not some sort of international tribunal" (p. 160), charged with arbitrating the activities of international trade and of multinational enterprises and, besides this, a system of social values recognized internationally. "The basic asymmetry between multinational enterprises and national governments may be tolerable up to a point, but beyond that point there is a need to reestablish balance through accountability to a governing body multinational in scope. If this does not happen, some of the apocalyptic projections of the future of multinational enterprise will grow more plausible" (p. 162); " . . . there is a considerable possibility that the multinational enterprise problem will find itself shortly merged in a very much larger issue: how advanced nations can live side by side in a world in which physical and cultural space is so rapidly shrinking. This issue involves not only the multinational enterprise but all forms of international movements, of goods, of capital, of people, and of ideas. It may be that in dealing with the overwhelming problems that are arising from forces such as these, the problem of multinational enterprise will have been solved as well" (p. 197). See, too, pp. 31–32, 154–155, 160, 166, 200.

# XV

# THE DEMOCRATIC CONTRIBUTION: PUBLIC LIBERTIES

Socialism, because of the very nature of its ends, high work productivity and equal distribution of revenue, tends to establish an economic power strong enough to bring privileges to an end and put a reasonable limit on private powers. If life's objectives were purely economic, nothing would need to be added to this outcome. Marxism takes its stand from this unique perspective, seeing the political as only a superstructure on the economic. But the principles of social existence are more than an economic rationale; they also pertain to political reason. Although efficient production and equal distribution impose strong disciplinary measures, political society is built on a basis of liberties. Socialism must come to terms with a need that contradicts its own logic, and, in its turn, democracy must accept settlements that do not have their origin in its own depths. The crises taking place in both socialism and democracy are centered in this conflict. Looking around the world, we see socialist regimes aspiring to "liberalization" and democratic regimes moving toward "socialization." The most "progressive" socialist countries grant concessions to freedom, the most conservative deny them. The most "progressive" democratic countries call for some control over the economy, the most conservative oppose it.

Socialism does not intend to allow its adversaries a monopoly on democracy, which costs human beings so much energy and blood to win. So it presents itself as logical democracy, real democracy, which puts no value on *formal* liberties (universal suffrage based on the party system) but on *real*, quantitative, rights (equality in one standard of living for all). For its part, democracry claims to make the objectives of socialism its own. A real relationship between the two ideologies explains this pussin-the-corner game. It is taking place on the talking level only and, on the existential ground level, economic imperatives and political liberties remain unreconciled.

What place can liberties, so dearly bought, have in a society where the necessities of life and social ideals impose strong disciplinary measures?

## The Democratic Conviction

Marxist socialism has so denigrated "formal" liberties and treated them with such irony that people reach the point of questioning their timeliness and value. Do civil liberties, exercising the right to information, to association, to the election of government officers, to religion, still mean something?

It cannot be denied that, by challenging the divine origin of power, Christianity created for democracy and for socialism as well a milieu favorable for their birth and growth to fruitful maturity. By setting themselves against the worship of Caesar, martyrs have waged and continue to wage a war that proves instrumental in confining the organization of the city of man to the proportions of a human work and, at the same time, in forming an idea of it as a creation of a whole people gathered together in a society without discrimination. The secularization, the laicization, of power contravened all the ideas of the pagan world and was necessary for the development of the democratic idea.

Not without reason did this idea first emerge in theology at the time the New World—the East and West Indies first—was discovered. It was not yet called the third world. It was in response to a question asked about the American Indians that the great Spanish theologian Francisco de Vitoria formulated for the first time the democratic principle: no one, not even the pope, may decide the Indians' political organization; that is their concern and their concern alone. So it was that reflection in the theological order laid the foundation for the modern principles for both civil and international law as its logical outcome.[1]

If there is a theology of liberation, then unquestionably Vitoria's is it. It did not find acceptance all at once. It went dead against all the principles of the medieval society in which it sprang up. It was far from serving as the inspiration of the

Spanish conquest in America or the Portuguese conquest in India. Each of these was an open contradiction of it; each legitimatized itself by appealing to "holy" causes. The missionaries themselves, who set sail with a crowd of conquerors, did not always conduct their apostolate according to the new ideas that the great theologian had drawn up for them from the wellspring of their faith. The popes intervened, limiting the arbitrary will of princes by establishing the papacy as the supreme authority from which they held their rights, but, at the same time, sanctioning their conquests. However, careful historians[2] who deal with the history of the Church in Latin America point out plainly the actions of bishops and missionaries who defended the Indians against their unjust aggressors and tried to organize their society. The Jesuit initiative in Paraguay is famous: the Indian reductions there had a history of nearly two centuries. It took nothing less than the suppression of the Society of Jesus to bring them down. The missionaries can be reproached for not having succeeded in organizing a strong lay group capable of surviving once they themselves were gone; but the extraordinary success of these communities based on unanimous consent cannot be denied.[3]

The democratic idea is rooted in soil prepared by the faith. Initially, it met with opposition in the Christian world, at least in Italy and France, but the wars for liberation that it provoked in Spanish America found numerous sympathizers among the clergy and even in the hierarchy. To be astonished at the aggressive resistance of the Christian world in general would mean forgetting that, from the start, the French Revolution had been inspired by an antireligious philosophy which, at first sight, prevented its affinity with Christianity from being apparent. For the vast majority of believers of that time, the revolution was diabolical. Not content with attacking the alliance between the altar and the throne, it aimed at subverting the very principles of the faith. Good minds were not lacking[4] that were capable of discovering in this outpouring, mixed in with the inevitable dross, a deposit of Christian origin.

After the first condemnations of freedom of speech and of thought, which today seem so abnormal to us, Christian thinking recovered its self-possession. A slow work of elaboration gradually brought about a reconciliation between democracy and the faith. During the pontificate of Leo XIII, the papacy itself did not hesitate to take a stand against the monarchist convictions held by the majority of the upper echelons of the French clergy in order to counsel reconciliation.

Since that time, the Church has kept moving in the same direction in spite of some sudden halts,[5] partly explained by the excesses of "modernism." The elaboration of doctrine that took place during the pontificate of Pius XII at the end of World War II, was, in large part, the fruit of reflection on democracy. The intent to put up a barrier against the invasion of Marxist socialism can be detected in this development, but there is much more to it than that: the Church's recognition of fundamental principles that have their origins in the faith. Power, once liberated from the fetishism inherent in it, is a service and its organization must be the work of all adult citizens, without any discrimination. Means must be opened up for all to participate in this common work by freely coming together to think it through and work it through; such sharing groups have their justification and their high mission within the city of man.

## *Democracy Today: Its Content and Condition*

At the very time when public liberties no longer cause any difficulty in the Christian world, they are being disputed in civil society, especially wherever Marxist ideology has penetrated. Is it going to be necessary to throw overboard the doctrinal contribution that has done its utmost to reconcile the faith with the truths deducible from it? What modifications in this contribution are being introduced by the socialist critique of formal liberties? What is the content and condition of these liberties within industrial society, which an economic power cannot dispense with?

Democracy means, first of all, the delimitation of a private domain protected against public intervention; it is also some sort of participation by all citizens in the choice and control of their officials. This participation and choosing are the great victories of the bourgeoisie against the absolute monarchies and the aristocracies of the nobles and clergy. Now that monarchies and aristocracies have disappeared, do they still retain their significance when favored classes utilize and manipulate them against the common people? When they oppose the new power that Marxism conceives as "the revolutionary dictatorship of the proletariat"? Or when they are invoked against military dictatorships and one-party regimes brought about either by the threat of Marxism or simply by the chaos spawned by an anarchical conception of democracy to be found everywhere in the third world?

These are surely urgent questions. Democracy has become a rare exception in developing countries. Only a few nations in Latin America still accept its normal functioning. In Africa, a plurality of parties does not seem compatible with the governmental stability that a one-party system sometimes succeeds in ensuring. In Asia, a few countries still have democratic institutions—not counting Japan, which cannot be included in the third world. But the picture as a whole is enough to unsettle the firmest convictions. Could it be, as the example of antiquity seems to show, that democracy is a highly unlikely system except in entirely exceptional economic and political circumstances?

*Defining the private domain.* First of all, democracy is defined by beginning with two concepts that socialist countries reject—public and private. Does the definition of a private domain still retain some value today? And if it does, can it be made in accordance with the same criteria?

What the revolutionaries of 1789 found insupportable was the arbitrary intervention of kings and nobles in their personal possessions and lives. Doubtless "serfdom" had in large part disappeared; the "list of grievances" objected to the lord's hunting rights rather than his authority over the marriage of his serfs, a right that had fallen into disuse. But the people who launched the revolution, peasants and craftsworkers, felt themselves bound hand and foot by the network of rights and privileges accorded to the two estates, nobles and clergy, which constituted the *Ancien Régime;* they wanted a private domain where people would be in authority in their own homes and a public domain in which the law would apply to everybody without discrimination. Feudal law was based on the out-of-date notion of unequal personal status. From that time forward, there was to be a private sector of life and something public, the republic.

This distinction is just what is disputed today, not in the name of feudal principles but in the name of economic needs. The economic is all-pervasive, respecting no frontiers, transforming the state, entrusting it with power to perform entirely new functions, which liberal thought had explicitly excluded. It threatens private life. Nothing resists its law, neither urban nor rural property, nor the media, nor the environment. In cases where the state is still inspired with a certain "liberalism," the economic is no less obsessive; publicity penetrates every domain of private life, takes an agressive stance, and recognizes no other morality than the ethic of efficiency.

Socialism is characterized, more than other systems, by the importance it places on the economic, giving it, as it were, the keys to the city of man. Marx made it a principle that the economic structure determined the whole political superstructure. The development of the forces of production and the organization of social relationships in relation to these, in other words, the structure of economic society, condition the structures of political society. The first revolution began from the opposite principle, subjecting everything to the necessity for organizing public liberties. The Marxist critique reversed this position. In Marxism, the political no longer has any specificity; it is a function of economic structures, that is, of the class struggle and the dictatorship of the proletariat. The nation itself is defined as a social class.

Is it necessary to go to these lengths in making concessions to industrial society? Must political thinking be subject to that extent to an economic rationale? Pushed to the extreme, is the private domain to be absorbed by the public sector?

Christian conscience resists this thrust, judging the democratic idea to be not just an incidental presumption but a conviction that wells up from what is most essential in Christianity, the destruction of fetishes and faith in God. It recognizes that socialism is ineluctable. It yields to the necessity of organizing economic society in its productive and distributive processes. It admits the attribution of a new mission to the public powers. But it does not define the political simply by economic ends; and it will not support the disappearance of the private domain.[6]

The private domain is the area of personal relationships and is grounded in equality. It is the locus for contracts: no persons can be obliged to bind themselves without their own consent. It is the place for exchange: to each according to contribution. Equality is king there. In the public domain, on the contrary, the person is confronted by a power which people themselves have created together and which is imposed then on them in a sovereign manner and, if need be, by coercion. In relationship with that power, the person is in a situation of radical inequality.

Marxism finds it easy to show how this fine order has been destroyed. Relationships are not equal between persons, or in the market, or within enterprises. Relations between buyers and sellers and even more so between employers and employees are free only under set conditions. In other ways, uncontrolled freedom causes crises in the functioning of the market and of any enterprise. Therefore, the public domain must absorb the private in order to reestablish equality and order in social existence.

We need to recognize that the economic does not lend itself to interpretation according to traditional categories. The operations of production are neither entirely public nor entirely private services. Thinking in terms of the market and of business has come to conceive of a structure that does not fit into classic concepts. The new doctrine is inclined to mark off an area of industrial and commercial relations, in which individuals do not operate with the same freedom as in their properly personal sphere, their home. There is an economic society. Its activities originate in individual initiatives—buying, selling, investing, managing, etc.—which have their source in the private domain but include immanent ends that go beyond the scope of individuals and are answerable to the public.

It is equally dangerous, therefore, to define the economic as private, for that means forgetting its finality, or as public, for that means introducing into a realm where choices definitively remain those of individuals, a power that dominates them from the top to bottom and admits of no discussion. The first kind of definition implies anarchy and inequality; the second, dictatorship. The very term "political economy" avoids both oversimplifications.

If we want to preserve public liberties while ensuring economic efficiency and equality, the traditional distinction has to be maintained, but laws proper to the economic must be defined. Much has been done along this line; neither legislation nor jurisprudence concerning the economic can be interpreted any longer with the help of traditional concepts. This irresistible thrust must not be allowed, however, to do away with a definition that remains the basis for democracy.[7]

*Participation in politics.* The other question raised by the development of techniques in production is no less grave: are the tasks entrusted to centralized power in industrial society compatible with the political participation of its citizens? Are they compatible with a plurality of parties?

Marxism-Leninism gives a categorical answer: there must be but one party and it must have supremacy over the government. Other dictatorships and one-party systems make no attempt to offer theoretical justifications for themselves but act for purely empirical reasons; the anarchy in which democratic regimes are foundering and, in the face of this anarchy, the threat of Marxism.

The thrust that is shaking the very foundations of dictatorship, from whatever source it may draw its inspiration, wells up from the depths of human consciousness. It clashes with all the forces of coercion and repression used by those in power to impose their views. Although there may be only a few who, having overcome their fears, possess the courage to stand up against power at the risk of their liberty and their life, their peaceful resistance is no less irresistible. They are the proof of how deeply the idea of freedom is now anchored in people's minds. They no longer want notions and decisions imposed upon them in which they themselves have had no part to play.

It often happens in third-world countries that an uprising for freedom is inspired by Marxist thinking; the guerrilla in Latin America most often takes his place in this perspective. Between Che Guevara and Camilo Torres, on one hand, and Solzhenitsyn and Dubcek on the other, there seems to be, at first sight, a contradiction. In reality it may well be that a real relationship exists between them. Those who combat military dictatorships or capitalism have, in the depths of their souls, a concept of freedom that they believe can be realized apart from Marxism; they are hoping to cure Marxism of the evil that corrodes it, its idea of dictatorship. They have in mind their own kind of rethought

Marxism, quite different from the Marxism of socialist countries. They explicitly reject the Soviet, the "Stalinist" regime, and put their faith in the Chinese system.[8] And they are exposed to the same rude awakening that the Marxist "progressives" in France during the 1950s experienced at the revelations of Khrushchev's report in 1956. Today it is just as difficult for any criticism of Chinese Marxism to gain a hearing with certain segments of the public as it was for any criticism of Stalinist Marxism to win a hearing in certain segments of the public in 1950. Does that show that many Marxists are not basically Marxist? And if it does, then what are they? Is it possible that, by rising up against military dictatorships or against "institutionalized violence," they may be unconsciously joining forces with those who dare to take a stand against dictatorship in Marxist regimes? Both groups prove that freedom is not dead, since it leads them to resist the absolutisms that seek to destroy it.

*The plurality of parties.* Perhaps in Africa the one-party system is a necessary transitional phase[9] when the mentality and customs of the people are not yet ready for democracy, and provided that the one party does not lose sight of the end that justifies its existence for the time being. But there is no full and final freedom that does not accept plurality. The people who attempted to open up socialism to freedom in Czechoslovakia were well aware of that. It was the whole order of Marxism-Leninism that they exposed to questioning: the dictatorship of one class identified as the nation, the primacy of the party over the government.[10] They had the right idea: there is no freedom without pluralism. And there is no pluralism if information is managed, if the media are tightly controlled, if association is forbidden, if the domain of private life is violated.

Parties, therefore, have a mission but they can fulfill it only if they are alert to all the internal hazards that hang over them.

The first of these stems from private power and privilege when these attempt, against all reason, to enlist in their service what should be at the service of all—free information and communication and, ultimately, the political parties themselves. The intrusion of private interests into the democratic function corrupts it. No party can claim a right to exist if it does not accept what conscience requires—the abolition of all improper privileges and powers.

The second danger is the opposite of the first. It comes into existence when the party thinks that the only way to put an end to improper privilege and power is to suppress the liberties that people of power and privilege are utilizing for their own benefit. This is just another intrusion of the interests of a particular class into the democratic process and it destroys it just as effectively as the first, no matter how legitimate its purposes may be. No party has any justification for existing if it does not accept another principle of conscience—that the party is not identified with the nation.

In both cases, Christian doctrine shows the limits within which freedom operates and beyond which it becomes violence. It affirms the necessity of building a society according to a pluralistic model in which no political party can claim to usurp every role and to interfere in the internal life of basic communities, the economic organism, and educational institutions. Should a party succeed in doing that, the authorities in these various groups would lose their own proper purposes, distinct from those of the party, and would be gradually destroyed by permitting themselves to be taken over by a partisan spirit.

Another internal threat, although less extreme, is no less a danger to democracy itself: it is the tendency of parties to become transformed into sects. Here we have an example of fetishism that often goes unnoticed. Perhaps we people have not reflected enough on the heavy burden that democracy imposes on those who enjoy it—the enduring readiness of parties to try to overcome the passions and sectarian ways that make the proper exercise of power impossible. It is said—with some humor—that it is a fundamental democratic right to overthrow the government. To abuse that right will not fail to paralyze any exercise of power. Whatever the government formula, parliamentarian or presidential, democracy is possible only if the opposition is capable of imposing restraint upon itself and of collaborating with the party in power in all that is needed for the common good of the nation. The English call it fair play. The way they conduct their political affairs perhaps explains the stability which their democratic institutions have experienced up until now, even in the great crises of their history.

Certainly good intentions alone do not make good politics. The action needed to get hold of power and to exercise it demands a certain hardihood. It is normal that in electoral campaigns, the criticisms of the opposing parties are honed to a sharp edge, for the voters have to be able to make their options on good grounds. It is also normal for the opposition party to expose the mistakes of the party in power. But if these attacks are biased and unrelenting, if they have nothing to do with truth, they can, in the end, paralyze the action of those in power by obliging them to face, in addition to the overwhelming demands of their normal functions, the added difficulties arising from the traps laid in their path. The democratic process can become simply impossible if parties do not observe restraint in using their rights. Sectarianism in either the opposition or the party in power can be democracy's worst enemy.

In order to avoid it, it is important that both parties refer their conduct to truth and justice as their ultimate authority. The unfortunate thing is that some doctrines, such as the opposing ideologies of Machiavellianism and materialism, support the thesis that in political conflicts truth and justice are not to be appealed to because truth and justice are just what the rationale of the state or the interests of a class define them to be. There are just two powers facing each other; they themselves are their own justification.[11] Certainly, if these doctrines prevail, they make democracy impossible, as those who hold them well know. Their logical penchant is for dictatorship.

Democracy has a Christian origin and can be sustained only when rooted in the rich soil that made it fertile: the unshakable conviction that right exists and that it has primacy over might, that truth exists and can overcome falsehood. Yet any reference to a supreme authority of truth and justice cannot be a mere formality; it must constitute for both those in government and those who want to dispossess them in a legitimate way, a call to discern the play of emotion and passion in their thinking and doing and to rise above the collective drives that often actuate them. In the long run, they have a stake in doing this, if they want their cause to succeed. Violence, as an unreasoning refusal to look at matters from the viewpoint of truth and justice, brings only immediate returns. It is neither tactic nor strategy that effectively motivates people to practice self-control; it is the conviction that nothing is to be gained in a struggle that rejects on principle any wisdom, any loyalty, any impartiality.

Obviously, self-control on the part of opposing factions presupposes that they have a common conception of truth and justice as their reference point, a supreme authority that judges the established law and the law that seeks to replace it, discerning the elements of justice and injustice involved in each. This is the preeminent role of Christian prophecy in the midst of factions contending for power, just as it was Christ's: not to avoid action and struggle and the choices that they include but to keep involved, all the while remaining conscious of the bias and incompleteness that are part of contending viewpoints and groups in order to keep before the minds of all what being human means.

But is there such a thing as a human nature that all people share? Is humankind in any sense universal? This is the ultimate question of democracy. It was not an accident that the founders of democracy believed in reason and mankind. It is true that today we are better able to discern the irrational and inhuman elements covered over by that faith when it refuses to recognize social inequities. Too, from the structuralists we have learned of the radical differences between cultures.[12] These are definitive acquisitions of conscience. However, even if it were proved that cultures have nothing in common, the fact remains that the consciences of people everywhere react to the assassination of an innocent person, even of an entirely different culture, as an insupportable iniquity. Humankind is not, therefore, dead —because God is not dead; for believers, every person, just by being a person, is an image of God. Perhaps all the lines of force are divergent, but they mysteriously converge toward one common end—toward humanity, that is, toward God. Christian faith, in the measure to which it addresses itself to the one true

God, preserves the common ground where humanity finds its definitive, its indestructible unity.

Many people who are not believers, or are even professed atheists, join with Christians at this point.

What is essential is that the efforts of all those who believe in justice and truth as goods common to all humanity should join forces. On the day when faith dies, democracy has lost its last chance. The death of public liberties is ultimately the death of humankind itself, for it signals the death of God by the deification of power.

Happily, the Christian idea has taken such deep roots that it cannot be eradicated. Again and again it rises to rebirth from its own ashes. In opposition to the violence of every dictatorship, just when it is least expected, the authentically prophetic voices of martyrs are raised. And their accents find an echo in the hearts of people not deafened by a priori ideologies to the appeal, not of any ideology but of humankind, as it wells up from that *given* which comprises humanity's whole dignity, the divine likeness. Wherever the Church has not had to return to the catacombs, wherever it enjoys liberty and is even perhaps too much at home, it must have the capacity to pour out such testimony from its innermost self. Not only democracy depends upon its fulfilling that mission, but every ideal of liberty and justice which people possess today and which find their best chance of being recognized and reconciled through the Church.

## NOTES

1. Francisco de Vitoria, O.P. (1483–1545), *Relecciones Teologicas*. Edición critica del texto latino, versión española (Madrid: Teofilo Urdanoz, 1960). Of special interest are the first two *relectiones, De Indis* and *De jure belli Hispanorum in barbaros,* available in an English translation (Washington, D. C.: Carnegie Institute, 1917). The same two are analyzed in James Brown Scott, "Francisco de Vitoria's Law of Nations" in *The Catholic Conceptions of International Law* (Washington, D. C.: Georgetown University Press, 1934).

2. For example, Enrique Dussel, *Hipotesis para una historia de la Iglesia en America latina* (Barcelona: Estela-Iepal, 1967).

3. See Louis Baudin, *L'État jésuite de Paraguay* (Paris: Editions Génin, 1962); Maxime Haubert, *La vie quotidienne au Paraguay sous les jésuites* (Paris: Hachette, 1967.

4. For example, J. A. Emery, superior general of Saint-Sulpice. Imprisoned during the Terror, he was later freed and became the accepted guide of the clergy. Anxious to avoid the de-Christianization of France, he advocated recognition of the new regime by the Church.

5. During the pontificate of Pope Pius X, for instance, due much more to the existence of an unofficial power tolerated within the Church than to interventions by the hierarchy. To become acquainted with a concrete case of the difficulties met by those who defended the new ideas, see Paul Droulers, *Politique sociale et christianisme* (Paris: Editions Ouvrières), pp. 232 ff.

6. It is noteworthy that Francisco de Vitoria gives an important place to the distinction between private and public in his treatise on civil power. Cf. Stephen J. Reidy, *Civil Authority according to Francisco de Vitoria* (River Forest, Ill.: Aquinas Library, 1959).

7. It seems that it is in this sense that the famous statement of Pope Pius XII should be understood: "Actually it is the mission of public law to serve private rights, not to absorb them. The economy is not of its nature—no more, for that matter, than any other human activity—a state institution. It is, on the contrary, the living product of the free initiative of individuals and of their freely established associations." "Address to Catholic Employers," May 7, 1949, *The Catholic Mind* 47 (July 1949) 447.

8. The Marxist schema reduces the political problem to the relationship of the party to the people. Marxists studying the question see clearly the necessity to invert this relationship by returning to the people the power which, to their minds, the party has usurped in socialist countries of the Soviet type. For that reason they turn to China and its cultural revolution. But as long as the people remain an unorganized mass, they cannot exercise any control over the party. The Chinese example is no exception. The "leap forward" of the young was possible at the time of the cultural revolution only because of the all-powerful intervention of Mao, concentrating complete power in his person.

9. See Jean-Yves Calvez, *Politics and Society in the Third World,* trans. M. O'Connell (Maryknoll, N.Y.: Orbis Books, 1973), ch. 6, "The Role of the Single Party," pp. 93–106.

10. The measures for democratization proposed by the Czechoslovak Communist Party Presidium in October 1967 included: greater participa-

tion by the people in national activity (economic, social, and political) together with mechanisms that would assure the people of the most information possible; freedom of opinion and the right to express it publicly; the right to criticize; the right of association; the right of parties other than the Communist Party to be established and enjoy equal rights; separation of the functions of the party from those of the government; the party must have independence enough to pull together the cares and interests of the people in general; recognition of the role of the "intelligentsia" in the country's direction, lacking at the present because of government directives; rejection of bureaucratic centralization; the establishment of a federal system throughout the country. See *Czechoslovakia's Blueprint for Freedom,* introd. and analysis Ello Paul (Washington, D. C.: Acropolis, 1968), *passim.*

11. Some people, not materialists, bring water to the mill when they say that there is no ethic without guile, every ideology is partisan and that, consequently, it is useless to try to discern what is right.

12. See A. Jeannière, "La rencontre des cultures," *Projet* (January 1972), p. 7.

# XVI

# THE PROBLEM OF VIOLENCE

As the preceding thoughts were developed concerning the difficulty in reconciling public liberties, central planning, and basic communities, some doubts must have arisen. Is it possible to realize, while respecting "human rights" and the necessary autonomies, the ideal of an equalizing rise in the standard of living that would benefit a whole people?

Here the problem of violence enters in. Capitalism, when inspired by a purely liberal doctrine and marked by the institutionalization of social inequities, and, above all, when it establishes a dictatorship for its own benefit, has chosen violence. Marxism, too, chooses violence, since, to its mind, the masses' standard of living cannot be raised and equalized with that of the upper classes if freedom and community participation are maintained.

Between the two extreme theories, both holding it to be impossible to reconcile elements of justice and freedom, governments founder. Some are more inclined to leave industry, trade, and speculation free and to accept the social inequities involved in freedom. Others are more concerned with equality, are loath to reward initiative and investment, and fail to promote what growth requires. Ineffectiveness characterizes them both, the first in the social sphere, the second in the economic and, ultimately, in both spheres at once, for the social and the economic cannot make progress independently of one another. The opposition that they meet from public opinion and, as a result, in government assemblies, often leads them to suppress public liberties.

Is it possible to break through this circle, to escape this dilemma, to give the third world a chance?

The only way out seems to be to build a society that allows

freedom under the three forms defined by the three successive revolutions: democracy, socialism, community.

Skeptics will not be lacking to object that such a proposal is vain. One group will treat it as neocapitalist, the other, as crypto-Communist. Yet it may be that the future of the third world hangs on the answer to this question: will people be capable of disregarding the attacks that cannot fail to be made on them from both directions? The double objection assumes, it is true, a prestigious ideological guise. Liberalism, on one side, and Marxism on the other, demolish in advance, with a sort of implacable irony, the very idea of getting out of the tragic impasse. There is, however, no other way to go save by the route of the three freedoms. Between the two dictatorships, the one of unjustifiable privilege and power, sometimes still masked by the appearance of formal democracy, the other a system of one-party supremacy over government, there is no other solution. The free and responsible construction of a new society from which private privilege and power, and, therefore, the source of social conflict, will be excluded is the price that has to be paid. Once this narrow path is departed from, no other way lies open except the two opposing philosophies, both committed to violence. To admit this is not to define a third party but simply to point out the path to justice and freedom.

But the most difficult barrier to cross is perhaps not the combined conflagrations lit by those who have made a real choice of violence, whether they are inspired by liberalism or by Marxism. The most dangerous opposition comes, without a doubt, from those who elect violence without assuming the consequences. Many still adhere to liberalism, that is, to the traditional principles of a free society and of free enterprise, because, in the back of their minds, the thought lingers that this way does not exclude some kind of social equality. Others accept Marxism because they are persuaded that this way out does not necessarily include violence and dictatorship. By such mental devices, people are able to be liberal or Marxist at very little cost, thanks to their skill at intellectual editing. Neither the liberal nor the Marxist philosophy justifies any such hope. Both have to be granted their coherence and both include violence as part of their logic. In a sense, the opposition of leading liberals and Marxists seems preferable: they know what their choices involve and do not mince words. The former are well aware that a society derived from their principles will always be unjust. The latter are just as cognizant that the dictatorship of the proletariat will have to rule for ten thousand years. The most subtle objections come from those who do not really accept the responsibility for all the violence implied in their choice.

Some will say true, but, taking everything into consideration, we prefer the first to the second system of violence. Why does a believer refuse to be hemmed in by such a dilemma? Why believe in a third world?

Hegel and, after him, Marx, have said that the social reality never presents people with problems that they cannot solve. The Christian adds—that they cannot solve in regard to people themselves, to all people, and to all human rights.

The arguments of the two systems in confrontation with each other finally come down to just one: violence can be overcome only by violence. One side says, the violence of the dictatorship of the proletariat can be defeated only by capitalist violence with the dictatorship that it requires. The other side says, only the violence of the wage earners can get the better of the violence of the privileged, and an inverse dictatorship is a necessary phase of that violent action.

Are people really saved, is injustice really put aside, when they allow violence to take possession of them?

Christians refuse to be caught in this snare. They denounce political breaking and entering to the extent that it lies within their power. And they know why.

Force is sometimes necessary in the service of justice;[1] violence, never. In what does the intrinsic malice of violence consist? In being its own justification and a law unto itself. Violence is repression or revolution when they no longer attempt to be responsible to any higher authority of justice and truth, but simply assert their own authority, with no other end in mind than effectiveness, claiming to define the means to be put to use simply in function of their ends. Violence is either reaction or rebellion when they refuse a priori the possibility of either a just society or a free society and often of both, thus prohibiting, in the name of realism or materialism, any appeal to the ideals inscribed in the human conscience.

No one has refuted so penetratingly as Solzhenitsyn the objections poured out upon those who still believe that peace can be established by peaceful means. He faces them without fear:

> Well, let us not forget that violence does not have its own separate existence and is in fact incapable of having it: it is invariably interwoven with the lie. They have the closest of kinship, the most profound natural tie: violence has nothing to stand on but violence. Everyone who has once proclaimed violence as his method, must inexorably select the lie as his principle. At its birth violence acts openly and even takes pride in itself. But as soon as it is reenforced and strengthened, it begins to sense the rarified atmosphere around it, and it cannot go on existing except by befogging itself with lies, cloaking itself in hypocritical words. It does not always nor invariably choke its victims, more often it demands of them only that they participate in the lie.
>
> . . . So be it that this takes place in the world, even reigns in the world—but not with my complicity.
>
> . . . And as soon as the lie is dispersed the repulsive nakedness of violence is exposed, and violence will collapse in feebleness.
>
> . . . One word of truth outweighs the whole world.[2]

If there be prophetic words, the Russian writer has spoken them and they evoke in our minds the words of Jesus to Pilate and help us to understand them. "I was born for this, I came into the world for this: to bear witness to the truth."

People are not lacking to respond to Solzhenitsyn as Pilate did to Jesus, "Truth? What is that?"

Certainly believers have no way of knowing if their testimony will find any acceptance. They may simply be ground under. They may be obliged to live in a system not of their choosing. Their choice continues to be made—not to accept one of the two alternatives.

Believers do not put aside a priori the use of force, a renunciation that does not spring directly from the gospel, but force is called upon only after and through the mediation of political analysis.

Any people who refer their actions to the gospel think of two things. First, before people launch into a war, which in the case under consideration would be a class war, a civil war, with all the risks that involves, and, above all, before allowing themselves to be taken over by a philosophy not based on right but on violence, they must weigh, through an analysis of political realities, the enormity of the evils that would be engendered and the chance that they might simply replace these with still greater evils.[3] Second, conscientious action can open up a way inaccessible by any other route. On this point the Christian position is diametrically opposed to both Machievellianism and materialism: it believes in conscience, puts its hope in conscience.

When we observe, over the last ten years, the repeated failures of violence all over a continent, failures acknowledged and analyzed by the very people who believed in the effectiveness of violence, can we not believe that the energy and heroism expended in this way without any effect could have opened up a way to the realization of their hopes? If purely political analyses lead. us to that conclusion, how much stronger the conviction would be had the analyses been carried out under the light of faith?

Does not an action of this kind, in which many people would be involved, deserve, more than any other, the name of revolution? Of liberation?

Why are we waiting to put it into effect? To be positively sure of success? To be certain of a short-term solution? Since when have conditions like that been required to begin any undertaking at all?

## NOTES

1. Pope Paul VI, "Message on Peace," November 30, 1969; "That strife can be necessary, that it can be the arm of justice, that it can rise to a noble-hearted, heroic duty, we do not deny." *The Pope Speaks* 14 (1969) 313.

2. Solzhenitsyn, an address that was to have been given on receiving the Nobel Peace Prize, 1972. *New York Times,* October 7, 1972, p. 33, col. 2.

3. The Second Episcopal Conference of Latin America at Medellín, 1968, expressed itself as follows in regard to the situation throughout the continent: "If we consider, then, the totality of the circumstances of our countries, and if we take into account the Christian preference for peace, the enormous difficulty of a civil war, the logic of violence, the atrocities it engenders, the risk of provoking foreign intervention, illegitimate as it may be, the difficulty of building a regime of justice and freedom while participating in a process of violence, we earnestly desire that the dynamism of the awakened and organized community be put to the service of justice and peace." *The Church in the Present-Day Transformation of Latin America in the Light of the Council,* ed. Louis Colonnese, 2 vols. (Washington, D. C.: Latin American Bureau, United States Catholic Conference, 1970), Vol. 2, p. 80.

# XVII

# THE "VIOLENCE" OF THE CHURCH

> *The kingdom of heaven has been*
> *subjected to violence and the violent*
> *are taking it by storm.*
> MATTHEW 11:12

Are political forces alone enough? Must not higher energies also be called upon?

However important may be the task of the political person, the party person, it cannot and ought not reach into the innermost recesses of the person, there where the ultimate combat takes place between good and evil, justice and inequity, liberty and slavery, truth and falsehood, life and death. Neither equality nor liberty nor participation can be effected without a transformation of conscience, which does not fall within the compass of political authorities alone.

In countries where Christianity is alive, its first mission is to awaken consciences. If it does that, it achieves it not by means of political motivation but by an impulse welling up from what is deepest within it. All that has been said on the theology of liberation, on the necessity of contesting the social fetishisms of wealth and power, on worshiping the one true God in spirit and in truth, leads to one conclusion: the Church must lead this action under pain of being disavowed.[1]

Of all the Church's missions today, is this the most urgent? Is the Church aware of its role? And ready to assume it? Above all, is the Church conscious of what must be changed in itself and in its way of acting so that it may measure up to fulfilling its role?

The conditions required are weighty.

First, the Church must escape from the tyranny of collective passions. Every great spirituality has made clear how necessary it is to bring discernment to bear on the forces that have weight in the making of decisions and, less consciously, in the forming of convictions. Such insight is acquired only through an inner warfare to the death against everything that acts as an obstacle to truth and love and life in the human heart. But the passions that perpetrate confusion and disorder and serve to block the intuitions and impulses of the Spirit are not principally those due to a person's individual history but rather the collective passions that result from race, class, and nation. These divide humanity by irreconcilable enmities. They enslave people and pit them against each other in ruthless conflicts in which a sense of justice and, even more, any pardoning of injuries become veritably impossible.

It is surprising that in spiritual "exercises," in the review of life, and in those exchanges that Christians today love to have recourse to, so little attention is given to this new aspect of the discernment of spirits. Do not the social class to which we belong, all our spontaneous reactions, all the decisions and convictions built up in us during the course of our history enter in—before any judgment of reason and faith—to form prejudgments in the literal sense of the term? And do not these put obstacles in the way of freedom of spirit and the work of deliverance? What means do we have for breaking such powerful attachments?

It is not in solitude, surely, although that is a necessity too, that such a liberation can be worked out. Since we are concerned with collective phenomena, what is needed is communal deliberation, not the kind where each one is allowed to follow his or her own spontaneous tendencies and conclusions are reached by reconciling individual considerations and baptizing them "spiritual," but the kind where each person is disposed to open up personal prejudices and choices to questioning and to listen to what comes from above in order to overcome the passions which cloud the mind and hamper the will. Tradition has carefully preserved individual privacy but has often forgotten the role of the community when gathered together, so little inclined has it been to enter into this logic of "violence" and death, without which there is no discernment of spirits either by the individual or by the community.

Only in the Church is this kind of discussion possible. Groups can be brought together by ideological affinities. They are then exposed to partiality, especially if they rigidly exclude all those who do not fall in line with their partisan position. They are often conditioned by a small number of the group, more strongly bent than the others on the extremes that constitute the unifying feature of the group. Then it is no longer the faith but an ideology that is the principle of discernment, and collective passions, far from being overcome, risk becoming further inflamed.

Prayer and reflection are the desiderata for bringing together people who represent different points of view, not on the basis of political opinions but on the one criterion of the faith. Their unity will be expressed visibly by a sign that does not deceive: communion with the pastors of the Church. When this sign is lacking, doubts can be entertained about the spirit animating the community and the conclusions that it reaches. When it is detectable, the word of the Gospel can be verified: "For where two or three meet in my name, I shall be there with them" (Matt. 18:20). Then the positions adopted no longer represent a mean between the extremes of the various opinions in the group or some sort of summary of their personal statements. They represent something else, for the assembly reaches up into a reality that is completely above it.

This is the first form of the Church's "violence": to maintain itself in a state to surmount the collective passions that divide the human race and provoke confrontations in its own ranks, composed as it is of human beings.

Second, this achieved, the Church will really be a sign of liberation, inviting people to become channels of unity, conduits of lasting peace. This means not ignoring unjust acts of violence caused by conflicts but, on the contrary, denouncing them in order to prevail over them. It does not mean uniting oppressors and oppressed in one body; it does mean denouncing the oppression of the one and the violence of the other.

Yet the Church must also invite people to accept necessary coexistence. We have seen how each social category and each philosophy which provides their inspiration are excommunicated by the other, so that reconciliation, which would be a source of cohesion and peace in society, is impossible. Together with all the world's peoples, the Church has a mission to resist this schism in order to reduce the two violences, the two dictatorships that are threatening humanity. A peaceful revolution, an interior conversion to the living God, freedom from every idolatry, liberates human beings from the forces that oppress them and the injustices that divide them.

In the Church's work of unity, the violence of poverty is needed, for it overthrows the fetishes of wealth and power, which are forever being reborn. The Church must first press forward in its interior struggle to offer to the world the very image of Jesus, the poor man, the stranger, humiliated and oppressed, the man who renounced all worldly prestige and took his stand on the strength of the spirit alone. To reach that height, not only have the first steps been taken at the base of the mountain but they have set out for the summit; yet the journey still stretches out far into the distance ahead. Many have courageously undertaken it so that the Church may show its true face to the world.

Third, itself converted, the Church can then witness to the truth. And in other ways than in words. Like Jesus, it must not be afraid to confront wealth and power with no weapons save those of the spirit and at the risk of life itself. In this way it will change the course of history. Only this kind of violence can finally prevail over violence itself.[2]

People are called in many different ways. All will not have the courage to risk ruin, imprisonment, and death. Even if they are not lacking strength of soul, Christians must also be "cunning as serpents and yet as harmless as doves" (Matt. 10:16). They are not to rush into useless provocative actions. They are to know how to be silent sometimes and to live in the catacombs. At the same time, they have to keep in mind that you don't pull a lion's teeth by patting him on the back. The hour can come when false gods are to be defied—power when it would have itself adored, wealth when it enslaves human beings.

Is the Christian community ready to go that far in testifying to its faith and taking the offensive against every kind of violence? Is it ready to be despoiled of its own riches? its own power? Is each Christian, whether lay person, minister, or pastor, prepared for demonstrations that do not jeopardize authority, since they are unarmed, but risk ending in prison and death because they seem to disturb public order, although they are really trying to re-establish it by modifying unjust laws and ways of acting?

Situations are of many different kinds and discernment is needed to meet them. The Church does not have the same obliga-tion to be open with powers that frankly call themselves atheistic as with those that claim to be Christian. In different circum-stances, the Church will, therefore, take different forms of action.

In countries where the Church is free and embraces the vast majority of the citizens, its social vocation will have the best chance of being realized. Think of the potentiality of a com-munity, strongly built by its pastors, and capable of mobilizing many lay, priestly, and religious lives totally devoted to the service of the Church's mission, capable of actualizing many fruitful initiatives among the faithful. Truly, if such a Church, with its lay people, religious, priests, and pastors, awoke to its primordial function—the education of a social conscience in the leisure classes and in the masses of the people—political condi-tions would all be changed. What is at present impossible would become possible.

Vatican Council II, the Latin American Episcopal Conference at Medellín, and regional and general synods have shown the way. On both theoretical and practical planes much remains to be done to involve the whole Christian community in depth.

Where Christians are only a minority, their activity will be more limited, although fervor can compensate for lack of num-bers. They serve as a leaven. Who can estimate the effect of their hidden irradiation upon mind and actions when the day comes that their faith attains to its "political" dimension?

In Communist countries, where Christians are heroic in keep-ing their faith under persecution, or at least discrimination, evangelization has to assume the values of a hostile world, adopt-ing its modes of thought and life, its "rites" in everything that does not go contrary to the gospel message, following the tradi-tion of great missionaries throughout the ages and the example of Jesus, who took upon himself everything human save sin (Heb. 4:15). After all, to hold goods in common, to share in the same condition as other people, ought not to be anything to frighten Christians but, rather, something to gladden their hearts. Who first preached this sort of communism? And if the Church must continue to be aware of the violence of Marxism, it must also implant the gospel in this new world—and the Church can do that only by recognizing the values of the gospel.

In countries that have so far escaped dictatorship, where free choice still exists, Christians can do nothing else but keep on trying to break through the circle of the two violences. Whatever be the circumstances, woe to us if we do not evangelize. And the gospel will lead some of us to bear heroic witness.

No matter what the situation may be, this is the "violence" of the Church. If the Church does not go to these lengths in the discernment of spirits, will it not fail in its mission? Should not do its part in changing the terms of the dilemma in which the third world and humanity are foundering?[3]

## NOTES

1. See Pope Paul VI, *Populorum progressio*, no. 13: "Sharing the noblest aspirations of men and suffering when she sees them not satisfied, she (the Church) offers men what she possesses as her characteristic attribute: a global vision of man and of the human race" (Boston: Daughters of St. Paul, 1967), p. 10.

2. See Jacques Ellul, *Violence: Reflections from a Christian Perspective*, trans. C. G. Kings (New York: Seabury Press, 1972); Jean-Marie Muller, *Stratégie de l'action non violente* (Paris: Fayard, 1972), which includes a bibliography on nonviolence; and, by the same author, *L'Evangile de la non-violence* (Paris: Fayard, 1969). Among the great figures of active nonviolence the following stand out: Gandhi in India, Martin Luther King in the United States, both of whom lost their lives in the contest, and Dom Helder Camara, archbishop of Olinda and Recife, Brazil.

3. In treating of the "violence" of the Church, I have limited myself to discussing those actions which the whole Christian community, together with their pastors, can assume as one. The laity, acting as individual persons, have another duty: to put into effect the policies and politics needed to transform society, doing this in the light of the ideas about society that stem from their faith, although their personal options in intervening in the political order do not involve the Christian community as a whole.

# CONCLUSION

The third world is a scandal to the entire world because it cannot be liberated without the creation of a new model of society, and not one of the great powers can offer it that.

Turned away from the doors of the nations, the third world puts an obligation on the world to level its structures in order to receive and welcome it.

Today the questions being asked have to do with humankind itself. Has the Church an answer?

The silence of the Church or its complicity leads to contestation within itself. People lose their faith in it, in its dogmas, in its rules, in its rites, in its instructions to the extent to which it seems incapable of playing its part in the revolution that must take place. In proportion to its failure, men and women no longer recognize in the God it preaches the face of humankind. According to Christian faith, there is no other image of God.

Contestation nowadays is not ordinarily simple protest. It is in part expectation, disappointed perhaps, yet still alive. It is a summons to the Church to be for the world what it is in truth.

No other spiritual force can be to the world what the Christian faith is: the source of the renewal that is changing the face of the world today. "The world as we know it is passing away" (1 Cor. 7:31). There is but one revelation: that humankind and God, time and eternity, have formed an indissoluble union. And the Church is the only one to bear witness to it.

It has taken centuries for the world to come to realize what the Incarnation means for it. Not only deliverance from all credulities, all prohibitions, all superstitions that weighed down humankind—as Lucretius expressed it, the bent and bruised knee of religion—but liberation from all the servitudes that do harm to freedom.

As long as religions divinized might and glory, power and wealth, some portion of humanity was condemned to slavery. Even the greatest philosophies of antiquity did not succeed in shaking off that appalling yoke: there were more slaves than free persons in the Athens of Pericles, and sages pronounced a slave "unworthy of love." There were perhaps a hundred slaves to every free person in Rome at the time of Christ.[1]

What the highest forms of philosophy and religion were unable to do, one person accomplished, knowingly becoming the off-scouring of humanity, revealing God in that sort of abasement, in humiliation itself making himself recognized as the Son of God. God made human took on the condition of a slave. Since then, one person is of equal worth with any other. "All baptised in Christ, you have all clothed yourselves in Christ, and there are no more distinctions between Jew and Greek, slave and free, male and female, but all of you are one in Christ Jesus" (Gal. 3:27–28).

Here is the source from which all the great revolutions of our contemporary era originate. No distinction between Jew and Greek—culture and race are not privileges; between slave and free—the manual worker is not an inferior being; between male and female—there is no second sex.

For centuries, for almost two thousand years, the Church has been proclaiming the faith to a religious world which did not receive it, which was unprepared to receive it. Today the Church's mission is no longer to break a path through a thicket of gods; giants with feet of clay, they have tumbled down of themselves in a world desacralized and laicized by the faith itself. Today the Church's mission is to testify against the profane powers that are laying claim to adoration. The witnesses killed today are not those who refuse to offer incense to idols; they are those who stand up against false gods of wealth and power in all the forms of violence and falsehood with which they oppress and divide human beings.

The mission of the Church is to announce to the poor the good news of a society that is really free, really equal, really loving; a society in which power seeks to be put at the service of the people, in which wealth is shared, and the community holds the individual person responsible for personal decisions. The mis-

sion of the Church is not to become laicized, much less politicized. What justification would it then have for existing? Its
mission is to reveal to the world the One who alone is holy and to
lead the battle against the "principalities and powers" which
usurp divinity, to be in the vanguard of those who fight the evil
forces that people use to crush other people.

The Church has entered an era new to it, a time for the renewal
of structures, beliefs, laws, sacraments; a time not to reject the
good grain with the tares but to discern the old and the new, what
is dying and what is coming to birth through a return to its
sources.

People may turn to ideologies for a revelation of their destinies.
And these have no answer to give to the great questions about
life, for they move in a space strictly circumscribed by death. Or
they may turn to the light that is in the world but not of the world,
the only one that illumines their history, the only one that gives
meaning to their history by inaugurating the new times.

Of all that still remains to be changed in the Church we know
almost nothing, even after the profound renovations already
undertaken. We only know that the Church must be faithful to
Christ, who remains throughout the centuries God's Word to
humankind, that it must not be an accomplice of the forces of
death which hold onto the old and misjudge the new, but must
ally itself with all the forces of life that have their source in the
Spirit.

Obviously a gap exists between the analyses and options
which are trying so hard to determine the choice of a society and
that Word which is proposed to us as the way, the truth, and the
life. No one can pretend to obliterate the distance between them.
But the nature of Christian faith is to enter into the very texture of
history. Faith has need of analyses and options, however tenta-
tive they may be. For the world is waiting for the gospel. And the
good news that comes from heaven is confided to the earth as a
seed. Patient and never-ending labor makes it germinate.

The third-world revolution, taken in its full dimensions, is
really a world revolution. The faith is not in possession of its
secrets but enters into the depths of its mystery. Consciously or
unconsciously, the world needs a Church transparent enough

and "violent" enough to help bring a new society to birth. The whole Church is moved, is shaken by this call. Here is the Church's mission, a mission not issuing from any force, however noble, of this world but poured out by the Spirit sent by God to renew the face of the earth.

## NOTE

1. In just one instance, Caesar brought back a million Gallic slaves. Jacques Ellul, *Histoire des institutions* (Paris: P.U.F., 1958), Vol. I, pp. 108, 284.

# Index

Acculturation: process of, 14; problems of, 15–19; confrontation during, 18–19

Adoration (Worship), 74, 76, 92, 93, 98–99, 117, 119, 122, 126, 129, 149, 246, 272, 296, 300

Advertising, 252, 254

Africa, 3, 5, 13, 21, 24, 33, 40, 56, 62, 194, 238–239 n. 9, 261, 275, 279

Agrarian reform: cooperative movement in, 225; difficulties of, 225–226; in Latin America, 224–226; first mission of, 221–222; peasant organization in, 222–224; in third-world countries, 224–226; in today's world, 234

Agrarian society: characteristics of, 22–23, 26 n. 5; disintegration of, 15–18; work in, 17, 18, 155

Alienation, 84, 90, 97–99, 109, 126, 161

Allende, Salvador, 65 n. 13, 179, 186 n. 12, 225, 269 n. 17

Analysis, Christian and Marxist, 13. *See also* Marxism as an analysis

Anarchy: an adversary of democracy, 46, 93; and basic communities, 237; and the cultural revolution, 219–220; in the economy, 56, 277; in the international economy, 256–264; and multinational enterprises, 264–266; of permanent revolution, 58; in rebellion, 194; in Western contestation, 63

*Ancien Régime,* 41, 45, 120, 182, 247, 275

Andean Pact, 259

Arbitrage, 55

Argentina, 259

Art, 25, 104–105, 162, 192, 252–253

Asia, 3, 5, 21, 24, 25 n. 1, 33, 40, 56, 275

Atheism, 150, 193, 208, 272, 283

Basic communities, 59, 201, 204, 221–222, 237, 238–239 n. 12, 243, 280

Belgium, 36–37 n. 14

The Bible, 83, 88, 94–95; and commitment, 143; judgment in, 133; and nature of the kingdom, 117; and relationship of man and woman, 82–85; theology of, 103; world of Old and New Testament in, 81

Bigo, Pierre. *See La doctrine sociale de l'Eglise*

Bolivia, 224, 259

Bossuet, Jacques Benigne, 98

Bourgeoisie, 42, 46, 121, 182; in China, 189, 190; in "national regimes," 194; victories of, 274

Brazil, 3, 37–38 n. 17, 62, 209, 259, 261, 298 n. 2, 209

Brotherhood, the goal of the Third Revolution, 60

Business leaders, authority and power of, 245–246

Camara, Dom Helder, 298 n. 2

Canada, 260

*Capital,* (Karl Marx), 150, 153, 165 n. 10, 167, 172

Capital, 30, 32, 50, 55, 167, 231–232, 233, 234, 235, 236, 252,